Joseph Okechukwu Offor

Community Radio and its Influence in the Society:
The Case of Enugu State – Nigeria

DATE DUE

Joseph Okechukwu Offor

Community Radio and its Influence in the Society:

The Case of Enugu State – Nigeria

Ethik – Gesellschaft – Wirtschaft 14

IKO – Verlag für Interkulturelle Kommunikation

Die Reihe **Ethik – Gesellschaft – Wirtschaft**
wird herausgegeben von:

Prof. Dr. Johannes Hoffmann
Fachbereich Katholische Theologie
Universität Frankfurt am Main

Bibliographische Information Der Deutschen Bibliothek

Die Deutsche Bibliothek verzeichnet diese Publikation in der Deutschen Nationalbibliographie; detaillierte bibliographische Daten sind im Internet über http://dnb.ddb.de abrufbar.

©   IKO-Verlag für Interkulturelle Kommunikation
       Frankfurt am Main • London, 2002

       Frankfurt am Main   London
       Postfach 90 04 21   70 c, Wrentham Avenue
       D - 60444 Frankfurt   London NW10 3HG, UK

       e-mail: info@iko-verlag.de • Internet: www.iko-verlag.de

       ISBN: 3-88939-661-5
       Ethik – Gesellschaft – Wirtschaft, Band 14

Umschlaggestaltung: Volker Loschek, 61184 Karben
Herstellung: Verlagsdruckerei Spengler, 60488 Frankfurt a.M.

Distribution for
North America, South America, Asia, Australia, New Zealand and Africa by

Transaction Publishers,
Rutgers, The State University,
35 Berrue Circle, Piscataway,
New Jersey 08854
United States of America

DEDICATION

My Mother Roseline

TABLE OF CONTENTS

1. Acknowledgement:

This research work could not have been a reality without the immense contributions and assistance of some people. First, I give special thanks to Almighty God for His guidance and sustenance throughout my studies in Europe.

My gratitude goes also to Their Lordships, Rt. Rev. Dr. M.U. Eneja and Rt. Rev. Dr. A. Gbuji for giving me the opportunity to further my studies in Europe, and for their fatherly care and concern throughout my studies.

To my moderator, Professor Dr. Johannes Hoffmann, whose encouragement made the realisation of this research work possible, I am sincerely indebted. He not only painstakingly moderated my work but has equally been a father to me during my studies at Frankfurt University. I will ever remain grateful to him. Equally, I wish to express my gratitude to my second moderator, Professor Dr. Obiora Ike, whose inspiration and academic advice contributed to the success of this research work. I am thanking him most sincerely for his disposition, availability and brotherly concern all through my studies.

I am grateful also to the diocese of Limburg, especially His Lordship Rt. Rev. Dr. Franz Kamphaus, the bishop of the Diocese, for his care and concern throughout my studies. I am equally grateful to the "Weltkirche" of Limburg diocese for her assistance during my studies in Frankfurt.

I extend my gratitude also to Rev. Fr. Michael Weis whose brotherly care and concern will ever be remembered and the entire parishioners of St. Anna and St. Raphael parish Hausen Frankfurt am Main. The same thanks go to Rev. Fr. Robert Nandkisore and his parishioners of St. Anthony's parish Rödelheim in Frankfurt am Main, Rev.Fr. Franz Maywurm and entire parishioners of Liebfrauen parish Eislingen for their love and concern.

I must acknowledge that I owe great debt of gratitude to other people for their moral support and solidarity. Their helping hands have made this work a reality. I will continue to be grateful to Sr. Eunice Offor for her kindness and concern all these years. Her solidarity and moral assistance will always be remembered.

On the same note, my thanks go to Rev. Dr. Raphael Affah who has been my companion all the way through my studies in Europe. His brotherly advice has kept me going all these years.

I am deeply grateful to Rev. Dr. John Nwafor and Rev. Frs. Ambrose Agu and Geoben Emefiena Ezeani who painstakingly proof-read this work and made immense positive contributions.

The same appreciation goes to the following: Rev. Dr. Geoffrey Aguigwo, Rev. Fr. Victor Onyeador, Rev. Dr. Stanley Anyanwu,

Rev. Fr. Anthony Onyekwe, Rev. Fr. Celestine Aniakor, Dr. Michael Anyaehie, Mr. and Mrs. Max/Marion Housa, Mr. David Eromosele, Mr. Remmy Koleoso. and family, Mr. Anthony Sagoe and Mrs. Brigitta Eberhardt, Mrs Dorothea and Mr. Klaus Winter , Med. Dr. Roland Reuff, Mr. Eugen Abele and Family, their solidarity and assistance during my stay in Europe will never be forgotten.

I am also grateful to Ingo Brüggenjürgen, Director of Domradio, in Cologne, and all his co-workers. They were so helpful during my practical exposure at the radio station. The same appreciation goes to members of Enugu Broadcasting Service especially Mr. Edward C. Ogbonna for their immense help during my research work at Enugu.

My thanks go also to my mother, Mrs. Rose Offor, my uncle Mr. B.O. Offor and family , my sister Mrs. Elisabeth Anukanti, and my brothers for their solidarity und understanding throughout my academic stay in Europe.

I wish you all God's abundant blessings.

Joseph Okecchukwu Offor
Frankfurt, July 2002.

1.1. Aim of the Research Work.

It is a well-known fact that communication is fundamental in human life. From the onset of creation, communication has been seen as an inalienable right of every human being, a right without which a human person cannot be complete. Communication relates people to one another. Thus, it makes social intercourse possible and fosters the dynamism and well-being of humanity at all level. They make available information about issues and events, office holders and candidates for office. They enable leaders to communicate quickly and directly with the public about urgent matters. They are important instruments of accountability and exposing immediately incompetence, corruption, and abuses of trust, while also calling attention to instances of competence, public-spiritedness, and devotion to duty. The impact of media can hardly be exaggerated.

According to Pope John Paul II, "the media can be used for good or for evil—it is a matter of choice. The media can at times reduce human beings to units of consumption or competing interest groups, or manipulate viewers and readers and listeners as mere ciphers from whom some advantage is sought, whether product sales or political support; and these things destroy community. It is the task of communication to bring people together and enrich their lives, not isolate and exploit them. The means of social communication, properly used, can help to create and sustain a human community based on justice and charity; and, in so far as they do that, they will be signs of hope"[1]

So, there is need for a balanced communication not only between nations but also between governments and the governed and between different communities of poeple. The only medium that can bring about this equity and sustain it in the present day African context is radio. However, it must be radio which has been changed from being a means of dissemination of information to a means of communication; radio that is not only capable of transmitting to people but also of receiving from them; radio that will allow rural listeners not only to hear but also to be heard. It is this simplest and commonest means of communication in Africa, the "community radio", that is the concern of this research work. The focus in this work is limited to the Igbo society in southern part of Nigeria.

---

[1] Pope John Paul II, Message for the 32nd World Communications Day, Rome 1998.

1.2. NOTION AND TYPES OF RADIO STATIONS.

There are millions of radios broadcasting existing over the world. They go by different names and operate with different systems. This research takes note of the fact that there exists also in Nigeria varieties of radio broadcasting both federal, state and few private ones. However, not even one is community radio. What are the types of radio stations?

1.2.1. Community Radio Station.

Community radio goes by many names. It is called popular or educational radio in Latin America, rural or local radio in Africa, public radio in Australia and free or associative radio in Europe. All these names describe the same phenomenon: that of gaining a voice and democratising communication on a community scale. For one to understand the meaning of community radio station, a clear distinction between it and government-owned stations is necessary. The phenomenon of private ownership of radio is not common in developing nations, especially those of Africa. In most of African countries, the governments own the broadcasting facilities and operate them as well. Hence, it is not uncommon to see these radio stations totally controlled by the ruling government. They are mere mouthpiece of the government of the day. This has nothing to do with local radio. What is actually community radio? Lloyd, defines it as: "A small, low-powered station organised in such a way as to be responsive to the specific needs of the grassroots community. These stations often operate with a minimal staff and budget; responsibility for management, programming and financing the stations rests with the local community".[2]

In recent times, community radio has been developed as a distinct alternative to both government, commercial and public stations. Some of the characteristics of community radio include:

---

[2] Lloyd Libby, Towards a Democratic Radio Broadcast Media in South Africa, Montréal, AMARC 1991, p.11.

a). The avoidance, as much as possible, of commercial advertising. This is because going into commercial advertising may hinder the common man from having access to the station. This stems from the fact that "he who pipes the flute dictates the tune."

b). It seeks support primarily from the contributions of users with supplementation by grants from community organisations, foundations, etc. The major objectives are to encourage widespread community participation in broadcasting and provide an opportunity for horizontal communication between individuals and groups in the community.

c). It provides an active voice for less powerful majorities of the community and to give minorities a chance to make known their alternative views and styles of life.

d). In community radio volunteers play an important role in the production of programmes; the distinctions between "professional staff" and ordinary users are played down. Every user contributes effectively to the running of the station and is a potential producer.

It should be clearly noted that these stations have normally a low transmitting power. They serve only a very limited geographical area. They are owned and operated by a group of interested citizens. Very often the managers and announcers are volunteers who freely give their service to the local community. From this study, it is clear that through community radio people become part of the decision making of the community or nation where they live. Community radio allows people to participate in making decisions; audience can write letters, stations can conduct regular interviews with the audience, live presentation of popular festivals, major moments of human sufferings, news of epidemics and celebrations, are made known to the people.

1.2.2. Public /Commercial Radio Station.

In most cases, public and commercial radios are interchangeable. In some instances, not all-commercial radios are public radios. Public broadcasting station is normally set-up by law or arranged in such a way that the public participates in one-way or another in the station operation. Such broadcasting stations have their board of directors partly appointed by the government of the day. The government controls the content and kind of programs of such public radio stations and uses it as an instrument of propaganda. Examples are Federal Radio Corporation of Nigeria, (FRCN), the British Broadcasting Corporation (BBC) in London. Some African countries like, Ghana, Malawi, South Africa, Zambia and Zimbabwe have such public stations. This means they are supported by public funds but their day-to-day operation is the responsibility of a board of directors appointed by the government or determined by statute. However, the independence of this board varies from country to country.

1.2.3. Local/Rural Radio Station.

Local radio stations are common in Africa where some governments have set up alternative stations in the interior of their countries to transmit development messages with regard to the language and culture of the people. These stations are often taken to mean the same as community radio. The objectives of this local broadcasting are identical in all African countries. However, the initial experimentation of the use of local broadcasting station was first carried out in the United States of America. At that time much emphasis was placed on local community. The ideal policy behind setting up such station according to White is that, "radio should be owned and operated by people within the local community and that it should emphasise as much as possible, news and events of the local community."[3] Local radio stations made dialogue possible between peasants and the public powers, and also among peasants themselves. Some of the African countries are reaping the fruits of the rural radio stations. Here are few examples of local radios in some African countries.

Benin Republic: Radio Clubs: Objectives:

i). To sensitise "popular masses".
ii).To create, using widespread and carefully planned dissemination of information, conditions favouring progressive transformation of Benin society through social and economic development.

---

[3] Robert .A. White, *Community Radio as An Alternative to Traditional Broadcasting*, in *Media Development*, 30(3), London 1983 p.4.

iii). To find the means for an ongoing educational and mobilisation of the population in close collaboration with the state and political organisations.

Mali: Kayes Rural Radio. Objectives:

i). To promote the active participation of the population in the establishment and maintenance of local infrastructure.
ii). To transmit the knowledge necessary for the management of programs working toward nutritional self-sufficiency and the improvement of the local standard of living.
iii). To broadcast rural development experiences at the local level.

Burkina Faso: Local Radio in Burkina Faso: Objectives:

i). To inform, train and entertain in view of a true participation of the people in development.
ii). To help the people to participate in the creation and production of local development projects, and social life.
iii). To use local languages to create an atmosphere, which facilitates constructive discussion.
iv). Recreate the palaver tree (a place for exchanging ideas), to ensure that local radio workers "come with new ideas on how stations should be managed, administered, and financed.

The local radio is meant to give the rural people the opportunity to know what is happening within and outside their environment. For instance, a problem facing people in a village in India might happen to be a similar problem facing people in a village in Nigeria. If one group manages to solve the problem, then with an effective information flow, the other group can copy solutions to solve similar problems. Moreover, information brings awareness of new things, which happen in other places, and thus enables people to change for better in their way of living. News and information are not only important at the international level but also within national and regional boundaries. According to Macbride Sean the greatest challenge facing the third world communicators is to try alternative media that take root in the rural communities given that "communication is a sine qua non for all economic, social, and cultural activities between groups, peoples and nations".[4] Macbride Sean has made a very important remark, and I am therefore of the view that, it is time to heed this advise and find an alternative or local broadcasting station for the people of Enugu State.

1.3. FEATURES OF COMMUNITY RADIO.

1.3.1. Active Participation.

Ranking foremost among the features of community or local radio is the *active participation* of the people. It is a known fact, says Ansah P.V., that:
"The nearer a radio station is to the people, the easier it finds it to put out programmes that reflect the concern of the people in the area. With the establishment of private radio stations, community stations can spring up to serve the needs of the surrounding community and it can be used as an instrument for reinforcing social cohesion and harmony and promoting socio-economic development. Programming will take into consideration the basic needs of the people and deal with matters that are relevant to their concerns. Church organisations, Non-Governmental Organisations (NGOs), and other interest groups to promote or advocate specific causes for the general local interest can run such stations".[5]
The "active participation" as practised in African traditional society is something worth incorporating into community radio system of communication. In traditional society, people are called for a meeting by the town crier in the village square to deliberate upon issues of community interest. Each point is debated before a consensus is reached. It is then that the final decision is taken. Due to its nature, says Melkote, a lot should be borrowed from traditional media because: "The newer concepts of development such as grassroots participation, and two-way communication led to a re-examination of the

---

[4] Macbride Sean; Many Voices One World, Paris 1980, p.39.
[5] Ansah P.V., *Privatization of Radio – Implications and Challenges* in Karikari Kwame (ed.) Independent Broadcasting in Ghana, Ghana 1994, p.26.

advantages of the traditional media as vehicles for information, persuasion, and entertainment of the rural masses. Clearly, the folk media have several advantages: they are part of the rural social structure and, hence, credible sources of information to the people. They have proved useful in generating grassroots participation and a dialogue between the performers and the audience. Many of the folk media formats are flexible, thus facilitating the incorporation of development-oriented messages in their themes".[6]

There should be a steady access of this media to the local people. In rural Africa, no development communication strategy is likely to have a good chance of success unless it truly takes into account the basic principles that underline the system of traditional communication namely – the supremacy of the community, the utility of the individual and the sanctity of authority. This is the most distinguishing characteristic of community radio. This type of features is lacking in commercial stations. McQuail D, in his book *Towards A Sociology of Mass Communication*, identifies five means of democratic participation in local media:

"Individual citizens and minority groups have rights of access to the media (Right to Communicate) and rights to be served by the mass media according to their own determination of needs;

The organisation and content of the media should not be subject to centralised political or state bureaucratic control.

The media should exist primarily for their audiences and not for media organisations and professionals or for the clients of the media.

Groups, organisations and local communities should have their own media of mass communication; and

Small-scale, interactive and participative media forms are better than larger-scale, one-way, professional media."[7]

Macbride Sean, gave his own résumé of the features of community communication. This is on the basis that communication is considered in its broadest sense. The main functions of communication in any social system may therefore be identified as the following:

Information: the collection, storage, processing and dissemination of news, data, pictures, facts and messages, opinions and comments re-

[6] Melkote Srinivas; Communication for Development in the Third World. Theory and Practice from 1950's to 1990's, London 1991, p.226.

[7] McQuail D., Towards A Sociology of Mass Communication, London 1983, p.96.

quired in order to understand and react knowledgeably to personal, environmental, national and international conditions, as well as to be in a position to take appropriate decisions.

Socialisation: the provision of a common fund of knowledge which enables people to operate as effective members of the society in which they live and which fosters social cohesion and awareness thereby permitting active involvement in public life.

Motivation: the promotion of the immediate and ultimate aims of each society, and the stimulation of personal choices, and aspirations; the fostering of individual or community activities, geared to the pursuit of agreed aims.

Debate and Discussion: the provision and exchange of facts needed to facilitate agreement or to clarify differing viewpoints on public issues; the supply of relevant evidence needed to foster greater popular interest and involvement in all local, national and international matters of common concern.

Education: the transmission of knowledge so as to foster intellectual development, the formation of character and the acquisition of skills and capacities at all stages of life.

Cultural promotion: the dissemination of cultural and artistic products for the purpose of preserving the heritage of the past; the development of culture by widening the individual's horizons, awakening his imagination and stimulating his aesthetic needs and creativity.

Entertainment: the diffusion, through signs, symbols, sounds and images, of drama, dance, art, literature, music, comedy, sports, games etc. for personal and collective recreation and enjoyment.

Integration: the provision to all persons, groups and nations of access to the variety of messages that they need in order to know and understand each other and to appreciate others' living conditions, viewpoints and aspirations.

Self-reliance, cultural identity, freedom of speech, respect for human dignity, and participation in the reshaping of the environment are also other features of community radio. [8] Other features of community radio station include the following:

---

[8] Macbride Sean; op.cit. p.14.

1.3.2. Informal Education.

Boeren defines education as a notion that includes all "situations in which people learn, with or without a teacher. He goes further to write, "It includes education at school and out of school. What people learn from parents, peers and through experience. Through education, people are stimulated to learn the knowledge, skills, values and attitudes which they need in order to be successful in life, and ideally, education develops curiosity and an eagerness to learn in such a way that people will continue to learn through out their lives."[9] Education indeed plays a very important role in the transition and development process. Paulo Freire in his book, *Education: The Practice of Freedom,* speaks of education that places a great deal of importance on: "Stimulating students to become a creative influence in their environment rather than simply learning formulae in the conventional way. To him, the first condition for becoming creative is for individuals to reflect upon their situation and to become aware of themselves as distinct from environment. It is better for individuals to become conscious of their unique contribution to history, which is being made around them".[10]

The way this education is imparted should be diversified and the part played by educators is indispensable to the whole process. The education needed is one, which would lead people to take a new stance towards their problems, one oriented towards research and not to repetition of irrelevant principles. Education should offer opportunities for the analysis and debate of problems, or for genuine participation. The use of radio as a dialogical medium both in formal and non-formal education, for instance in adult literacy, will in a way guarantee greater access to the rural sector. The end results of such informal education through community radio, according to P. Christensen are:

"It will enhance the quality of teaching and learning, particularly in primary schools where classroom teaching is adversely affected by lack of textbook and other teaching materials.

---

[9] Andrew Bowren; *The Cultural Dimension of Communication for Development,* Hague 1974, p.207.
[10] Paulo Freire; *Education: The Practice of Freedom,* London 1967, p.27.

It will help students in open secondary classes; compete favourably with regular secondary schools for places at the senior secondary level.

It will provide correspondence students with extra, useful information to supplement printed lectures and information regarding their studies.

It will provide teachers with up-to-date information on teaching of subjects such as science, information on curriculum development and on the teaching profession in general."[11]

People strongly believe that access to and control of community radio will help to reduce this number of adult illiteracy in the country, of which women contribute greater percentage. "The introduction of community broadcasting will help the women who are in the minority of users of media in Africa. The education of the women through community radio is very important because, they are great contributors to any development process. It is mainly men who often discuss matters that affect them. In Latin America, Africa, Asia and North America, men have always dominated the radio medium. Owing to this domination, women are relegated to the background in the use of radio medium. In a workshop of popular promoters of communication, some women argued that they are often absent in radio speech. It is not easy for women to participate in radio, not only because of lack of familiarity with the radio profession, but because men have made women believe that the word of a woman is not valuable, that only the educated, the cultured men can speak. Women further lamented that some people take advantage of their passive attitudes and, without consulting them, speak for them".[12]

Community radio can help to break such barriers. It can help people identify the type of changes they wish, and what type of education that suits them. It can also help train people in particular skills and provide specific knowledge. It is not only women who can be beneficiaries of community educational broadcasting. Broadcasting such as daily or weekly radio programs aimed towards specific target groups such as farmers. Such courses through the community media are known as

---

[11] Christensen Philip; African Conference on Radio Education Harare, Ministry of Education and Culture, London 1990, p.123.

[12] Marita Mata; Pillar Radio, Women in Grassroots Communication. London, 1994, p.295f.

non-formal education. This type of non-formal education especially for adults can be referred to as: "Any organised educational activity outside the established formal education system, whether operating separately and independently or with government involvement and support. The courses offered are varied; they are short, practical, and part time, often with no rigid entry requirements and many are non-certificates oriented".[13]

Anthony Bates believes that "there are so many advantages of this type of non-formal education through broadcasting, which can also, "motivate people for social action, community development and to raise their political consciousness. The intention here is to help people to make the best of their situation or to improve their condition within the existing social and political framework"[14] This non-formal education should help to combat some of the unfortunate side-effects of development, such as the drift to the towns and the impoverishment of rural life. Up to now in many Nigerian villages, no amount of media programming that have painted the true picture of urban life seems to dissuaded the youth from moving to the cities in search of greener pasture. This means that community radio should be able to educate the youth to overcome passivity and hopelessness in the rural areas.

1.3.3. Promotion of Social Change.

When one looks at a country like Nigeria, just like many other countries in Africa, one sees the need for a change in the life of the people and especially of those living in rural areas. It is surprising that most Nigerians living in rural areas are content with their environment and see no need for change. This is for the simple reason that they are afraid of what change will bring. Development and change for better living should not mean for them feeding well in their communities. This is almost the same in the whole of African society. However, there is no life that does not require social change. Rocker a sociologist, distinguishes factors embedded in the notion of social change:

---

[13] Naran Kala K., African Conference on Radio Education, Ministry of Education and Culture, Harare -Zimbabwe 1990, p.23.
[14] Bates Anthony; Broadcasting in Education: An Evaluation, London 1989, p.71f.

"Social change affects the way of life, attitudes and beliefs of a whole community, or a major part of it.

Social change is a change in the structure and organisation of a community, so that it is possible to indicate the chain of change.

Social change occurs over time. This most obvious point implies that we observe change in relation to conditions in the past.

Social change does not refer to any temporary change that occurs in a community. The change involved must be lasting."[15]

According to Bloom and Ottong, social change "does not come only by improving the quality of life. It should be accompanied by changes in economy, politics and social infrastructures: roads; schools; power in leadership; and communication and information flow. Through participation in decision making, rural people are able to break the power structures that prevent them from free thinking and process in learning and knowing more about the world they live in."[16] Social welfare services embrace so many things which include: good water, free education, provision of good roads, electricity, public parks, peace and stability, decent housing, employment opportunities or unemployment benefits, etc, all measures designed to mitigate inequalities by assuring everyone access to basic necessities of life.

It is not only the government that should provide the social amenities, but that individuals should be encouraged through community radio to help in establishing social services as well. Where such schemes had succeeded, they tend to foster community identity and development ideology. Self-help schemes have played large part and will continue to provide amenities, which the government is unable to provide as quickly as they are needed. Community radio is one of the most effective means of making rural people see the need of positive social change. This results in a change in attitude towards policies even at the national level. With social change, people become more aware in political, economic and cultural life.

---

[15] Rocher G., Changing Africa: An Introduction to Sociology, London 1992, p. 236f.
[16] Bloom and Ottong; Changing African: An Introduction to Sociology, London 1992, p.241.

1.3.4. Promotion of Culture.

Promotion of culture is other areas where the community radio can bring about change, include culture and industry. Radio, to be interesting must be sensitive to the culture in which it is built. Culture lies at the basis of a people's existence, and must therefore be at centre of their everyday activities. It follows the rhythms of life. "Radio articulates the culture of the people, their stories, their music, their holidays and so forth. Radio is part of every important event: elections, disasters, problems; it carries the human dimension of life. It is an extension of ourselves. And finally, radio in a sense creates public events by making them public; it creates culture by articulating it".[17]

Educating the masses on the importance of culture is very necessary. Nigeria is richly endowed with beautiful cultural heritage. The community media can do the much-needed job of identifying some of these rich cultural heritages, and popularising them in the rural areas, and motivating the people to make full use of them. Through this coverage, the community radio will set the cultural agenda for the people by convincing them to take pride in their cultural values. This can enhance the chances of the indigenous culture to contribute to the enrichment of the people. The absence of this rural media, says Kwame Karikari, has continued to have a devastating effect on the development of local artistic and cultural creativity. He asks: "How would musicians improve their art? Who would know them – their recordings – beyond the confines of a local palm-wine or beer bar, or at best the homes of the few who can own record or audio cassette players? The storytellers, folksingers, dramatists, comedians – indeed generations of performing artists – are threatened with a silent death where no mass (rural) media exist to enhance their creativity".[18] Community radio is the backbone for the survival of local culture.

---

[17] White Robert A., Radio to Support Rural Organisation: Conditions for Success, Unpublished Lecture, Gregorian University Rome 1995, p.12.
[18] Kwame Karikari (ed.); Independent Broadcasting in Ghana: Implications and Challenges, Legon-Ghana 1994, p.4.

1.3.5. Promotion of Health Education.

In many countries especially in the developing ones, communicating broadcasting has been known to play an important role in health matters. The use of the radio for communicating health-care practices to rural communities is seen as justified because radio is the only medium of mass communication with which the rural communities are familiar. In comparison to other mass media, the radio is the most accessible in time and space. It is better used for the wide dissemination of information on such an important subject as health, which touches on the very existence, and survival of rural inhabitants. Health messages should cover such areas as:
"Immunisation,
Child nutrition,
Child care,
Nutrition during pregnancy,
General nutrition,
General cleanliness,
The management of infant diarrhoea."
Community broadcasting should provide a means for the solution of more serious problems of life. Consequently, radio personnel should develop methods of communicating with their audience on issues for urgent or general attention. For instance, when an epidemic of a disease breaks out, it may be necessary to alert everybody on how the disease spreads, what the possible preventive means are available, how to recognise the symptoms, what action to take if one catches the disease, and any other questions that can either originate in-house or come from the audience should also be given attention. There is no other media that can do this dissemination better as the community broadcasting.

The station can instruct one of its personnel or another medical expert to carry out research on such illness and means of preventing it. At least each week one of them could present a brief program, dramatising how one could prevent oneself from such diseases. Such programmes could arouse the interest of many people. However, individual's decision to continue to listen to such health messages, once it has captured his/her attention, will depend on his/her interest in the content of the information it carries. A community broadcasting station can answer common questions that arise in discussion in local communities. In general, the more a broadcast deals with specific questions that concern the audience, the more the audience will be satisfied by the broadcasting station.

1.3.6. Promotion of Traditional Health Education.

In traditional or rural societies, religion, medicine and social thought are blended together. People have the belief that spirits reside in animate and inanimate objects. The health or illnesses of people are at times attributed to these spirits. The sick person is generally believed to be the victim of some transcendental forces that exercise social sanctions. In order to diagnose the cause of illness, the traditional medicine man –the native doctor- quietly finds out from the patient whether or not he/she remembers having broken any taboos or had committed any offences against other people, or whether a member of his or her family had committed any offence. This is because; physical illness is believed to be caused by the offended spirits who have been provoked by human violation of some social norms and taboos. Thus the origins of disease are attributed not to natural causes, but to human actions, that is, human manipulation of an evil spirit or supernatural forces. Sickness is a punishment from an evil spirit for violation of a taboo or of taboos. Treatment of the disease is through dealing with the evil spirit either by propitiation or by casting it out. The best way to deal with such beliefs is, first to recognise and appreciate them. The next step is to use the community broadcasting to educate the people to be less superstitious. For instance Robert White says that; "there is one community radio station in Nicaragua, which did a survey on the use of traditional medicines in the region and then had these verified as useful by the traditional doctors. At least each week one of the traditional, inexpensive preventive health methods was presented in terms of a brief dramatisation depicting a traditional community herbalist, who received at his door a community resident who describes to him the symptoms associated with the respective sickness. The symptoms were carefully explained and confirmed by the herbalist who could then provide additional information".[19]

---

[19] Robert White; op.cit. p.11.

Andrew Moemeka also supported this idea of inviting the traditional healers into the studio to talk to the people. He says that: "these traditional healers or native doctors are physicians and therapists, as well as social norms protectors. They can be called upon to enlighten the people. They are not only concerned with the health of the individual but also with the welfare of the entire community. The native doctor is also a sociologist who knows what principles of human interaction protect the welfare of the entire society, as well as a physician with knowledge and skills in curing illness".[20]

Another important aspect is the health of the children. It is always said; "A healthy child is the wealth of a nation." The health-care of children should be given precedence. Immunisation of children, Child nutrition and Child-care are issues on which the people should be enlightened. Promotion of oral dehydration therapy among mothers should be encouraged. Dehydration caused by diarrhoea infections is by far the biggest single cause of child morality in the world. It is estimated that many children die of this disease yearly. The enlightenment and propaganda on these and related issues are some of the important functions that community radio can help to fulfil. The local ministry of health and community broadcasting station should undertake relevant researches and also promote oral dehydration therapy. The major educational objectives of this campaign should be:

i). "To train mothers to identify the signs of dehydration such as sunken eyes, loss of weight, dry skin, etc.

ii). To enable mothers to correctly mix a single sugar and salt solution.

iii). To train mothers to know when and how to administer the solution correctly, emphasising that they must breast feed their children and give them solid foods made from locally available ingredients.

iv). To enable mothers to regularly clean up faeces from the grounds of the family compound and dispose of them properly in a latrine.

v). To encourage the prevention of diarrhoea through cleaning of wells and washing of hands with soap and water.

vi). To encourage personal hygiene and environmental cleanliness. Such programmes should draw attention to the problems of waste disposal by urging the villagers to develop hygienic and systematic attitude towards waste disposal.

---

[20] Moemeka Andrew; op.cit. p.54.

Slogans should be developed in this line: For instance drumming such messages – *Relatives and friends, this message is for you. "A healthy child brings peace of mind to a parent"*. Other programme formats to be used are short dialogues, stories, interviews with mothers which should be used as testimonies; poems; questions and answers using a health authority expert; quizzes; straight talks, drama; musical compositions by local artistes using local musical instruments; and demonstrations in the villages square where possible. The whole community should be involved at all levels – these should include religious leaders, village leaders, mothers, fathers, grandmothers and health personnel and traditional birth attendants.

Community broadcasting should also cover such areas as nutrition, the use of locally available foodstuffs, and family planning. Other areas to be looked into include methods of food preservation, breast feeding, essential first aid skills, good water supply and water treatment, women's rights and privileges, juvenile delinquency, income generating activities, etc. The format for such programmes should include interviews, talks, and letters from listeners, serialised discussions, drama, sports and advertising jungles. The service of all agencies engaged in such area of development programmes in the rural areas should be utilised.

The rural people should be made to be aware of such communicable diseases like dysentery, measles, small pox, typhoid fever and diarrhoea. A primary strategy for prevention of these diseases by modern methods is to be encouraged. This will break the chain of transmission by preventing the carrier from reaching and infecting a new host. Sanitation and immunisation, which are the first and commonest steps in reducing the danger of contact and the spread of such diseases, are to be emphasised. The success of such non-formal educational activities geared towards knowledge and utilisation of modern medical practice must take the socio-cultural environment of the rural communities into account.

1.3.7. Promotion of Religious Tolerance.

Nigeria is not only known as the most populous country in Africa but also as the most multi-linguistic, multi-cultural and multi-religious country. In it are different denominations of Christianity and Islam. There are also the traditional religionists. The existing media houses have not properly addressed the issue of religious conflict among the people. Many people believe that with the establishment of community radio, opportunity will be given to various religious denominations or sects to enlighten the public on their activities and tenets. It will be also an open forum for religious dialogue between members of various denominations. Prominent leaders of these religious denomination or sects should be invited often to the studio for dialogue and exchange of ideas. When their fanatic members hear such program, they will come to believe that religion is not a do or die affair. Community radio will play a serious role in promoting ecumenical spirit especially in Enugu state with multi-cultural and multi-religious dimensions.

1.4. METHODOLOGY

This research work is unique in itself. Due to its uniqueness, this research will use empirical, descriptive and historical dimensional approach. This research deals with a critical analysis of the social, political and administrative structures of the traditional Igbo society. This is necessary so as to understand their way of life and how they communicate with one another.

Further, the research examines the various means of communication in the traditional Igbo society. Prominent among these media include "*Ikoro*", "*Ekwe*", and "*Ogene*", instruments. There were also some agents of communication used in traditional Igbo society. They include "*Town crier*, and "*Village orator*". They were highly proficient in the art of communication. They knew what was interesting to their audience and had the gift of exciting and sustaining the attention of their hearers. They could be seen as the prototypes of the modern newscaster. News circulated with great rapidity through their media to different parts of Igbo villages. They were the principal means of communication and information.

Again this work reviews the coming of the Europeans in southeastern Nigeria. Their arrival brought about the need for new means and method of communication. A common vehicle of communication was needed to bridge the communication gap between the indigenous people and the *"whiteman"*. The *"whiteman"* on arrival in Igboland could not communicate with the people because of language barrier. What means or agents did the Whiteman employ in order to communication? The desire to learn about the local people whom he had come to live and work with, made the whiteman to employ other means of communication quite different from the traditional ones.

Again the research looks into the communication media after Nigerian independence in October 1, 1960. What happens when the whiteman left?

He set-up certain infrastructures of communication like radio station, which he used as a propaganda machine. What happened to these radio stations after the country's independence? Obviously the indigenous people took over the control and management of these infrastructures. How did the various governments (civilian and military) managed these media left behind by the whiteman. Did they use them for their own selfish end and for propaganda purposes like the whiteman? Broadcasting, they claimed was very useful. Was it useful to all or only to the government? These are matters to be considered in this research work.

The research suggests an alternative to government owned broadcasting media. Indeed, for genuine and proper development to take place in any society and especially in Enugu state, "community radio" becomes then a sine qua non. This medium should be the people's parliament, where the voice of the people could be heard. For it to bring about development, it has to explain issues properly and in the context in which they can be understood by the people. People can be involved in development through active participation. This can be done through community radio station.

Further the research takes cognisance of the problems the community radio might face. These ranges from closure of such private broadcasting media by the military government, press control in Nigeria, multilingualism in the society to ethnic conflict and unavailability of electricity. Things being equal, community radio should be the best thing that will happen in Enugu state where there are only two radio stations, each belonging to Federal and State governments respectively.

This work ends by concluding that there exist certain continuity and similarity between traditional Igbo system of public communication and the modern means of communication. Each should complement the other. For effective communication in our society today, the two systems should be harmonised. Each needs the other.

This research (work) is indeed a "pilot-project" as regard the area of "community radio" in Nigeria general and with special reference to Enugu state. Empirical method is applied in this research. The data collected are analysed and evaluated from different perspective. This gives a vivid situation of radio broadcasting in Nigeria and in Enugu state in particular.

Due to the importance attached to the empirical data of this research work, the researcher visited Nigeria twice for data collection. He was in Nigeria from February - March 1996 and again in March – May 2000. During these periods, the researcher conducted interviews and distributed questionnaires to the people to ascertain their opinion as regards to radio broadcasting in Nigeria.

The questionnaires are very important to this research. The answers given by the people can be said to be the mirror/mind of the society as regard radio broadcasting in Nigeria and the necessity of community radio in Enugu state. It was indeed a qualitative Questionnaires and interviews. The analysis and end result of the analysis of the questionnaire forms major part of this work.

The questionnaire is divided into two parts. The first part "Questions 1-9" deals with personal data like age, family status and ones profession while the second part of the "Questions 10-44" deals with such issues as: Have governmental media live up to peoples expectations? Should government continue to monopolise broadcasting media in Nigeria? What actually is community radio? Should community radio be set up in Enugu state? What should be the contents of such broadcasting medium? The questionnaire is meant for all different age groups. Truly opinions of these age groups will surely differ from one another. People were categorised in the following groups:

Grouping	Age in Years	Questionnaire Returned	Questionnaire Returned in Percentage.
I	18 – 30	405	40.18 %
II	31 -50	297	29.46%
III	51 and above	306	30.36%

In all one, thousand, two hundred (**1200**) questionnaires were distributed. One thousand and eight (**1008**) people responded by way of returning their filled questionnaires. This means that 84% of the people responded while **192** people, representing 16% did not return their questionnaires. Nevertheless, despite the fact that 16% did not return their questionnaires, the number that responded are quite sufficient for this study. It is generally hoped that this study will not be adversely affected. This empirical method is an attempt in building up a unity between theory and practice. See the questionnaire in Appendix I of this research.

Like every research study, the next method that will be intensively used is data collecting through library research. This method of data collection through library research took the researcher to many libraries. These include: Catholic Media Council (CAMECO) in Aachen/Germany, Deutsche Bibliothek in Frankfurt, School of Oriental and African Studies library (SOAS) University of London, World Association for Christian Communication (WACC) in London, Catholic Institute for Development Justice and Peace (CIDJAP) Enugu/Nigeria, Media Service Centre: Training Department Kaduna/Nigeria.

Some of the radio stations visited by the researcher include: Federal Radio Cooperation of Nigeria (FRCN) Enugu/Nigeria, Enugu Broadcasting Service (EBS), Radio Vatican in Rome and Domradio in Cologne/Germany. Apart from the above-mentioned source of information, there are other historical secondary documents: periodicals, newspapers, and magazines.

With the help of these documents, it became possible to apply concepts and theories of various broadcasting media in comparison to the area of research (Enugu State). This type of application gives this study a conceptual framework and general theoretical orientation.

1.4.1. Limitation of this Research Work.

There were obstacles and limitations encountered by the researcher during the period of this research. "Limitation" however here has nothing to do with the limiting of the area of research, but the constraints, obstacles and difficulties encountered during this research. In this regard, the researcher has to acknowledge that the greatest constraint in this study is the excessive scarcity and dearth of literature and previous studies on the theme of this work. There have been no official documents or books that have made attempt to study the possibility of establishing community radio in Enugu state. This is indeed the first of its kind.

Another limitation encountered during the research is the deplorable problems of data collecting in Nigeria. Apart from the regular interviews conducted by the researcher and the questionnaire filled by the people, the researcher regrets the non-availability of documented materials and information in Nigeria. This non-availability of materials is already a known problem among the Nigerian academicians. Alex C.K. Nnwere once expressed this problem when asserts: "One would not obviously escape either laughing or sighing for this country [Nigeria] when one reflects on the way records are kept and information processed and disseminated. Some of the records where they are available are grossly falsified, mutilated or unreliable. But more often than not the records are not available. Sad to say most data on Nigeria are those kept by foreign agencies".[21]

This research been the first of its kind will serve as an insight into the real nature of radio broadcasting in a developing country like Nigeria. It will also going to give a new light of aid to further research works in Nigerian in the area of community radio.

---

[21] Nigerian Statesman, Wednesday November 16, 1983, p.3.

2. AREA OF RESEARCH AND THE PEOPLE.

2.1. Brief Socio-Cultural and Historical Background of the Igbos of Nigeria.

For one to appreciate and understand the communication media (traditional and modern) in Igbo society, an exposé of the socio-cultural and historical background of the Igbos is necessary. The Igbos with the Hausas and Yorubas, number amongst the three major ethnic groups in Nigeria. It is estimated that nearly 10 million or more Igbo-speaking people live in South Eastern Nigeria. Mainly found on the left bank of the Niger, they stretch to the Delta, where some of them have filtered through the flat belt of tropical forest and into the rolling orchard bush country that lies North of it. Their most striking characteristic is what has aptly been called their social fragmentation.

For many centuries before the Europeans arrived, the Igbos had settled in their present home. According to historians, the Igbos started emerging as a distinct people between 3,000 and 5,000 years ago. One of the perennial problems encountered in tracing the history of Igbo people is the absence of written documents by the early settlers which gives room for many versions of information. There was lack of interest among the early writers and researchers to study the origin of Igbo people. In this respect, E. Afigbo pointed out that: "Far behind research into Yoruba or Edo culture history. .. Of all African ethnic scholarly research, Igbo cultural history has lagged nationalities, of about their numerical size and general dynamism, the Igbo are the least studied, the people we know the least about their main landmarks and their cultural evolution".[22]

Virtually every researcher who has worked among them admits that the Igbo people attach much importance to their traditions of origin. Elizabeth Isichei noted in her book: "No historical quest arouses more interest among the present day Igbos than the enquiry, "where did the Igbo come from".[23]

---

[22] Afigbo A.E; Ropes of Sand, Ibadan 1981, p.2.
[23] Elizabeth Isichie; A History of Igbo People, London 1976, p.3.

She also confirmed the difficulty in researching into the Igbo history: "It is like gazing at the bottom of a deep gorge from the top of a high mountain, the objects seen are veritable, but their true nature is blurred by distance."[24] For Ottenberg Simon: "The question "who are the Ibos"? is one to which a satisfactory answer has not yet be found, mainly because no definitive study of Ibo history exists. Some anthropologists who have worked among the Ibo groups believe that there are distinguishing characteristics of Iboness. Others believe that the Ibo nationality can only be based on language. It has been suggested that this apparent uncertainty is due to the considerable variations existing in Ibo culture".[25]

An interesting persistent belief among many writers is that the Igbos are related originally in some way to the Semitic world. This belief in the Semitic origin of the Igbos is held not only by non-Igbo writers but also by the Igbos themselves. Instances are cited of similarities of origin and culture between the Jews and the Igbo. Olaudah Equiano (1789), an Igbo ex-slave also the first Igbo historian and ethnologist, was the first to pose the question of the origin of the Igbo people. In answer to this question, he appeals to the old Testament in which he: "Compared cultural similarities between the Jews and Igbos, especially in areas of circumcision, confinement of woman after birth and purification rite thereafter ... and draws the conclusion that the Igbos are one of the lost tribes of Israel".[26]

Basden G.T, also adds his voice to this hypothesis of the Jewish descent: "By giving reference to marriage customs, observance of new moon and attitude towards landed property... and above all the similarity between idea of "ofo-na-ogu" to the Jewish "Lex Talionis" as contained in the Torah".[27]

Whatever may be the truth about the origin of the Igbo people, one thing is indisputable; that they settled on the bank of the River Niger. How far then did the Igbo people try to organise themselves into a community, an ethnic group and a nation?

---

[24] ibid., p.3.
[25] Simon Ottenberg; "Ibo Oracles and Intergroup Relations" in South -Western Journal of Anthropology vol XIV, 3, London 1958, p.295.
[26] Afigbo A.E; Towards A History of the Igbo Speaking People, In Igbo Language and Culture, Ibadan 1982, p.13f
[27] Basden G.T; Niger Ibos, London 1966, p.411f

2.1.1. The Igbo People as a Community, Tribe and as a Nation.

From the beginning, the Igbos lived in small village communities, often described as village "democracies". These political units were also known as the "village-group" consisting of lineage segments bound together by the belief in the common descendant of one ancestor. They had a corporate unity derived from a single lineage genealogy. The most crucial questions in all these are obviously the solidarity of the group as a political unit and the formulation of rules and standards of social behaviour. These make them a community.

Is the Igbos a community? Yes, a community could be described as a special kind of group of individuals, intimately bound together by specific ends and natural forces. Webster's Third New International Dictionary sees a community as: "A body of individuals organised into a unit. People living in a particular place or region and usually linked by common interests. An interacting population of different kinds of individuals constituting a society or an association or simply an aggregation of mutually related individuals in a given location. A group sharing a particular economic or political or social belief and living communally".[28]

As a community, the Igbo people are bound together by series of factors. These binding factors basically include, blood affinity, permanent geographical residence in a place where the ancestors too had lived, having a common traditional religion, belonging to the same clan, and having a sense of common belonging, identification within the kindred group or village, and an awareness of solidarity and interdependence. Based on the above parameters, one can say that the Igbo people are indeed a living, dynamic and organised community.
In the words of R. Emerson: "The Igbo communities constitute one major ethnic and linguistic group; nevertheless they differ by modifications in culture, social orientation and thinking. This diversity may be minor but it is still strong enough to affect the political life of the people".[29]

---

[28] Wester's Third New International Dictionary of the English Language, (1768), vol. 1A-G, Encyclopaedia Britannica, Inc., Chicago, Merriam Co. Publishers, 1981, p.460.
[29] Emerson R., From Empire to Nation, Cambridge 1982, p.102.

Many writers have described the Igbo society not only as a community but also as a tribe and a nation. Toeing this line, Goulb and Kolb defined a tribe as: "A system of social organisation which includes several local groups – villages, districts, or lineages and normally includes a common territory, and a common language and a common culture."[30] Meek C.K is of the opinion that the Igbo people are a veritable tribe because: "They speak a common language, occupy a common territory and on the whole share a common culture and a common outlook of life."[31]

However, not all the scholars see the Igbo people as a tribe. For instance, Starling Anyanwu disagrees with Meek on the description of the Igbo society as a tribe and suggested instead the term "nation". He writes: "If a compendious term is required, then nation is at least as descriptive as and certainly less reprehensible than tribe".[32]

It must be noted however, that some confusion may result from the application of, "nation" to Igboland, since "nation" is also applicable to Nigeria as a whole. Whatever may be the case, the Igbo socio-political system is today a very complex one when compared with what obtained centuries ago. For a better understanding of the communication media that exist in the traditional Igbo society, one should be acquainted also with the administrative system of this people.

2.2. The Political-Administrative System in Traditional Igbo Society.

Recent researches show that indigenous African societies have been basically classified as operating mainly two broad political patterns. The first group consisted of those societies with a centralised authority, having a King or Monarch or chief, with an organised and strong administrative machinery, which included judicial institutions. Among societies that belonged to this group were the vast empires and fallen kingdoms of Ghana, Songhai and Mali, Kingdom of Congo, the Zulu empire and those of Kanem and Bornu in today's Nigeria, and

---

[30] Gould and Kolb William; (ed.) A Dictionary of the Social Sciences, New York 1964, p.279.
[31] Meek C.K., Law and Authority in Nigeria Tribe, London 1950, p.1.
[32] Starlin Anyanwu , The Igbo Family Life and Cultural Change, Marburg 1976, p.57.

the kingdom's of Oyo and Benin. Foreign influence, especially from Europe in latter times, subdued these nations finally, and the central authority fell to the colonial government of France, Britain, Germany, Belgium, Spain and Portugal in the 19th and 20th centuries.

The second group of political pattern of government in traditional African society refers to societies without any centralised authority, and lacking any concentration of political power in the hands of a political, military or judicial group. These societies were not controlled by direct decrees from any central structure, except those they voted to represent them. Power belonged essentially to the people. The leaders can rightly be described as figureheads. An example of such kingless societies is the Igbo group of Nigeria and the Tallensi of Northern Ghana. The basic approach to our classification of the Igbo system hangs on some basic questions: how many are involved in its authoritative decision-making processes?

In what manner are they involved, how do they play their role? Can people share power and contest power freely? What structures take control of decision-making? This is very important in the life of any political society. The Igbo traditional and administrative machinery is very complex and difficult to understand. U. Nwala sums up the traditional administrative system of the Igbo society thus: "In Igbo traditional society, the political units (recognised for political purposes) are the family (ezi), the compound (obi); the village (obodo) and the village group or clan".[33]

The first European travellers to set foot on Igbo soil expected the type of monarchism that they had been used to in their own country, and indeed, the type they had come across in other parts of Nigeria. Nwabara S. N writes: "Clapperton and his party were impressed with the royalty they met in Badagry, where Adolee, a king honoured their visit with all the pomp and barbarous magnificence of Africa royalty and was mounted on a diminutive black horse, and accompanied by almost one hundred and fifty of his subjects who danced before and behind him".[34]

The Igbos are democrat. They consider their democratic participation from the following values:

---

[33] Uzodinma Nwala., Igbo Philosophy, Lagos 1985, p.165.
[34] Richard Lander, Records of Clapperton's Last Expedition to Africa, London 1830, p.18.

i). Respect for individual Personality
ii). Equality of all individuals
iii). Justice for all
iv). Rule by Law
v). Popular Sovereignty
vi). Popular Consultation
vii). Direct Participation

This democratic spirit is an important element in Igbo traditional political system and philosophy. According to Neal, this type of democracy denotes: "a way of life in a society in which each individual is believed to be entitled to an equality of concern as regards the chances of his participating freely in the values of that society".[35]

All these values are sustained by deep belief in the community, which treats the people well and commands their loyalty. The people respect the community and deserve her protection. In this bilateral balance the Igbo people participate fully and freely in all decisions, which affect their individual and collective lives. It has been said that the Igbo are distrustful of authority and do not look kindly to individuals who try to impose personal rule over them.

In areas with more "advanced" systems like Onitsha, Oguta, Abor, Osomari, Arochukwu, etc. the people accepted institutionalised authority as a matter of course. The republican spirit actually prevailed in areas where this separate and institutionalised authority had not emerged. In such areas the people defend their right to be part of the decision-making process. But they actually have to constitute themselves into pressure groups and traditional social forces (example, age-grades, secret societies of titled men, women organisation) in order to be effective in the general political process. The effect of this primary democracy on the more feudal formations was to limit the powers of the chief or king and make him just a constitutional monarchy. Personal decisions of the rulers are not always kindly welcomed because such decisions strike against this primordial republican spirit. Expressions like:

"Ochichi gi agafego oke" – You are becoming too authoritative and autocratic;

---

[35] Gould J. and Kolb, W.L. (eds.)., A Dictionary of the Social Sciences, London 964, p.187.

"Onye obula bu eze na be ya" – Everyone is king in his compound or chamber;

"Igbo enwe eze" – Igbos have no king portrays the spirit of democracy among the traditional Igbo society. Although the last expression says that the Igbos have no king expresses the general disposition of Igbo social and political spirit. Some areas in Igboland do have kings. Nwala suggested that in such areas: "The idea of kingship is not original with the Igbo and may have been borrowed from their neighbours of Benin, Igala, and Calabar areas. At any rate wherever we find the institution of kingship, we find that they do not enjoy and may rarely have enjoyed any personal or absolute rule. They are just presidents of communal councils and symbols of communal power and authority in the state".[36]

Given a more explicit picture of this Moemeka A. writes: "Among the Igbo of the East, Kingship as a system of government was until very recently unknown, and is in fact, regarded with some amount of suspicion at present. The Igbo by nature, are republican and regard the concentration of political and religious power in one individual as immoral. In each separate side of life, whether economic, military, supernatural or legal, there is no concentration of power in any one centre. The Igbo are very much against authoritarian rule; they demand to be involved in everything that concerns their welfare. Their regard for authority is conditioned by the willingness of the man in authority to recognise their right to participate. A leader is supported by his followers as long as he does not "govern too much". ... He holds office at the pleasure of the people and is expected to render public service to a level that is satisfactory to the people. He can be removed from office by a consensus of the people".[37]

Going further he says: "...Sovereignty of the people expressed through the assembly recognised in the state is supreme.... the presidency of the "Obi" at the council sitting is a matter of routine since the council can proceed without him as the case may be but decisions automatically bind him."[38] This means that the consensual aspect of Igbo political behaviour militates against regimentation or very secure

---

[36] Uzodinma Nwala, op. cit., p.172.
[37] Moemeka A, *Socio-Cultural Environment of Communication in Traditional Nigeria An Ethnographic Exploration*, in Communication Socialis, 16(1983) Grünewald, p.336.
[38] ibid., p.245.

self-perpetuated leadership. The Igbos follow a leader in times of risk for as long as he can carry their reasoning and conviction with him in a venture. The individual who starts off with a large following must budget all the time for desertions, which are bound to result from personal calculations subsequent to decisions made on the spur of an emergency. This means that among a democratic people decisive political status is open and contestable. Chieftaincy in such a situation has to leave the function of taking major decisions to the generality of the people and content itself with the role of a symbol of unity and harmony. Giving credibility to the political structure Anaynwu S, writes: "The Igbo belong to those societies known anthropologically as a cephalous groups. These groups constitute independent villages and have designated local heads but have neither centralised leadership nor central authority in their social organisation".[39]

Certainly, there were some political and social arrangement which gave the various heads of families, elders of the clan, priests and medicine men among others, some special duty in the affairs of the society. Commenting on the same issue Jones writes: "The traditional government of communities in the Eastern Region (of Nigeria) depended on the general will of the component segments of the groups as expressed through their representatives at a general meeting of the tribe. This does not mean that communities in the Eastern Region have no chiefs.... It means that the functions they were required to perform differed. Every local community has some person or persons whom they refer to by a term signifying head or chief".[40]

However, the pattern of political and social organisation differed from place to place. In some localities, the unit of government began with the kindred, and then moved on to the village and lastly the clan; in others the clan exercised authority, which descended to the village and the family kindred, but with varying functionaries and duties. A common denominator in Igbo political organisation at all levels, however, was consultation and consensus. Moemeka .A. confirmed this point: "In the East, ... the leader is not allowed the right to make personal decisions that would be binding on all. The Igbo are very much

---

[39] Nwbara S, Iboland: A Century of Contact with Britain 1860 – 1960, London 1977, p.22.
[40] Jones G.I, *Report of the Position, Status and influence of Chief and Traditional 'Rulers in The Easter Region of Nigeria*, Enugu 1957, p.7.

37

against authoritarian rule; they demand to be involved in everything that concerns their welfare. They abhor handed-down orders. The first taste of this abhorrence was made manifest to Europeans at Aba in 1929 when Igbo women were instigated by their husbands to riot against taxation and the imposition of warrant chiefs by Britain.... Government at the village level in the East is an exercise in direct democracy. It involves all the lineages and requires the political participation of all male adults; people are free to discuss with whom ever they want; between compounds, between quarters and between villages. The village is autonomous in its affairs and accepts no interference or dictation from the town or any other village". [41]

This means that when an issue has been exhaustively discussed, the president gathers all the points in a summary for all to endorse. However, not to be allowed to speak may mean a rejection of one's voice and all it stands for, namely one's personality and one's own existence. Everyone, no matter who he is, must be both seen and heard. People that demonstrate such a high degree of democratic consultation in policy making may be presumed to be correspondingly and essentially democratic. Groth A.J writes: "In a democratic society, then, we are concerned about the flow of appreciation, of clarification; of consultation- for these are the specifics of deference. When men and women are deferred to, they are appreciated, clarified and consulted. Whatever practices interferes with the flow of mutual respect, and arouses destructive impulses; endanger the fulfilment of a democracy". [42]

Lambert Ejiofor gives a vivid picture of what happens in the traditional Igbo assembly: "Every issue starts with a spirited debate by the members of the assembly. Everyone has a voice in decision-making. One who is unfamiliar with Igbo politics would imagine that a consensus was impossible and that discussions would finally collapse in pandemonium; for so it looks. In the end, there is order and agreement on most matters, a few being amended or dropped.... Every participant strives to express his views. It is impressive to observe the serenity with which individuals accept a defeat of their views in public meet-

---

[41] Moemeka A. op. cit., p.340
[42] Groth A.J, Comparative Politics, A Distributive Approach, London 1971, p.11.

ings. In the end every decision is made to look like a compromise; and a most partisan view assumes the cloak of a consensus".[43]

Nwala S. supports the above assertion: "Democracy whether primary or representative was the bulwark of the whole Igbo political system. Unanimity and the rigorous processes and compromises ("igba- izu"= period of consultation) that lead to it are all efforts made to contain the wishes of the majority as well as those of the minority. In short, they are designed to arrive at what may be abstractly called the 'general will of the people or community. Unanimity becomes desirable since the Igbo conceive of politics and government not as the means whereby the stronger or the many impose their will on the rest but as 'the process of regulating normal life among brothers".[44]

This differs from the type of democracy being practised in the western democracy. The governments take decisions that many citizens disapprove of, even among those that elected them. Minorities, even large ones, have little hope of having their political ideals put into practice. In the western world, the average citizen has effectively no power to alter the network of regulations that govern his life. One of the things that always struck the first Western visitors to Igboland, was the extent to which democracy was truly practised. One thing stands in the centre of all political process: decision-making. All political activity hinges on rational action and this subsumes a deliberation on facts and ideas which, lofty as they might be, are translated into programmes and projects only after the agent shall have decided to do so. Decision-making is the engine of all political life and, when followed up, it becomes the classificatory principle of all political systems. In a democratic society, regimes can be classified into authoritarian, liberal, or democratic, according to the number of those involved in the key decision-making processes and the manner in which they are again open or restricted that is the degree of readiness with which they admit those in whose interest the decisions are made.

The Igbo society remains decentralised and sturdily 'democratic' in the special African sense of the term. This 'democracy' must be emphasised. Authority is further limited by its distribution between the component groupings. There is also the distribution of authority be-

---

[43] Ejiofor Lambert, Igbo Kingdoms Power and Control, Nigeria 1982, p.51.
[44] Nwala S., op.cit, p.168.

tween coexisting leaders, senior elders, priests and titled men. The women, in their more restricted sphere, have their own organisations. By the allocation of important duties to special groups of middle-aged men and to age-grades, all members of the community, down to quite young children, have their active social responsibilities.

Search must be made for those persons and groups in Igbo traditional society who perform the governmental functions and the particular manner in which they perform them. This democratic system of government is carried through different organs.

2.3. Organs of Government in Traditional Igbo Society.

2.3.1. The Council of Elders.

The council of elders is made up of "fathers" of component family segments. The elders were fundamentally the representatives and mouthpiece of the ancestors. Their sacred staff of office, called the "ofo", symbolised the authority of the ancestors and was venerated as the embodiment of the supernatural world and all the spirits of the ancestors. Each elder possessed domestic authority because he was the intermediary between the family and the ancestors. This council was not a legislative body in the real sense of the word. The meetings of the elders were neither formal nor frequent. The elders met when it was necessary to take a common action like sacrifice or war, or to settle an internal dispute which if allowed to continue would undermine the solidarity of the community. There was no institutionalised judiciary. Judicial proceedings were informal and were aimed at restoring solidarity. Within the family group, trial was a matter of conciliation and a purification ceremony. In inter-lineage dispute, the elders met, but technically nobody was excluded from their assembly.

This is what Nwara S. means by asserting: "Power and authority belongs to all, but by the virtue of their seniority and ontological status, knowledge, moral and intellectual qualities and economic status, some individuals are known to exercise greater power and influence than the others. This was thought necessary in order to ensure an effective political system".[45]

In Igbo traditional society the elders are a standing group. They are supposed to be versed in the traditions and the laws of the land. Difficult and reserved cases are sent to them, although they are still under the authority of the entire community. Elders are believed to be closed to the divinity and as such expected to live the truth and apply it to all situations. Corruption is less tolerated in them than in any other group.

They constitute the last conscience of the community and when they collapse in their role it becomes a shocking event. Old age is trusted because, it is also identified with patience, diligence and experience. These are also the qualities of a good judge. The judgement of the elders is trusted and they deliver it with equal solemnity. The entire community may decide to over-rule their decision. In extreme situations they can be disciplined. This emphasises the supremacy of the entire population as a judicial body.

This council is the predominant political structure among the majority of Igbo towns. The Elders include the heads of the various families in the villages who hold the symbol of authority "**OFO**"[46] representing the collective will of their people in truth, justice and faith. The elder who was advanced in years, was supposed to possess wisdom and experience having spent long years on earth and being on the brink of joining the ancestors. He had to behave with integrity to command respect. The onus of organisation, jurisdiction and planning rested on the council of Elders.

The elder may be at the same time the lineage head, one who governed his family, spoke on their behalf in public, and controlled recalcitrant and issued warnings or even punishment to incorrigible members. The elder therefore had to be objective and impartial in family quarrels. The elders met often privately in their various homes. Lambert Ejiofor asserts: "They (elders) are respected for their age, integrity, and link with the past. Their legislative power is really confined to the level of invoking the traditional laws of the community and, if

---

[45] Nwala S., op. cit., p.168.

[46] "OFO", is usually the legal seal and symbol of authority. It must be present during the deliberations of the assembly and it must be used to give approval and sanction to the rules, decisions and laws. Every major decision whether of a legislative or judicial nature has to be reinforced by invoking the ancestors and the earth goddess.

necessary, reformulating them in keeping with the demands of the time. They are really there to regulate the community according to the taboos and customs of the people".[47]

At times they held general meeting on the village level; but this was an exceptional occurrence, being held only when it was necessary to take a common action against an external enemy, to offer community sacrifices to the supernatural in order to rid the village of some disaster, pest or abomination, or they met to settle internal disputes of land, marriage or affairs which could threaten the peace of the community.

In Igbo society, old age is honourable, and the old men and women are treated with dignity and respect. It is expected that nothing but words of wisdom and good counsel should come out of the lips of the aged. The aged is given a place of honour in the government of the community and their advice is generally not easily set aside or ignored. At the meeting of council of elders, one had the right to free speech or disagreement on issues raised, but once a decision was taken, he had to withdraw his private opinion, and not only conform to the decision, but also allow his entire family and kin to do likewise. Decisions were often taken on broad majority basis. Commenting on this S.N. Nwabara writes: "When a decision is to be taken after taking statements from the plaintiff and the accused, witnesses were also called and swore on the "OFO", that they would give true evidence. When the council was satisfied that it had all the facts of the case, the litigants, the witnesses and relatives were asked to leave the council while the council deliberated. The deliberation might last for an hour or more before a decision for guilt or innocence was returned".[48]

There was no voting for an elder's membership into the village council, since his status, age and membership to a family automatically qualified him to this group. An elder could not be withdrawn from the council, except through death, illness or if he committed a heinous crime, which merited for him the wrath of the judicial sanctions from the village community. The village council of elders had to send emissaries or delegates to certain groups or to foreign villages to settle matters or convey a village option when the situation called for it.

---

[47] Ejiofor Lambert, op. cit., p.149.
[48] Nwabara S.N, op. cit, p.47.

2.3.2. The Village Assembly.

The village assembly was a meeting of the male grown-ups in the entire village, which held public meetings in the market place (Afia), or in the village square (ilo), or at the premises of the village shrine (lhu ani). It cannot be understood as a parliament or a senate in our modern understanding of these ideas, even though it followed largely the pattern of democratic principles seen in the modern democratic countries of the world. This point is confirmed by Basden when he says, "Igbos are highly republican and democratic."[49] Onwubiko maintains like many other historians that: "The lgbos have intense love for personal freedom and very strong resentment for autocratic government over them. As a result, they preferred living in small village republics where every grown-up male is regarded as important as everyone else in the village".[50]

Each mature lgbo male had an inalienable right of speech at the village assembly, since his vote on any issue was necessary to effectively carry out the community decisions peacefully. Questions are asked and answered. Should all who want to speak not have their opportunity the same day, the issue may be adjourned for as often as it is necessary to hear all speakers. It is against the people's tradition to ignore a would-be speaker. The aim is general consensus; there is no formal voting. Nwabara gives a vivid picture of it all when he writes: "All laws were debated and passed by the "Oha" – the congregation of all the adults of the village. As in the ancient Greek polis, every adult participated in the deliberation. Each law and decision passed by the "Oha" was debated first in the "umu nna" assembly, which also consisted of all male adults. The laws so passed became the laws of the land- "iwu-ala" and any infringement of the law was punished accordingly".[51]

Lambert attests to this democratic spirit when he writes: "Neither the community nor the individual is an onlooker in the affairs of the people; neither is merely a recipient or a critic of the products of local politics. Individuals, groups, and the community are involved in the

---

[49] Basden G.T, Niger lbos, op. cit., p.209.
[50] Onwubiko K.B.C, A History of West Africa 1800- Present Day, Book 2, Nigeria 1976 p.78.
[51] Nwabara S.N, op.cit., p.32.

political process. Decision-making becomes a mass affair in so far as either the entire population takes the decision directly or those delegated to decide are directly responsible to the entire community. There is no anarchy. Political decisions are as much the responsibility of individual participants as they are of the collectivity".[52]

However, women were excluded from the rights of participation at the village assembly meetings, since the Igbos, a highly patriarchal people, regarded certain meetings only for men, and others for women only, depending on the nature, substance and type of gathering. In modern times, such practices of excluding women could also have certain constructive suggestions to make. In as much as a defence for such a criticism will be avoided here, suffice it to mention that in precolonial Igboland, women were very powerful in their different families, and could therefore influence their sons or husbands to think in a particular way and vote in a particular way on a certain issue in the village assembly. They were therefore indirectly participating in the decisions at meetings through their men. Besides, women had their own special meetings where men were not allowed to participate. Lastly, matters raised in the village assembly pertained sometimes, if not often, to the political order and to external affairs, while women in their own meetings discussed matters considering domestics, market affairs and internal order and cleaning. It is a type of division of labour.

The village assembly met when the town crier (announcer) summoned it. The town crier got his mandate to summon the village from either the village council of elders or from the eldest man in the village. Extraordinary events, such as war, natural calamity, a serious abomination within the community or the murder of a fellow villager necessitated an immediate "ad-hoc" meeting. At the village assembly, custom and tradition, ritual and religion, war and social or legal sanctions were often deliberated upon.

People's natural talents qualified them to certain roles within the village assembly, so that an orator would be asked to open up discussions on an issue, and a wrestler or warrior, or a diplomat or man of wisdom would be delegated depending on circumstances to represent the village. The basic spirit behind the village assembly and also the Elder-Council was to ensure that "Omenala" (customs and tradition)

---

[52] Ejiofor Lambert, op.cit., p.113.

44

was observed, laws and order were kept and that the village adhered to the wish of the ancestors, worshipped the village deities and preserved a general harmony within the community.

No single individual could impose his will on the whole village assembly. Such a move would be challenged and opposed. The people made laws for themselves directly and bound themselves to it. They also dictated punishments for breaches of the law and got young people and age grades to carry out the demands of the law on offenders. It is a fact that certain influential people played essential roles in deliberations towards a consensus at meetings. These included men with titles or relative wealth, men of honour and wisdom as a result of age or as a result of extraordinary services offered to the village in its hour of need, priests of the deity and great warriors. General consensus prevailed, and dissidents were privately approached by their colleagues to change their views in favour of general opinion in the spirit of communitarian harmony.

2.3.3. The Family.

The family is the smallest unit in the lgbo traditional society. Nwabara describes the lgbo family as normally consisting of: "the father, his wives and the children from all his wives. There is also the extended family, as above, plus the children of the man's daughters and sons, maternal and paternal uncles and their families".[53]

It is necessary to emphasise again that the father is the voice and cornerstone of the family, who absorbs all shocks and forces coming on the family from the outside. He takes direct charge of his own family and does not accept dictation or direct interference from even his own father or brothers. He is blamed squarely if any member of his family is unjustly treated or denied any rights in the community. The father becomes at alert once there are extra-family conflicts and strives to resolve them. The family household, although not in itself a political unit, was the foundation on which all more complex lgbo institutions were based.

The lgbo people developed a system whereby they lived in groups of kinship ties of extended families of varying sizes. The extended family is made up of a man and his wife or wives, their children and close

---

[53] ibid., p.24.

relations such as the uncles, nieces, aunts, cousins and other distant or near relations. Such a group of general close relationship constituted the kindred. The kindred (Umunna) might live in a compound or in adjoining compounds separated by mud walls, and they are all united through the decendancy of a common ancestor, they could form a local group (ogbe) and become the subdivision of a village. Nwala gives his own picture of Igbo family: "The most important ancient form of government is that found in a family and the family seems to be the core from which state and government in ancient and traditional communities emerge. In Igbo traditional society the political units (recognised for political purposes), are the family (ezi), the compound (obi) the village (obodo) and the village group or clan".[54]

The typical Igbo village group usually thought of itself as a lineage, and commonly supports this with a genealogical charter, which traces its origin to a single male ancestor, whose son founded the component villages and whose grandsons founded its village sections or kindred. This means that the family is the nucleus and live wire of the Igbo society where each individual belongs.

2.3.4. The Individual and the Community in Igbo Society.

Having seen the political structure and system in a traditional Igbo society, one begins to pose many questions regarding the fate of an individual in a traditional Igbo society. In Igboland, it appears that the individual has no role, no part to play and is not important, except with, and in the society. One tends to pose the question, was Igbo traditional society a totalitarian community where an individual is not really reckoned with or is of his individuality, only to become a depersonalised clog in the ever-tuning wheel of the community?

What remained of the individual's independent, autonomous action within the community? Were his personal rights guaranteed, including his freedom of speech and communication? For there to be an effective democracy, the above rights of the individual must be guaranteed. The traditional Igbo society being a democratic one, the rights, privileges and personality of the single individual were preserved. Many writers have tried in their various works to prove that there is always a cordial relationship between individual and the community in tradi-

---

[54] Nwala S, op. cit., p.165.

tional African societies. The concept of the individual and the community should never be misconstrued or compared with ideological conflicts between the East and the West, the former as "communism" emphasising the society; the latter as "capitalism" emphasising the individual and his role within the society. The English philosopher, John Stuart Mill, paints the picture of man in a society as having an absolute freedom: "The individual is not accountable to society for his actions in so far as these concern the interests of no person else but himself.... Neither one person, nor any number of persons is warranted to say to another human creature of ripe years, what he shall not do with his life, for his own benefit, what he chooses to do with it. ... Society should not interfere in the private affairs of the individual.... In all such cases, there should be perfect freedom, legal and social for the individual to do the action and stand the consequences".[55]

The above view of this English philosopher appears absurd and unattainable for an ordinary Igbo man who would pose the following question(s): "How can the conduct of a member of society be a matter of indifference to other members of a society? Is there any person who is entirely an isolated being? It was the attempt to answer such questions that Professor Mbiti comes up with the core of African philosophical perspective to the conflict, by saying, "I am because we are; and since we are, therefore I am". He goes further to say: "The individual does not and cannot exist alone except corporately. He owes his existence to other people, including those of past generations and his contemporaries. He is simply part of the whole.... only in terms of other people does the individual become conscious of his own being, his own duties, his privileges and responsibilities towards himself and towards others. When he suffers, he does not suffer alone but with his kinsmen, his neighbours and his relatives whether living or dead. When he gets married, he is not alone, neither does the wife belong to him alone. So also the children belong to the corporate body of kinsmen, even if they bear only the fathers name. Whatever happens to the group happens to the individual".[56]

Due to this intertwining of each individual with the fate of the entire community, a rupture in the normal functioning of this relationship not only endangers this shared reality, but threatens existence itself.

---

[55] Mill J.S, The Liberal Arts Press, New York 1956, p.xviii.
[56] Mbiti J.S., African Religions and Philosophy, London 1977, p.100.

Ejiofor supports this view: "In as much as the results of an action or policy are realised in the individuals so much are the individuals understood to bring themselves freely to promote the aims of the collectivity. That is, the community policy is accepted if it benefits individuals, and individuals' actions are accepted if they benefit the community".[57] He continues: "A prosperous community must benefit its individual persons, and prosperous individuals must benefit their community. One is then a prop to the other. The two may be distinct but they need not be separate."[58] Expressing the same view Greene, M. writes: "In Africa, the community takes precedence over the individual, but depends on him for its existence. The desires, wants and needs of the individual are subjugated to those of the community.... In general, if what an individual has to say is not in the interest of the community, no matter how relevant and important, it is to the individual, he would be bound by custom to "swallow his words. He may of course, whisper his complaints into the ears of those he can trust and who can help him in other ways that would not hurt the community".[59]

Membership in an Igbo community is not a matter of free choice for the individual, but is a destiny because an individual is born into a specific family, and is initiated into the structures of community while he is still a child. Greene M. M. noted this community attitude in the colonial days: "Any form of solitude is looked upon by the Igbo with mistrust, for no one could exist outside the community, just as fish could not live outside water. An attempt to extricate oneself therefore from his community was worse like death, for whereas, there was continuity and relationship between the dead and the living, being ostracised or willingly extricating oneself from the group means living without a 'locus standi' in traditional society".[60]

This means that the individual's importance in society is dependent only on the welfare of the community. He sees himself not as a slave of the community but as part and parcel of the community which he serves and whose peace good government and progress will eventually be of direct benefit to him. He has a legitimate right to say how he thinks the community should be run. When public issues are

---

[57] Ejiofor Lambert, op. cit., p.110.
[58] ibid., p.110.
[59] Green M.M., Igbo Village Affairs, London 1964, p.78.
[60] ibid., p.20.

thrown open for discussion, he is given a hearing if he wants to contribute. It is only after a decision has been taken, and given a ritual binder that the individual's views and opinions become irrelevant. Before then such views and opinions are regarded as very important. It is the synthesis of such individual views and opinions, which forms the basis of community decisions. This means that a true community gives no room for alienation of its members. This is because all members have a common feeling of central belonging, and approach their affairs without fear or anxiety. The community should therefore play the precious role of an enlarged home, and people generally strive to do something for their home. In all matters of decision-making, the entire population must be involved. Communication must be vertically and horizontally strengthened if the citizens are to maintain community integration. Basden also adds: "Under the old system, every person knew the "Head" to whom he or she was attached, and they realised their mutual allegiance and responsibility, hence, there were in past days, no homeless vagrants in lgboland, the family being responsible for the less fortunate relatives".[61]

An average European will have difficulties trying to understand this strong community consciousness among the lgbo, which however did not mean loss of individual freedom. Commenting on this Sofola asserts: "The type of community life and cohesion which exist among Africans is a source of puzzlement for non-Africans and almost all European scholars of African society noted the existence of a corporate life which contrasts sharply with the individualism of the westerner".[62]

In traditional lgbo society, there is always a concept of the individual, his rights and his role within the community. From the concept of person as a being with definite rights and duties, the lgbo built up their worldview. Here, the community accords regard and respect to the individuals, while the individuals pay homage and loyalty to the community. S. Ottenberg confirms this: "Individualism was very strong among the lgbos of Nigeria, for while a man was dependent on

---

[61] Basden, G.T., Niger lbos, op. cit., p.121.
[62] Sofola J. A., African Culture and African Personality – What Makes an African, African? Nigeria 1973, p.69.

his lineage and residential groups for support, strong emphasis were placed on his activity to make his own way in the world".[63]

This explains why the Igbos lay great emphasis on individual achievement and initiative. Everybody struggled to make an impact on the world, to show that he could do it better than the other. Farmers or traders competed among each other. One's personal effort was appraised, and not simply that of his father or other relations, for each person was considered on his own merits. On this, T.A. Dunn remarks: "A man was esteemed for himself, his achievements and his value to the community, and not for what his father was. The Igbo settled everything political by argument and discussion... and thus were regarded as highly argumentative and individualists".[64]

We now see that there was a deep interrelationship between the individual and community. Uchendu V.C adds: "Igbo individualism is not rugged individualism; it is rooted in group solidarity... There was a great emphasis on communal co-operation and achievement."[65] Going further Uchendu says: "Community spirit is very strong among the Igbo. Almost from the first, the individual is aware of his dependence on his kith and kin and community. He realised the necessity of making his contribution to the group to which he owes so much. He seldom, if ever, becomes really detached from that group, wherever he may live".[66]

Professor Obiechina adds also his voice when he says: "Of necessity, the hold, which the community has over the individual, cannot be so understood that the expression of his individuality is completely frustrated; the individual cannot be so individualistic in his outlook that he regards, his interest as entirely independent of those of the community within where he lives".[67]

This community spirit that exists between the individual and the society provides a healthy platform for inter communication among them. How and what means of communication that are available in the traditional Igbo society will be discussed in the next chapter.

---

[63] Ottenberg S., *Ibo Receptivity to Change*: in M.J. Herskovits, ed., Continuity and Change in African Cultures, Chicago 1959, p.136.
[64] Dunn T.A., Notes on Things Fall Apart (Chinua Achebe.), Essex 1981, p.13.
[65] Uchendu C.V., The Igbo of South-Eastern Nigeria, New York 1965, p.2.
[66] ibid. p.2.
[67] Obiechina N.E., *Amos Tutuola and Oral Tradition* , in Presecence Africaine No.65 , New Bilingual Edition, Paris 1956, p.95.

3. THE COMMUNICATION MEDIA IN IGBO TRADITIONAL SOCIETY.

3.1. The Communication Media in Igbo Traditional Set-Up.

Since Igbo existence as a people, they used simple forms of communication, which have been enhanced, extended, refined, and are still in use today, despite the continuous invention of new technologies and the increasing sophistication and complexity of interaction between people. This traditional form of communication and particularly interpersonal communication is vital among the people. Moreover, the majority of people in the rural areas today, comprising as much as fifty to sixty percent of the population, continues to impart and receive messages through these channels of communication. It is easy to comprehend completely the advantages and limitations of modern media if they are treated as factors separate from the interpersonal communication. Obviously, communications networks grow cumulatively, with each new form adding, to but not eclipsing the older systems. What are these organs of communication available in the traditional Igbo society?

3.2. The Traditional Broadcaster.

"Go-di-di-go-di-go. Di -go-go-di-go. It was the ekwe talking to the clan. One of the things every man learned was the language of the hollowed-out wooden instrument. Dim ! Dim ! Dim !, boomed the cannon at intervals. The first cock had not crowed, and Umuofia was still swallowed up in sleep and silence when the ekwe began to talk, and the cannon shattered the silence".[68]

Here Achebe gives a vivid description of one of the media of communication used in traditional Igbo society. He is known as the famous "Town-Crier". In early times especially before the advent of colonialisation, the "Town-Crier" also known as the "Village broad-

---

[68] Achebe Chinua, Things Fall Apart, London 1958, p.109.

caster" or "Traditional Broadcaster" enjoyed widespread popularity in various parts of Nigeria.

The Traditional broadcaster was not necessarily an executive member of the governing council described in the previous chapter; however, he maintains regular communication contacts between the ruling authorities and the rest of the community. In his role as a liaison officer, he gives the society vital information. On some occasions, he takes part in the meeting of the village assembly or council of elders but only as a partial observer, whereby he takes records of the important decisions. The message he disseminates is not his making; he gives the information in the same way he received them. This means that he acts according to the instructions given to him by the administrative circle. Even though the traditional broadcaster is called "the News caster" in the modern sense of it, he does not read his messages from script like his counterpart in the radio or television houses. He logically memorises his message and other items of information with admirable accuracy that is without undue mistakes or omissions. Resonant in voice, he could be heard even in remote corners of the village. In this case, he could reach his audience without any groups being isolated. He is a man of courage and patience because most of the time he has to cover distances, even at odd times at the risk of his life.

3.2.1. His Personality:

In most cases, the interest of the society takes precedence over his personal pursuits. He always relinquishes his personal assignment and attends to that of the society at any time he is called upon. He is always loyal and dedicated to his duty. Certain qualities and decorum are expected of him. According to Frank Ugboajah, the traditional broadcaster, as a communicator is supposed to be a person who:
i. "Knows his culture
ii. Interprets his culture to fit the objectives of his society
iii. Is not only respected and revered but perceived as authoritative and credible and the notes from his communication medium, the gong or

the drum are decoded appropriately and received attention from, from the specific audiences to whom they are addressed."[69]

According to Fearing, this means that he is supposed to be: "a person who produces and also controls the production of information, signals or sign-symbols with the intention of cognitively structuring or influencing the behavioural landscape of specifically aimed interpreters who are presumably in specific need or demand of the producer's signals or sign-symbols".[70]

In the same way, Maletzke sees a communicator as: "Any person(s) concerned with the production of public statements or information through a normative usage of conventional mass medium with either creative, selective or controlling nature."[71]

The traditional broadcaster is not a social leader in the sense of a social crusader. He is simply an informant or informer who publicises the "given order". His message has objectivity because it is always free from his opinion and partisanship. He only communicates what he is told to say. He knows his audience very well. Before examining the functions of the town crier in different communities, let us first examine the instruments with which he executes his duties.

3.2.2. His Instruments.

The silence was broken by the village crier beating his sonorous "Ogene"[72]. He called every man in Umuofia, from the Akakanma age groups upwards, to a meeting in the market place after the morning meal. He went from one end of the village to the other and walked all its breath. He did not leave out any of the main footpaths.[73] This is the general picture of the functions and main instruments of the traditional newscaster. The custom of transmitting signals and information

---

[69] Ugboajah Frank, Communication Policies in Nigeria, Paris 1980, p.50.
[70] Fearing B.F., „Towards a Psychological Theory of Human Communication" in Journal of Personality vol.22, Chicago 1953, p.72.
[71] Maletzke G., Psychologie der Massenkommunikation, Uelzen 1978, p.43.
[72] Ogene is an instrument of communication which shall be explained shortly in this work.
[73] Achebe Chinua, Things Fall Apart, London 1958, p.177.

is a common one among Igbo society of Nigeria. There are different instruments used in passing information in the society.

According to Joy Nwosu Lo-Bamijoko, these Igbo instruments of communication follow a hierarchical order which determines the place and role of each of them. This means that all instruments are not equal. Their ranks are as follows:
i). Ikolo and Ekwe (Slit drums)
ii). Igba family of instruments (membrane drums).
iii). Odu, opi and oja (wind instruments)
iv). Ngedegwu (xylophone)
v). Ogene family of instruments (gongs)
vi). Udo family of instruments and ubo-aka (strings and thumb piano)
vii). Nyo family of instruments (shakers, rattles and clappers)[74]
This ranking, she said is according to the role each instruments plays in the music and communication system of the Igbo society. They are classified as:
i). Oke (leading instruments)
ii). Nee (second leading instrument)
iii). Nwa (time keeping).[75]

In this section of the work, we are only going to discuss those instruments used by the village broadcaster in carrying out his work. The traditional broadcaster's main instruments for communication and passing on information to the villagers are:
a). The "Ikoro" and "Ekwe" known as the Slit drums.
b). The "Ogene"
c). The "Oja" which he uses on rare occasions.

The Slit Drums:

Joy Nwosu also makes a vivid description of this category of Igbo instruments when she describes them as Slit Drums. The largest of this category of instruments is the "IKORO", while "ekwe" is generally known as the smallest slit drum.

---

[74] Lo-Bamijoko Joy Nwosu , Preliminary Study of the Classification and Tuning, London 1982 , p.31.
[75] Ibid., p.31.

54

The ekwe, being a very portable instrument, enables the village broadcaster to carry it along during his transmission of the local news to the people. Unlike the Ekwe, the largest slit drum "Ikoro", is not portable. This means that these Slit drums never play or perform similar functions. These drums are not only the most common musical, but the most important instruments used in transmitting information. These instruments have been described by many scholars as rhythm-melodic instruments. It is regarded among the people as the generator of everything happening in the society. Joy Nwosu describes it as: "The pulsating force, like the heart... which gives life and meaning to music. As a melodic instrument, it is regarded among the Igbos as possessing life, but this life is not life as we know it, of the mortal ephemeral type. The drum possesses the spirit of the gods. It is supernatural. For this reason, the drum can do all that a mortal can do and even more. It can talk, it can sing, it can do all of this in the way that only the gods can, the supernatural way. As in all Igbo musical instruments used for communication, one has to be schooled to be able to understand the language of the drum".[76]

a). The "Ikoro"

Ikoro is normally very large in size. Basden T. gives us a vivid nature of Ikoro :
"An Ikoro to be 10 feet, 2 inches in length, 7 feet, 10 inches in width and 8 feet, 5 inches in height."[77] Going further he adds: "The largest slit drums are not intended to be instruments of music, rather they are used for spreading information, for ceremonial purposes and at festivals".[78]

It was on this basis that Jerome argues that: "Since the Ikoro remains fixed in the place where it is housed, we can call this building the "broadcasting house" of the community which is in a way comparable with a radio or television transmitting station of today".[79]

---

[76] Ibid., p.36
[77] Basden G.T., Among the Ibos of Nigeria, London 1966, p.137.
[78] Ibid., p.359
[79] Okonkwo Jerome, The History and Some Problems of Television Service in Anambra State in Nigeria, Frankfurt /Main 1986, p.28.

This means that the message being transmitted through the Ikoro is not only meant for those living around but also for people living very far away. Basden in his book says: "The big Tom-tom (Ikoro) are not intended to be instruments of music, rather they are used for spreading information, for ceremonial purposes, and at sacrificial festivals. Meetings are called by their use and various announcements proclaimed. The beating of an "Ikolo" can be heard up to a distance of five miles and other villages are able to pick up the message and pass it on to those dwelling in the regions beyond".[80]

Consequently Ikoro is the most awesome and the most vibrant of all the instruments of the lgbo traditional information media. One traditional broadcaster in one village in Anambra state Nigeria told me how he swore to keep secret an arrangement made with some men on how they would kill one of their neighbours. According to him, after swearing with this group not to reveal the secret, but not wanting to have anything to do with the killing, he decided to inform the condemned man about the plot of the killing. He did not know how to do this without breaking his oath of silence (secrecy). However, that evening he waited for the condemned man whom he knew always went palm wine tapping every evening at that particular hour, and as soon as he saw him climbing the palm tree, he started sending him messages with the "Ikoro", telling him about the plan to kill him that night, and advising him to leave the town, immediately. He warned him not to even try to get home to say goodbye to his family because the killers were already spreading out a dragnet for him, and gave him directions on how to elude his pursuers. He ended by warning the man that if he did not do as he was told, his blood will be on his own head. By the time the killers were ready for their man, he was nowhere to be found. The assassins never knew how the man found out about their plot.

The Ikoro is normally housed in a special sanctuary built by the community. The traditional broadcaster has the key to this media house. He alone enters it and keeps things in order. On the command or order of the ruling authority of the community the traditional broadcaster uses the lkoro to announce the deaths of important people from important families, public spirited men, veterans and heroes.

---

[80] Basden G.T, Niger Ibos, London 1966, p.359.

Jerome goes further to paint the picture of the use of Ikoro, he writes: "The Ikoro announces also the beginning and end of serious tribal wars and peace treaties. On the vigils of important feasts of the year, the Ikoro bellows out burst-fully saluting the memorable dead and the respectable living. One has to pay a heavy stipend, indeed, to have his name or her name lipped by the Ikoro through the magic hands of the Town crier. The Ikoro is in simple terms the medium for the external "news broadcasting" service of the Igbo traditional community".[81]

An "Ikoro" is also in great request when a man is also preparing for the highest title taking in a village. When all has been done for this title taking for example, Ozo title, the fact is then communicated to the people by beating the Ikoro.

For the Yorubas, the Ikoro can also be called the drum. This drum has many functions. For example, every palace (Yoruba Afin) has a drum set at the entrance to the Afin, and it is the duty of this drumming set to announce each visitor as he enters the palace, so that the Oba knows who has entered, the drums also announce his departure, for the king that his visitor has left. The drum is also used to send messages. Messages which are clearly understood by those who learnt the language of the drum. According to Fred. I. Omu: "In addition of producing music for dancing, it also directs the movements of dancers and, at social gatherings, announced the appearance and departure of important persons. The 'freedom of the drum' enables it to recite and multiply praise-names and also to pour abuse as the occasion warrant. Apparently nobody in the kingdom was above drum criticism. Old Oyo had what can be called 'free-speech festivals' during which talking drums freely ventilated their opinion about the king and his government. For the drummers, who operated from outside the walls of the palace, it was one of the greatest events in their lives".[82]

At marriages and funerals, special and appropriate music is played on the drums, every visitor of importance is always announced, and if he happens to be a dancer, his favourite dance is played for him.

---

[81] Okonkwo Jerome, op.cit., p.29.
[82] Omu Fred, Press and Politics in Nigeria 1880 – 1937, London 1978, p.4.

b.) The "Ekwe".

Ekwe and Ogene are other instruments available to the village broad-caster for the dissemination of his message. These instruments are very portable. This enables him to carry them along to all corners of the village while performing his duty. The "Ekwe" is used to dissemi-nate news for internal consumption, which are not meant for other neighbouring villages. The traditional broadcaster uses the "ekwe" to attract the attention of the villagers before he gives out his message. In most cases the "ekwe" unlike the "lkoro" does not talk but send signals whose significant role is to attract the eagerness and attention of the people to the oral messages by the "news caster."

c.) The "Ogene".

Ogene also does the same function as the ekwe, that is drawing out the attention of the audience before the message comes up. O. Oreh sums up a typical message from the traditional broadcaster via Ogene:

> Go-gom. Go gom! Go-gom, go-gom.
> Men and women of obodo inyi-o
> Hear the words of the ndi-ichie. !
>
> Every able bodied man, one big yam.
> Every able bodied man, one big yam.
> Every woman five cassava tubers
> Every woman five cassava tubers
>
> Every village one tin of palm oil !
> Every village one tin of palm oil !
> First thing tomorrow morning.
> All for our soldiers.
>
> Whoever hears should spread.
> Whoever hears should spread.
> Go- gom Go- gom.[83]

---

[83] Oreh . O, *Modes of Communication* in Reading in African Humanities, Enugu 1980, p.106.

The traditional broadcaster not only keeps in custody all these instruments for the dissemination of information but he alone possesses the privilege to operate them at will. Achebe also paints similar picture in his book, Things Fall Apart: "Okonkwo had just blown out the palm-oil lamp and stretched himself on his bamboo bed when he heard the "ogene", of the town-crier piercing the still, night air. Gome, gome, gome, boomed the hollow metal. Then the crier gave his message, and at the end of it beat his instrument again".[84]

It must be noted that all these instruments used by the traditional broadcasters are made locally according to the taste of each community. These instruments have been consistently used to promote the sense of communication in African societies despite the low priority given to them. Scholars have attributed to the fact that society and community life in contemporary Igbo society are under-going rapid changes.

3.2.3. Duties of the Town Crier.

As earlier indicated, traditional means of communication is almost in oral form. This oral-media or folk media are grounded on indigenous culture, produced and consumed by members of a group. They are visible cultural features, often strictly conventional, by which social relationships and a world-view are maintained and defined. They take on many forms. One of these forms, is oral information dissemination. It is then one of the duties of the traditional broadcaster to disseminate this information to the people whom they are meant for. Asuzu is of the opinion that: "The position of the gong man in the ordinary life of the community is indeed an irreplaceable one in the realm of distribution of information, within the belief system of rural audiences in Africa. His expertise and effectiveness in hawking and transmitting information is precise and impressive".[85]

The traditional Broadcaster knows when best to disseminate his messages or make his local broadcasting. Many a times according to Jerome, "The Town Crier therefore goes about his job for example

---

[84] Achebe Chinua, op. cit., p.9.
[85] Asuzu Boniface, Communication Media in Nigeria Today, Paris 1987, p.26.

when the society has retired to houses after the day's toil. In this regard the "Ikoro" talks (Ikoro n'ekwu) and the Ekwe and Ogene or Alo "strikes" (n'aku) between 7p.m and 8 p.m. At this time most of the people are indoors, relaxed, refreshed and ready to listen and glean up flying views. Another popular time for the encoding and decoding is at 5 a.m when the night news is clearly repeated. The Town-crier purposely does his transmission a "double round" in a single night to make sure that all decode his message and respond accordingly to evade blame and punishment".[86]

For Duylie, "The announcer's (traditional broadcaster's) techniques are downright native both in content and in approach.... The intensity of the vibration of the talking drums, the clear voice, the confidence with which the message is delivered, the timing of the message, that means, delivering messages early in the morning and evening when the inhabitants are indoors, and his personality as a man of the people and also the manner in which he moulds his message to the capabilities of his audience, all help him to deliver messages with remarkable impact".[87]

This means that the traditional broadcaster feels at home with his message and knows his audience very well. He knows what to say any moment and how to say it. Thus the "Town crier" operates in his vicinity where he has no language difficulty and therefore does not use strange vocabularies unlike the case with the Western media and their special English. By implication, at times he restructures the message to suit his purpose but still retains the actual and total meaning of the message. It is on this basis that Dayo Duyile describes the traditional broadcaster as a "Gatekeeper". "The Town crier is not only an announcer, but also a "gatekeeper" in a sense because once he has listened to the Oba's message at the Palace, he sets out to disseminate the information to the people in his own words. If he likes, he can restructure the Oba's message to suit his purpose but still retaining the actual meaning of the message, and many times, he chooses to use words that evoke laughter from his audience, or use strong threatening language, depending on the situation in which the message falls. As a

---

[86] Okonkwo Jerome, op.cit., p.32.
[87] Duylie Dayo, Media and Mass Communication in Nigeria, Ibadan 1979, p.285.

gatekeeper he edits and reconstructs the message to suit the prevailing situation".[88]

It was not only in traditional Igbo society that the impact of traditional broadcaster was felt. Other communities made use of them as well. For instance among the Ashanti in Ghana, the broadcaster is appointed by the chiefs to serve as permanent palace messenger who carries the king's daily pronouncements to the sub-ordinate chiefs. He is an eloquent interpreter of his chief's messages, well tutored in Ashanti traditions and proverbs. His message is said to start from the chief's court and is transmitted to strategic points throughout the village. He also accompanies the chief's entourage during the village processions to sing his praises.

Among the Yorubas in Western Nigeria, the traditional broadcaster (Town crier) is called the "Omode-Owas". The chief messenger also servers as the peace liaison officer, providing a channel by which the views of the people may be expressed to the king. Other warnings are sent by the king to "broadcast" or "herald" the dates of traditional ceremonies, warnings, announcing of epidemics, dates for cultivation and harvesting. In most cases, this post among the Yorubas is hereditary. This means that at times the announcer trains his children for this post. This teaching includes studying the Oba's area of influence. According to Fred Omu: "In the Oyo empire, the state messengers and intelligence officers (Ilari) who carried information between the capital and the officials was the town-crier or bell man. With his loud-sounding gong, he announced the promulgation of laws and regulations, meetings, arrangements for communal work and generally spread 'official' information in the community. The town-crier is very much a crucial part of village society today".[89]

In another part of Nigeria, the Benin area, the chief town crier is the eldest among a group of twenty-one traditional chiefs in kingdom. Here the special assignment of the traditional broadcaster is to collect the king's taxes, and he assigns his colleagues to cover and disseminate the news of the kingdom. In the ancient kingdom of Benin the traditional broadcaster is very much respected by the people. They are excepted to behave while on duty. In Eziokpor village of Bendel state, the traditional town crier is always seen as "the telephone line" be-

---

[88] Ibid., p.283.
[89] Omu Fred, op. cit., p. 3.

tween the villagers and the chief. He gets the message from the chief and enriches this skeletal messages which the chief gives him with songs and riddles. His news is generally given in the early morning and repeated late in the evening. Again at occasional time, he may announce important newsbreak such as the death of an important villager. This he will also repeat in the evening when he is sure that the villagers have come back from farming. On the function of a traditional broadcaster Frank Okwu says: "In the little village of Ashipa-ilawo near Abeokuta in Ogun state, the village announcer is known as the Ashipa and has the status of a chief. Although he does not rule the village and is responsible to the most senior chief, the Ashipa's credibility is unquestioned. He strikes the Gong often before his announcements and also plays the" Gbedu drum" to emphasise the importance of certain messages".[90]

In traditional lgbo society, due to the tedious nature of his work, the village broadcaster is given certain concession. This enables him to carry out his work effectively. Asuzu has rightly noted: "As the chief editor, (the news broadcaster) he gives desired texture to the news received from the reporters. These reporters are men highly respected among the people. Because of the nature of their duty to the community, in season and out of season, they are usually dispensed from traditional community labour. This concession is granted to them in order that they may devote their energies to their own sphere of responsibility for the welfare of the entire community".[91]

He goes further to give us a vivid image of a Gongman in Hausa area where a Town crier is known as "Mai Shela". "He occupies a central position among the people. Indeed he is a legendary figure generally believed to have been appointed by Allah, but he is selected by the Sarki or ruler of the village. Revered and respected as a holy man, his body is inviolate and his announcements undoubted. The culmination of his yearly responsibility is his prediction and announcement of the date and time for the sighting of the religious Ramadan moon".[92]

---

[90] Okwu Frank, Developing Indigenous Communication in Nigeria, in Journal of Communication, 29(4) Chicago 1979, p.44.
[91] Asuzu Boniface, op. cit., p.24.
[92] Ibid., p.25.

Although there were few radio receivers in those days in some parts of Eastern region, most of the people interviewed by this writer indicated that their source of information regarding the affairs of their village community work, chief's decisions was always through the village broadcaster. Thus, the village broadcaster is regarded as the most dependable source of information in the affairs of the village. On the ground of the authentic and unquestionable reliance placed on the messages of the village broadcaster by the villages, efforts then should be made to integrate him into the modern means of communication. Means to realise this total integration will be discussed at the end of this chapter. Having seen the functions of the traditional broadcaster in Igbo traditional society, we then ask ourselves, whether there is anything that can be borrowed from him for use in the practice of modern communication? Before going further to discuss such problem, let us see other means of communication available in the Igbo society.

3.3. Traditional Igbo Orator.

Apart from the Igbo traditional broadcaster, there are other communicators used to get messages across to the audience to whom they are meant.

"In the morning, the market place was full. There must have been about ten thousand men there, all talking in low voices. At last Ogbuefi Ezeugo, stood up in the midst of them and bellowed four times "Umuofia kwenu", and on each occasion he faced a different direction and seemed to push the air with a clenched fist. And ten thousand men answered "ya", each time. Then there was perfect silence".[93]

Among the Igbos, an orator is respected and always called upon to put across messages especially during important occasions. For the Igbos of Nigeria, the art of public speaking or address is a cherished one, which continues to pass from one generation to the next. A good Igbo orator is a wonderful speaker and communicator. Igbo forbearers, community leaders and traditional chiefs are known to be great orators. Even in modern time, they have no use of microphones and ad-

---

[93] Chinua Achebe, op. cit., p. 8

dress large crowds of villagers at public squares. Ndiokwere writes that: "They do not read from the prepared texts but most often deliver their address with minimum number of punctuation marks and difficulty. They almost recite their speeches or address often interspersed with numerous proverbs, short stories and the like with on-the-spot comments from listeners. Community leaders who perfect in these arts of public speech making are respected and admired when they speak in public because they employ proverbs and other forms of expressions, often dramatising events, thus keeping their audience awake and listening. Astute, as they are, though un-lettered they can hold their listeners for hours while nobody complains of boredom".[94]

Often a ten-minute address can begin with a short story, which initially may seem not to bear any type of relationship with the topic being discussed. It may end up with some chains of proverbs.

Those who understand him nod in approval or disapproval, while the unwise continue to wait for further clarification. Dramatisation of an event or topic under discussion is another important feature of an Igbo orator. As we have seen in a quotation from Achebe concerning the gathering of the people of Umuofia, highlights Ogbuefi Ezeugo was said to be a powerful orator and was always chosen to speak on such occasions. From all indication, he is not only an orator but also a great actor and dramatist. Achebe describes him thus: "He moved his hand over his white head and strokes his white beard. He then adjusted his cloth, which was passed under his right armpit and tied above his left shoulder. "Umuofia Kwenu"!, he bellowed a fifth time, and the crowd yelled in answer. And then suddenly like one possessed he shot out his left hand and pointed in the direction of "Mbaino" and said through gleaming white teeth firmly clenched... He threw his head down and gnashed his teeth, and allowed a murmur of suppressed anger to sweep the crowd. When he began again, the anger on his face was gone and in its place a sort of smile hovered, more terrible and more sinister than the anger".[95]

Here Ogbuefi Ezeugo is seen as a great orator and actor. He succeeded in moving and inciting his listeners to resentment. This is the type of effect such an oratory or powerful public address is meant to produce

---

[94] Ndiokwere Nathaniel, The African Church, Today and Tomorrow, Enugu 1994, p.258.
[95] Chinua Achebe, op. cit., p.8.

64

immediate and decisive action on the part of the listeners. Achebe uses the above story to illustrate a real picture of Igbo traditional art of communication. The communicator or orator may choose to demonstrate by dancing, singing or may employ any other symbolic action to drive home his message which must provoke the desired reaction. Whatever art or forms of expression he employs proverbs, short stories, drama, the idea is to produce the desired effect and leave a clear picture or impression of the event. Oral tradition often creates the best atmosphere for imparting the message. The Igbo orator tries to impress his listeners with many other introductory words and phrases and at the same time make his point. At the end of the short story, imaginary or real, he tells his audience before continuing his speech. "nke a bu uka, obukwa ilu" (literally meaning this can be a simple story and at the same time a proverb). In other word, he is telling his listeners to draw whatever lessons they could from the illustration. Let each person interpret it according to his ability. According to Aylward Shorter African traditional oratory is full of expression and literary forms. He notes: "African stories may be "Just so" stories or tale stories about how things began, told in order to point out a popular social and moral lesson. Some stories are folk-tales, often of human cunning in animal disguise. These stories are chiefly told for amusement- then there are the solemn myths, the charters for world order or historic political structures. They deal with the basic truths of cosmology and the human condition. Many of them are religious and most are so encrusted with symbol that they require exegesis at different levels. Finally there are the straightforward historical narratives, which require the same kind of analysis as any other form of local history".[96]

African traditional oratory is unique in nature and is useful in communication. The art form is generally completely bound to the local language of expression. It may be impossible if not absurd to try to translate an Igbo proverb into English. It often does not bring out the real meaning. What looks like literal translation of the proverb or saying is a mere scratch on the surface of the original import of the said expression. It is carried out to satisfy the ignorant foreigner or listener. Only the gifted man can fully comprehend the story in its original setting. Such can be said of any other ethnic group or language group

---

[96] Ibid., p.133.

expression directly. A child grows up with them. Those who grow up in families of wise and traditionally brought up parents are normally good orators who equally can speak in proverbs. It must be noted that today, there is lowering of standards in the presentation of materials in public address or oratory. The memory is no more as retentive as in the past and has largely remained porous. If speeches are not written and rehearsed, if notes are not jotted down, the presentation is poor. The modern politician or learned community leader cannot speak long without notes that are carefully prepared. He is rarely heard or understood if forests of microphones are not scattered on the stage for him as in theatrical performances. He may not gesticulate or even look up at his listeners for a short while, as that would cause some embarrassment. He may miss a line of his speech or even the trend of thought. So generally, the presentation of the address remains poor and unimpressive. Worse still the speaker may not be described as an orator as he is not even sure of the language of his address.

Some people today found themselves in a desperate situation when it comes to the problem of his language. When they try to deliver an unprepared speech in Igbo language, they mix it up with English language. Perhaps lack of knowledge of proverbs, short stories and other forms of expression is responsible for the poor quality of speech delivery. Dramatisation, gesticulation, even dancing is well known forms that convey vivid expressions of events, and surely help to reduce verbosity.

3.4. Traditional Singer and Entertainer.

The traditional Singer and Entertainer used to sang freshly composed local songs as he roamed the village. Sometimes he sang songs of praise to honour great men and women of the village. He was a popular singer whose songs were woven with the fabric of the community's experiences – sad and happy ones. Everyone knew its impact on the imagination and behaviour of the villagers. During funerals, the village Singer sang to condemn the evil forces that destroy life. On the birth of a child, he celebrated new life in song and dance. During weddings, the traditional singer composed songs to the happiness of the marriage, to the continuation of life. The traditional singer was a free man who entertained the whole community with his songs. The members of the community knew him as historian and great singer.

3.5. Narrative Means of Communication.

3.5.1. Oral Tradition.

As has already pointed out in traditional African society, communication can be made through various means. Generally this is done through oral communication. Old people narrate their traditions to teach the younger generations of the land. This teaching and transmission of tradition can be done at various occasions such as informal meetings, at night around the family fireside, during the raining season and dry season, when people work less; or out in summer moonlight. Almost all old men and women take the opportunity to recount events in their traditional history. Such knowledge of traditional history and origins of their families and villages is part of the wisdom of the old men and women, which they are bound to hand over as legacy to their children. Chenjerai Hove gave a vivid description of such impacting of wisdom by old men and women in African society: "It is early evening, after the evening meal. Darkness is already engulfing the solitary village, abandoning it to the ogress and witches, which swell the night, according to the traditional beliefs of the village. But it will not be so tonight. The moon is already surfacing above the eastern horizon, above the trees, brightening the night and the minds of the villagers, young and old. It is time for a festival of music, story and dance".[97] Going further he describe again how: "The old woman awaits the coming of the children to beg her: "Please tell us a story. Later in the night, she is performing the tale, with the children harmoniously repeating the chorused refrain of their participation. The bodies of the children and the old woman sway to the music that accompanies the tale. And many more moral tales will be told in that same evening.

---

[97] Hove Chenjerai, *Oral Traditions Claim a Place in Modern Mass Media*, in Media Development, Journal of the World Association for Christian Communication vol. XLIV, London 1997, p.13.

Tales of how to be a dignified boy or girl, how to respect the weak as well as the strong, how to work hard for oneself and for the community are narrated".[98] However, people now lament that with the introduction of western education and media such as television and radio, the children were robbed of this type of moonlight scene.

The joys of moonlight have never been the same again since the introduction of new forms of education; technological media and the written word which demands a new type of 'home work' after formal lessons are done with during the day. We should appreciate that the oral tale has been a pillar of indigenous communication in traditional Igbo society. Through it, the values, the history and legendary tales were communicated to the young. Such information or oral tradition may be transmitted in the form of songs, riddles and fables, proverbs and story telling. Nwala describes such "oral tradition" as myths. For him: "Myths abound in stories, proverbs, idioms and songs describing the origin and nature of the universe, the various community deities, origin of all the created beings, life in remote past etc. These may not contain the true or actual stories (on their face value) of the original state of affairs but yet they embody certain central ideas and beliefs as ideological forces which influence the action and the life of the people and provide the intellectual and moral climate in which the people think and act".[99]

It is clear that Frank Okwu supports this observation. In his book he notes: "Folk media speaks to the common man in his own language, in his idiom and also deals with problems of direct relevance to his situation. "Oramedia" are made up of dialogue and verbal exchange; this entails almost constant presence of one or more surrounding listeners. It means that the function of Oramedia is to provide teaching and initiation, with the object of imparting traditional aesthetic, historical, technical, social ethical and religious values. They provide a legal code of sorts, which rests on stories and proverbs generated through the spoken word. They also play other roles in the village society such as mobilising people's awareness of their own history, magnifying past events and evoking deeds of illustrious ancestors".[100]

---

[98] Ibid., p.13.
[99] Nwala Uzodinma, Igbo Philosophy , Lagos 1985, p. 71.
[100] Okwu Frank, Mass Communication, Culture and Society in West Africa, Paris 1985, p.166.

Ndiokwere observes that: "Even though various peoples and cultural groups all over the world may have these forms of expressions, but the African is known to possess them in abundance and in almost their original forms in spite of the influence of modern communication media. Folk-tales have a still revered place in speech making or public speaking in Africa today".[101]

Oral tradition is grounded in indigenous culture and consumed by member of a particular group. It helps to reinforce the values of a particular group.

This means that such Tales are not written anywhere rather transmitted by word of mouth. Colins Nicholas tells that it is the same with the indigenous minority peoples of Peninsular in Malaysia. He says: "Traditionally, when the Orang Asli (the indigenous minority peoples of Peninsular Malaysia) wanted to disseminate a message it was done by word of mouth. One community was responsible for communicating a particular message to the next community, which in turn was responsible for doing the same again. In no time, a message could be communicated to all communities within a specified region – be it in a river valley or beyond a mountain range".[102]

With this type of communication system, secrets of the community's communication are kept secret unless where one of the community members decides to let the cat out of the bag. Below we shall examine some mythologies and see how the Igbo traditional society has employed them as media of their communication.

3.5.2. Story - Telling.

Folk-stories abound in Igbo life and literature of the Igbo people. They range from explanation of the origin of the world, man, animals, water etc. to the explanation of why certain things are and how they are (for example, there are folk-stories to explain why the sky and the earth are separated, why God went to live on high, why there is death in the world etc.) Besides there are numerous stories about the activities of

---

[101] Ndiokwere Nathaniel, op. cit., p.225.
[102] Colins Nicholas, Stealing Stories in Media Development, Journal of the Association for Christian Communication vol. XLIV, London 1997, p.10.

the gods, certain heroes among men, activities of animals especially of the tortoise that is the hero of most lgbo folk-stories. From these folk-stories, an insight into the number of basic beliefs of the people is gained or communicated.

Furthermore, fables and stories play a didactic role. They are used to "instruct while amusing at the same time". This method of story telling in traditional society was very effective in bringing up and socialising the children into the culture and belief system of the people. Emphasising the importance of story telling among the lgbo people, Basden has this to say: "The lbos, in common with other West African tribes, have a great fondness for fairy tales. They have a bit stock of legend and folklore.... The lbo is a good story-teller, with a faculty of putting reality into fables. He uses as illustration animals and birds in such a way that they seem to be endowed with human powers. He can conjure up an atmosphere, and carry his audience with him, and thus provide a thrilling entertainment".[103]

As already said, the lgbo people use these stories to explain why things are the way they are. Giving an explanation why mosquitoes always go to ears; Okonkwo in Things Fall Apart told the story narrated to him when he was a child by his mother: "Mosquito, she had said, has asked Ear to marry him, whereupon the ear fell on the floor in uncontrollable laughter. "How much longer do you think you will live"? She asked Mosquito? You are already a skeleton. Mosquito went away humiliated and any time he passed her way he told the ear that he was still alive".[104]

A story can also be used for a moral lesson, such as this narrated by Frank Okwu: "A wicked man had prepared poison to harm his neighbour. He did not wash his hands after handling the preparation and suddenly scratched his vital organ. His organ died".[105]

Lesson: The lesson of this story is that no one should plan evil against his neighbour else it might boomerang.

Story telling cannot be conveniently separated from folk cultures in whose context they are significant. One can perhaps look at stories as a medium but it is better to regard them as interpersonal medium speaking to the common man in his language and dealing with prob-

---

[103] Basden G.T, op. cit., p.422.
[104] Chinua Achebe, op. cit., p.68.
[105] Okwu Frank, op. cit., p.170.

lems that are relevant to his situation. Perhaps the best way to illustrate this is to take the way the villager often attaches importance to their stories. For instance; a story was told in Ashanti kingdom in Ghana: "A British Governor once sat on the stool of the King of Ashanti as a way of communicating his authority as the representative of Queen Victoria of England. The significance of the stool in the mind of the people of Ashanti was reverence, as being not an appurtenance of the kingly office, but of an embodiment of the nation's soul. They were insulted. They were provoked. They went home and prepared for war".[106]

The story illustrates the ignorance of the British Governor who thought every throne signifies power and authority, whereas the people were thinking about religion and the sacredness of a stool as well as its political symbolism. What resulted was a communication gap, which soon developed into hostilities. Stories can also be used to explain how animals behave the way they are doing.

The Igbos tell story of why Monkeys are good jumpers: "In the olden days, all the animals and birds enjoyed the fruit of a certain tree generally. At the head of the animals was the tortoise. He called a meeting to discover who was really the owner of the tree. Meanwhile, neither birds nor animals were to touch the fruit within the period of investigation. One day, however a monkey became hungry looked for something to eat, he went and ate the forbidden fruit. When tortoise the chairman of all animals noticed that someone has stolen the forbidden fruit, he called another meeting to discover the culprit. All declared that they were innocent of the charge. Not being satisfied with their denial, he called upon each to swear an oath and to undergo trial by ordeal. Each was to swear and then throw himself down from the tree. Any one who was innocent, no harm would befall him, if guilty, then he would perish. So all animals and birds assembled and proceeded with the trial. As each prepared to fall he said; "let me fall and die if I am guilty of stealing the fruit". All the birds and beasts passed safely through the ordeal until it came to the turn of the monkey to swear and fall. He, the guilty one, changed the words and said, "let me jump from tree to tree if I have stolen the fruit." He immediately became an expert jumper and has remained so till today".[107]

---

[106] Ibid., p.166.
[107] Obiora Ike & Ndidi Edozien, Understanding Africa, Eungu 2001, p41.

Lesson: people should always tell the truth and admit their faults when they do any thing wrong. Generally, stories have moral overtones, stressing one virtue or the other. They also stress the contexts of traditional custom and hence are important means of ensuring that "Omenala" (traditions, customs) are passed on and upheld from one generation to the other.

3.5.3. Proverbs.

Besides the wealth of folklore in the form of fables and legends, the Igbo has a generous store of proverbs which also they use to impart information to the young generation. They are at times so full of meaning that often it is impossible to understand the full meaning posed through proverb, which do not need a direct answer. Shorter says: "Proverbs play an important role in traditional African societies in the process by which the young are initiated to life or acculturated, that is educated to a cultural tradition. They teach young people to observe and to compare. They reflect the participatory character of experience encouraging the young to explore a given experience in the light of another related experience. They contain an often-cyclical philosophy, bordering on the humorous".[108]

Among the Igbos of Nigeria the art of public speaking or address is a cherished one which continues to pass from one generation to the next. Traditionally, eldest sons are expected to sit around their fathers and uncles to imbibe the wisdom of the ancients couched in aphorisms, folk-tales and proverbs and other forms of artistic expressions. An old man or an elder who cannot intersperse his public address or stories with proverbs is not regarded as a wise or intelligent fellow. He is despised and is rarely called upon to be the spokesman of the family or community at public debates or negotiations. As he cannot handle or interpret proverbs he is not seen as a sagacious man and may not be enlisted among the elders and judges of the people. Such fellows are ridiculed and classified as imbeciles.

In fact, among the Igbos one who fails to grasp the meaning of a proverb is regarded as an imbecile. The Igbo have a saying "one who

---

[108] Shorter Aylward, Songs and Symbols of Initiation, Nairobi 1987, p.50.

has been addressed in a proverb, and who awaits for an explanation or interpretation must realise that the dowry paid on his mother was a waste." This point confirms another saying: "Nze na amaghi okwu ekwu na asi na ya kwu ebe ibe ya kwu". (An elder who is a poor speaker only concurs with other speakers). Chinua Achebe in "Things Fall Apart" highlights the importance of proverbs in both style and colloquialism .He says: "Among the Igbos the art of conversation is regarded very highly, and proverbs are the palm-oil with which words are eaten".[109]

In the book, he illustrated this art in a dialogue between Okoye and Unoka (money lender and debtor respectively). "Okoye had spoken to Unoka plainly so far, but had to say the next half a dozen sentences in proverbs. He was a great talker and spoke for a long time, skirting round the subject and then hitting it finally. In short, he was asking Unoka to return the money he had borrowed from him more than two years before".[110]

Arinze Francis also confirms the importance of proverb among the Igbos: "The ibos love to use proverbs. For them to speak always in very plain and simple language is to talk like inexperienced, little children. "Inu bu mmanu eji esuli okwu" (proverbs are the oil for eating speech) say the Ibos. Hence the uninitiated could be present when the hoardy-headed discuss important matters and yet understand absolutely nothing".[111]

Ndiokwere says: "At present in Nigeria and among Igbo language experts, a big research project has been initiated by which efforts are geared towards recovering and studying some of the disappearing traditional folklore's which have only been handed down through oral tradition. Most of the wise old men who told most of the stories and remained the only sources and reservoirs of the cherished traditions, customs and beliefs of the ancients are dying off. Some have not got good retentive memories, but when they open their mouth to speak, researchers need tape recorders for a more meticulous account of the wise sayings and uncountable number of proverbs that emerge from a simple dialogue with the elders".[112]

---

[109] Chinua Achebe, op. cit., p.5.
[110] Ibid., p.5.
[111] Arinze Francis, Sacrifice in Ibo Religion, Ibadan 1940, p.3.
[112] Ndiokwere Nathaneil, op. cit., p.257f.

Some of the Igbo proverbs include:

"Egbe bere ugo bere"! = Let the Kite (a bird) perch, as well as the Eagle. This teaches co-existence of all people. We should live in harmony and peace with one another.

"Aka nri kwo aka ekpe, ake ekpe akwo aka nri." = The right hand washes the left, the left hand should also wash the right, so that both may be clean. It is natural and right to help one another.

"Onye rue n'ani anebe nti obelu nke ya tinye" = When one reaches a land where men cut off their ears, he should do the same. This means that one should comply with rules and regulations of a given land or organisation.

"Ome mma na mma zukwara"= May the just man be rewarded with good.

"Ebe onye bi k'onawachi" = It is the place one lives in that one repairs. That means charity begins at home.

"Echi di ime" = Tomorrow is pregnant

"Onye ma echi" = Who knows tomorrow. These are proverbs that portray condensed uncertainty about the future and the need to approach it with some apprehension.

In public affairs, the Igbos do not oversimplify issues or underrate persons. Their philosophy is loaded with proverbs to illustrate this point.

"Elelia nwa-ite o gbanyua oku" = If you underrate a small pot its steaming water extinguishes the burning fire.

"Anu kporo nku na eju onu" = dry meat that looks small but fills the mouth when chewed.

"Nkenke enyi na-achu igwe enyi oso" = a short elephant that chases off a herd of elephants.

Proverbs such as these are meant to warn people not to underrate the capacity of others for good or evil, not to reckon on sheer visible size but to consider forces and resources, which lie below the surface. It means that one must be prepared and be on one's guard for any eventuality.

Proverbs to show appreciation of achievements:

The Igbo people believe in gratitude as an important social virtue. Sometimes tokens of gratitude outweigh the favour received. "Ökuku adi elozo onye kwolu ya odu na udu mmiri" = A chicken never forgets one who pruned its feathers in the rainy season. It means that even minor favours done in times of need are never forgotten.

Having seen some of the Igbo proverbs, great attention will be paid to them for they often communicate more than an ordinary speech could convey. They reveal profound thoughts, the soul of the people. This field is often closed to outsiders.

3.6. Formal and Informal Gatherings.

3.6.1. The General Assembly.

It is true that the responsibility of governing and organising a village lies squarely on the village assembly and also on the council of elders, however when certain delicate issues come up the whole village is called upon to take decision on such matters. It can be internal or external affairs. The internal affairs are issues, which concern the members of the village while external affairs are issues dealing with inter-village relationship. This means the involvement of two villages. Chinua Achebe described such a situation where the whole village gathered to settle an internal squabble between two families: Uzowulu's and Odukwe's families:

"Large crowds began to gather on the village "ilo" as soon as the edge had worn off the sun's heat and it was no longer painful on the body... It was clear from the way the crowd stood or sat that the ceremony was for men. There were many women, but they looked on from the fringe like outsiders. The titled men and elders sat on their stools waiting for the trial to begin... Two little groups of people stood at a respectable distance beyond the stools. They faced the elders. There were three men in one group and three men and one woman in the other. The woman was "Mgbafo" and the three men with her were her brothers. In the other groups were her husband, Uzowulu and his relatives.... The hearing began and Uzowulu stepped forward and presented his case. He began, The woman standing there is my wife ,Mgbafo. I married her with my money and yams. I do not owe my in-laws anything. I owe them no yams. I owe them no cocoyam. One morning three of them came to my house, beat me up and took my wife and children away. This happened in the rainy reason. I have waited in vain for my wife to return. At last I went to my in-laws and said to them; "You have taken back your sister. I did not send her away. You yourselves took her. The law of the clan is that you should return her bride-pride." But my wife's brothers said they had nothing to tell me. So I has brought the matter to the fathers of the clan. My case is finished. I salute you.

Odukwe stepped forward and began his own side of the case. He said;" My in-law (Uzowulu) had told you that we went to his house, beat him up and took our sister and her children away. All he said is true. He told you that he came to take back her bride-price and we refused to give it to him. That also is true. My in-law Uzowulu is a beast. My sister lived with him for nine years, during those years no single day that passed in the sky without his beating the woman. We have tried to settle their quarrels time without number and on each occasion Uzowulu was guilty.

After the presentation of such cases, the elders usually retire in the inner chambers for consultation among themselves where they take an unbiased decision of the case before them, later they will make their decisions known to the public. On the above case it was the chief spokesman who delivered the verdict thus: "Our duty is not to blame this man or to praise that, but to settle the dispute. He turned to Uzowulu's group and allowed a short pause... he said, Go to your in-laws with a pot of wine and beg your wife to return to you. It is not bravery when a man fights with a woman". He turned to Odukwe and allowed a brief pause, he said, "If your in-laws brings wine to you, let your sister go with him."[113]

The case was then amicably settled without any bias. Similar matters may crop up in varied dimensions. It could be an issue of land dispute between one family and another. It could also be between

---

[113] Chinua Achebe, op. cit., p.84f.

kinsman and the other. If in such cases, they could not arrive at a compromise, the issue could be forwarded or tabled before the village assembly or the council of elders.

3.6.2. Inter – Village Gathering.

There could also be issues arising which at times need the attention of two villages. In most cases, the elders of the villages concerned meet at the appointed place and time to deliberate on the issue. The decisions at the meeting are usually communicated to the whole village through the usual way, the village broadcaster. This is to keep all informed on the deliberations of the councils of the two villages. An instance of such a case was the one between "Umuofia" and "Mbano" regarding the killing of the daughter of Umuofia by Mbano people. Achebe tells us that: "The whole people of Umuofia gathered at the village square to deliberate on the murder of one of their daughters by the Mbano people. When all have gathered, "many spoke, and at the end it was decided that they will follow the normal course of action. An ultimatum was immediately dispatched to Mbano asking them to choose between war on the one hand, or peace the other hand that means the offer of a young man and a virgin as compensation. When Okonkwo and other emissaries of Umuofia arrived at Mbano, they were treated with great honour and respect. The two villages went into discussion. At the end the Mbano people agreed to compensate the Umuofia village with a lad of fifteen years and a young virgin".[114]

In many cases this open dialogue on inter-village levels always bring peace and harmony among them. At times, two neighbouring villages in lgbo traditional society may go into pact never to think evil or inflict harm on their citizens. This may take the form of oath-taking or blood pact.

---

[114] ibid., p.11.

3.6.3. Inter – Family Visitations.

In African society, especially among the Igbos, no one lives for himself or herself. There is a strong sense of community and neighbourliness. This naturally increased the scope of interaction and news circulation among the people. It was virtuous to visit relations and friends in their homes, 'eat from the same pot' and exchange the latest information. The sense of kinship and community did not exhaust itself in one town or village; on the contrary, it was manifested in a much wider sphere in, the attitude to relatives in other communities, villages and towns. The extent of these connections and attitudes gives some idea of the scope of news circulation in indigenous Igbo society. Organised and spontaneous gatherings are fairly frequent in the African society. Death and burial ceremonies always attracted large congregations, which often included participants from neighbouring or distant places. These ceremonies often lasted quiet long and while weeping and wailing characterised the particular moments of death and burial, the intervening periods were usually occupied with gossiping, storytelling and general exchange of information. Town or village festivals, marriage and circumcision feasts, public meetings and assemblies, and several other events, which characterise the African way of life, encouraged similar results.

3.6.4. Inner Family Affairs.

The communication level in a typical Igbo traditional family is always cordial. In Igbo traditional set-up, it is the responsibility of the parents to train their children. Even as an adult one is bound to obey his parents and listen to their advice. No parents would give a misleading advice to their children. It is believed that whatever comes out of their mouth are words of wisdom. The education of the children by the parents could take divergent forms. This could take the form of advice, or story telling, recalling events of the past and genealogy of the family. It must be mentioned that the strongest affective relationship in the family is developed through such advice, education and communication. It is during this period of education that the bond of affection between parents and the child is formed. Often the man exercises most aspects of family decisions. It is he who decides in the first instance where the family is to live, how the house is to be built, who or where a son or daughter is to marry. In most cases, the man must approve of all the decisions taken or made by the wife. It is always said, that no Igbo man will ever honour the decisions or enter into serious discussions with any married woman in the absence or without approval of her husband. Any misunderstanding between husband and wife arising from such unapproved decisions or breach of family protocol are usually settled in public.

On the side of the children, they regard their father with respect, but often are afraid of him. They feel free in the presence of their mother because she is more indulgent and tolerating. Owing to such affinity between the mother and her children, she tends to have a strong influence on their decisions. The children seem to confide in her and she later communicates to her husband the wishes of their children. Children are brought up to regard their father as the breadwinner of the family. Beside such major function, the father is also consulted on all major matters. In this regard, male issues are expected to be close to their father and endeavour not to differ with him on certain matters. Their decisions in life should receive his blessings. Due to the fact that Nwoye Okonkwo's son, was not ready to emulate the footsteps of his father Okonkwo, that there ensured a misunderstanding between them. Okonkwo therefore, always wished that his obedient daughter Ezinma was a male. He considered it great tragedy in his family that his first son Nwoye decided to be a Christian. In the end Okonkwo overcame his sorrow and sent for his other male sons for consultation and admonition. He told them: "You have all seen the great abomination of your brother. Now he is no longer my son or your brother. I will only have a son who is a man, who will hold his head up among my people. If any one of you prefers to be a woman, let him follow Nwoye now while I am alive so that I can curse him. If you turn against me when I am dead I will visit you and break your neck".[115]

Although the father tends to use iron hand on the males in the family, he always has the responsibility for their well-being. He wants them to be men of integrity in society.

---

[115] Ibid., p.156.

On the other hand, there seems to be more communicational rapport between the mother of the family and the daughters. A daughter grows up in daily-unbroken intimacy with her mother. From her mother she learns all feminine skills and also derives her character from her. Her success in marital life will depend on how much she imbibed the good or bad qualities of her mother. On the other hand, the son confides in the mother on matters of whom to marry or how to handle his future wife. On matters regarding marriage, a mother wages a single-handed war against her husband, if he ever tries to force a daughter or a son into a marriage arrangement which the children do not like. Whatever may be the case, in lgbo traditional family everybody knows his or her functions and performs them with joy. At the end there is always a good rapport between parents and their children.

3.6.5. Market Square.

In the traditional lgbo society, trading is an important economic activity but is secondary to agriculture. This shows the important place agriculture occupies in the economy and social life of the people. An Igbo man is always proud to say that he does not depend on the market for his daily living. In the olden days everybody was self-sufficient. Surplus goods were taken to the market for sale. This was the practice before colonisation. In the words of Nwala: "There were internal as well as external trade going on with their neighbours in both the north and the south. Surplus yam and rice from the northern lgbo-land, products of craftsmen and pottery-markers from Awka areas, cattle, and horses from the north (beyond lgboland), salt from uburu, - these and many other commodities constituted important items which different sections of lgboland exchange among themselves and with their neighbours".[116]

This means that market square is generally speaking a commercial meeting place. There are four market days in lgboland (Afor, Nkwo, Eke, Orie). This enabled traders to know what days to meet for exchange of commodities. This exchange of goods was done on personal basis, people enter into dialogue themselves personally during mo-

---

[116] Nwala Uzodinma, op. cit., p.176.

ments of bargaining and exchange. This should be well organised by the group in-charge of market in any given village. Each village group therefore controls the market developed within its group and also the feast and ceremonies that fall within the market days.

That was why Uchendu says: "Each village ensures that their local market is well organised as to retain the confidence of traders from other areas. This they do by ensuring market peace, taking care of the rainmakers, making sure that the god of the local market is actively involved in the affairs of the market and in the peace and security of the goods".[117]

Each village sees her market as her own treasure because, it is not only her source of livelihood, but also gives a sense of pride and prestige. The villagers can also make it more attractive to outsiders by organising drinking parties of different age groups on the market day. The aim was that friends from other villages, whom they treated well, would feel bound to come back another time. Again each village ensured the safety of their trading with others from other villages by entering into trading agreements in the forms of "igba ndu" (blood pacts), which guarantees natural co-operation. These local markets were centres of importance not only for exchange of goods but also for exchange of ideas. They were also recreational, political and ritual centres. This is what Ugboaja Frank means when he says: "Market places in Africa, in themselves are veritable communication forums.... they are not just where people go to buy or sell but are diffusion forums for important social interaction... In some villages in the eastern part of Nigeria, a case of incest is censured by parading the offender adorned with a necklace of snail shells and live millipedes in the marketplace".[118]

Going further he says: "In Nigeria, mass communication in the village can be looked at in the context of the village market square as a web of group affiliations, a mode of information, a medium that attracts the mass of its audience physically and socially to itself to receive a socially mediated communication diversified according to need. The village market square is a powerful integration force, important news and gossip centre and a place of ceremonials and parade ground, a meeting place for relatives and friends from different localities and a

---

[117] Uchendu Victor, The Igbos of Southern Nigeria, New York 1965, p.22.
[118] Ugboajah Frank, op. cit., p.167.

place where people congregate to hear news from distant places. It functions therefore as a mass medium".[119]
This means that the market squares scattered in different villages are powerful integrative force, an important centre for news and gossip, a place for ceremonial parades and a meeting place for relatives and friends.

Achebe describes a typical traditional Igbo society market square thus: "The market place began to fill as soon as the sun rose. When Okonkwo and Oberika got to the meeting place (in the market square), there were already so many people there that if one threw up a grain of sand it would not find its way to the earth again. And many more people were coming from every quarter of the nine villages".[120]

Even in cities the open markets still play an important role and may compete with the mass media as alternative sources of information. Market squares among the Igbos are the most frequent and regular place for the assembling of a large number of people. In certain villages they use to decree that attendance to market is compulsory or they can divide themselves into village-groups. Certain groups must turn out for its own particular market time. Each village group can also control all the activities carried out within the market square that falls within their own jurisdiction. In one of the villages the writer visited, an informant told me that on Eke market day, a law had been passed that all men and women must come out regularly to Afor market or face the option of being fined. Women spent greater portion of their time in the market on any of the market days. Basden observed: "It is the practice of the women to spend a portion of each day at the market. A woman will visit the market if she can, whether she wants to buy or sell, or not because it is one sphere of entertainment in the ordinary life of the village. There she will meet friends, there she can learn the latest news, and share in the gossip of the hour. To be deprived of this privilege is a hardship".[121]

Giving more attestation to the importance of marketplace and its role in communication in traditional society, the intergovernmental conference on communication policies in Africa says: "The village market (places) represent ... strong integrating forces, as well as... meeting

---

[119] Ugboajah Frank, Communication Policies in Nigeria, Paris 1980, p.51.
[120] Chinua Achebe, op. cit., p.181.
[121] Basden G.T, Niger Ibos, op. cit., p.335.

(place) where people come to hear news of far-off districts... The open air markets still play an important role in communication and ... even compete with the mass media as alternative sources of information".[122] Put in a simple way, markets in Africa society provided a most convenient forum to meet friends and kinsmen and exchange news and gossip. While bringing together large numbers of sellers, buyers and mere visitors, some from distant places, they created an atmosphere of festivity and entertainment in which gossip and the exchange of information flourished. Some markets were also the terminal points of trade routes connecting different parts of one area with one another and with foreign lands and civilisations. The caravans who plied these routes helped to disseminate information. They gathered and relayed news as they passed from place to place communicating with fellow traders and collecting information on resources and prospects of trade. It is a well known fact, that in the communication set-up of the Igbo market square, there is no top-down or one-way traffic model of communication but a "free-for-all talk system", which is the modus of the Igbo community media. People meet regularly to exchange ideas and information without any hindrance or censorship.

3.7. In Defence of the Traditional Media.

3.7.1. Merits of Traditional Media.

Whatever may be the case, traditional broadcaster can still be integrated into today's modern means of communication. His services should not be discarded because there is always more discernible feedback in person-to-person communication in rural areas wherever the traditional broadcaster is used than the use of modern media. There is always a better opportunity to delivery a convincing message face to face. This could be attested to by sampling of opinion done in one rural area where the services of the traditional broadcaster are still in use: "In a given town, 13,500 taxable adults paid N15,000 (Fifteen thousand naira) as taxes to officials of the local government, when

---

[122] Intergovernmental Conference on Communication Policies in Africa „AFRICOM", Working Paper, Paris 1980, p.22.

the village announcer was introduced for the purpose of tax campaign drive. If this number is compared with the previous months in the same area, when the village broadcaster was not used, only 3,100 people paid N4,100 (four thousand, one hundred naira). Here the feedback becomes more glaring".[123]

There were other feedbacks in another village where the village broadcaster was used to summon people for their community work, such as: bush clearing, clearing site for their new market or summoning of the village assembly or Council of elders meetings. The feedback has been very wonderful. This is because his techniques are downright native both in content and in approach. It is true that today there are many radio and television stations all over, coupled with supplies of daily newspapers, most of the people interviewed in some rural areas, both literate and illiterate, said that their source of information regarding the affairs of their village community works and the council of elders' decisions was always from the village broadcaster, not the newspapers nor the radio. Thus, the village announcer is regarded as the most dependable source of information in the affairs of a village. Due to the authenticity and unquestionable reliance placed on the messages of the village announcer by the villagers, it is suggested that commercial houses, which have products for marketing in the villages and smaller towns, should explore the possibility of using village announcers on commercial basis. The effect of such commercial campaigns can be strengthened by the traditional indigenous qualities of the village announcer resulting in big economic boom for such institutions. Government functionaries, too, can experiment by making use of this traditional mode of communication to reach the villages with their messages effectively rather than relying on the use of printed messages, which has often proved unproductive. This system can be used in vaccination campaigns in the rural areas, in health campaigns and similar campaigns by the various ministries.

---

[123] Dylie Doya, op. cit., p.43

3.7.2. Limitations of Traditional Media.

Igbo society is indeed a homogeneous one. For a long period of time, they have organised means of communication among themselves. Those communicational media made it possible for consensus and understanding to exist among them. Those media through which they communicate cannot be waved by the way side because of the introduction of modern means of communication. Credit should be given to the "Traditional broadcaster" or the "Village broadcaster" who was their main organ of communication. Even though his work has been over-taken by western media, he should not be forgotten.

It is of particular interest to note and to recall here that news distribution in the Igbo village and towns was superbly carried out through the genius of the traditional broadcaster. The success of his work was not solely as a result of individual effort for he had the co-operation of the society as a whole. We cannot advocate here that this particular medium of communication because of its precious success in the Igbo traditional society should continued to be used without augmenting them with the modern means. We should also bear in mind that the success of the traditional broadcaster at that time has been attributed to certain factors which include:

In those days, the Igbo society was homogenous in nature. This means that all the people lived together. The news brought by the news-carrier is always meant for this particular group. Nowadays however, there is the problem of migration and urbanisation. There is free movement of people. Many villages have no longer homogenous faces but are made up of indigenous and foreigners. The information disseminated by the town crier that are supposed to be private matters, are longer possible.

When the population was smaller and the audience very well defined and limited, the "Village broadcaster" or the "Village orator " did not need to strain himself too much while carrying out his duties. At this time, the society was a communicative one indeed, and news travel instead of having to be sent. The instruments used for communication have a very limited distance range. This means that only a handful of people can hear them when they are in use.

Not minding the limitations of the traditional means of communication, its importance and usefulness should be recognised and acknowledged. Summing up their importance Ugboajah writes: "Traditional media linked to belief systems have been found effective as tools in development programmes of government. As entertainment media, they can attract and hold the interest of large numbers of people. As oral media in local languages, they can involve the poorest groups and classes who are often left out in development activities because of illiteracy or lack of understanding of the English language. As dramatic representations of local problems, they can provide a codification of reality which can be used by participants in analysing their situation. And as collective expressions and communal activities they create the contexts for co-operative rather than individual thinking and action and the possibility for peer learning".[124] Policy makers and communication specialist should double their efforts in their research to evaluate clearly the resultant effect of integration of traditional media with modern means of communication. We should not forget that these traditional means of communication are embodiment of the culture of Igbo society. Generally, national development is conceptually not possible without cultural development. Before any development is embarked upon, for example, the construction of a trunk road, the opening of civic centre, the citing of an industrial complex, the building of the village market etc., the effects of such a development on the culture of the people must be ascertained. If this is not done, the development positive though it may be, may bring about negative results. Therefore, all available means of communication both traditional and modern should be adequately used to educate the people on the pros and cons of such development.

---

[124] Ugboajah Frank, Mass Communication, Culture and Society in West Africa, op. cit., p.172.

4. MEANS OF COMMUNICATION IN COLONIAL ERA IN TRADITIONAL IGBO SOCIETY.

4.1. Introduction.

"The white man came and stayed. This was a transition period, a period of intense conflict between indigenous and western cultures. The old were dying and the new were born. Men experienced the changes with mixed feelings".[125] This feelings of an old man who experienced the advent of the white man is also the view of others. This quotation raises a fundamental question: when the white man came, was he able to adjust quickly by way of learning the language spoken by the people that is "Igbo" or were the people forced to adjust themselves in order to accommodate their visitors by way of learning the visitors' way of life especially their language? The colonial masters came and not only subjugated the people to their own way of thinking and speaking but stayed for a long time. This chapter then treats the communication media through which the colonial masters and the indigenous people were able to interact and communicate among themselves. Did the colonial masters continue to use the traditional media of communication or were they able to impose their own in other to communicate effectively with the people? Without effective media of communication, nothing works. Communication means a bridge that links people of different languages together.

4.2. The Berlin Conference.

The conference, the first of its kind held in Berlin between November 15th, 1884, and February 26th, 1885, to discuss outstanding problems connected with West Africa. It was attended by every power in Europe (except Switzerland) as well as by the United States – in all, fourteen world powers. Of these powers only five were of real importance: "These were: France, Germany, Great Britain, Portugal and an ambiguous body called the International Association of the Congo,

---

[125] Okafor-Omali Dilim, A Nigerian Villager in two Worlds, London 1965, p.77

which had no legal representation there at all, and which was in reality only a cloak to hide the ambitions of Leopold 11, King of the Belgians".[126]

It is indeed surprising to many especially to Gerard Wanjobi that even with the: "Abolition of the slave trade, one would have expected European countries to drop their interest in Africa. This, however, was not the case. In fact, these countries developed a new and more vigorous interest in Africa. This interest was so great that a rivalry arose among these countries for the possession and mastery of Africa. The rivalry gave rise to what has come to be called the Scramble for Africa. In order to put an end to this rivalry – or at least to minimise it – the European countries called the Berlin Conference in 1875".[127]

This unique conference went ahead in Berlin with the five mentioned famous great powers of the world at that time. Crowe admitted that from these five, "three were more important than the rest. They are France, Germany and Great Britain."[128] The period under consideration is one in which African and colonial questions generally were still subordinate to European in world of diplomacy. Actually, the history of the conference has to do with outstanding colonial conflicts between the three important world powers at that time namely: France, Germany and Great Britain. Not only was Germany dominant in Europe, she was desirous of having a lion-share of Africa. It is in this combination of circumstances that was the raison d'être of calling for the conference in Berlin only for the Europeans.

Jean Suret-Canale observed: *"Es war also ein im wesentlichen europäischer Kongreß. Die Debatte aber würde sich zum ersten Mal in der Geschichte um Afrika drehen, ohne jede Vertretung eines afrikanischen Volkes oder Staates selbst in Abwesenheit jener, die schon damals international von eben den europäischen Mächten anerkannt waren, wie das Sultanat von Sansibar oder das Königreich Madagaskar".*[129]

---

[126] Crowe S.E., The Berlin West African Conference 1884 – 1885, Westport 1984, p.5.

[127] Gerard Wanjobi, *Orality and Reading Tradition in African in the Context of the Emerging World of Social Communications* in Raymond B and Marcazzan T. (ed) Publishing at the Services of Evangelisation, Nairobi 1996, p.43.

[128] ibid., p.5

[129] *(It was essentially an European congress. For the first time in history, was debate centred on Africa without any African people or nation being represented. States like Sultanate in Zanzibar and Madagascar Kingdom were not invited for the conference,*

The consequent years after the signing of the *Berlin General Act* were characterised by more intensive scramble for colonial territory: All the colonial powers endeavoured to obtain the best territories of the unclaimed African continent. This resulted at the end the complete partition of the African continent. In his opening speech, Bismarck, the chairman of the General Act, formulated the aims of the conference thus: *"Es handelte sich nicht um die Aufteilung Afrikas, sondern eher im Gegenteil um die Suche nach Mitteln, mit denen eine Politik der "offenen Tür" durchgesetzt werden konnte, so wie es die europäischen Mächte und die Vereinigten Staaten in Fernost praktizierten".* [130]

The opening speech stated that the conference was only to open the way for all to have access into Africa, but what type of access does one need before travelling to the continent? The Berlin "West African Conference of 1885" was in many ways a turning point in the history of British relations with the present country called Nigeria. The Berlin Conference opened and secured for Britain international recognition of her paramount interest in the districts.

Giving a picture of the whole scenario Obiora Ike writes: "In the Year 1884 and 1885 some European greedy powers gathered at Berlin to take what belongs to others and to scramble for Africa without consulting the inhabitant of this great continent. This led to the eventual partition of the continent to suit the new conquerors. The boundaries of the new territories were drawn on a table in Berlin, not on the fields of Africa. ... Britain participated and thus got the large geographical territory of over 250 ethnic tribes, nations and languages under their authority. It must be made clear here that conquest was not by due invitation by the African people rather it was obtained by forces and by treachery". [131]

---

despite the fact that they were at that time internationally recognized by the very same European Powers): Frank Thomas Gatter, Protokolle und Generakte der Berliner Afrika – Konferenz 1884 – 1885, Bremen 1984 p.8.

[130] *(We are not dealing with the partition of Africa but on the contrary, we are looking for political means for all to have access to the continent, which was the appealed by the European powers and the United States in the Far East.)* ibid. p.35.

[131] Ike, Obiora., *The Social, Political and Economic Situation of Nigeria: A Critical Survey,* in Wer Befreit ist, kann befreien, Hoffmann Johannes (ed.) Band 5 Frankfurt am Main 1997, p.77

The long-term consequence of this infiltration pioneered essentially by Britain – the colonial power, and consolidated by other neo-colonial powers – has been among others, the dilution of elements of Igbo traditions. This influence is particularly noticeable in the areas of culture, education, politics and economy. They were able to achieve this through various communication means they introduced among the people.

4.3. The Arrival of the Colonialists in Southern Nigeria.

Before the Igbos of the Southern Nigerian knew what had happened concerning the Berlin Conference which gave the British government authority over them, they were in 1906 amalgamated with the colony and protectorate of Lagos. The new unit was renamed the colony and Protectorate of Southern Nigeria. The amalgamation was accompanied by internal administrative rearrangements as a result of which the whole unit was divided into three administrative provinces, Western, Central and Eastern. Under this arrangement, the Igbo people were incorporated in the central and eastern provinces. Finally in 1914, Lord Lugard the British administrator for Nigeria amalgamated both Southern and Northern Protectorates into what we know today as Nigeria. Giving a vivid description of the political scenario of the Igbo people, Ottenberg S. writes: "One striking characteristic of the Ibo peoples at the time of British advent was their political decentralisation. There is no evidence that any of these people or sections of them ever evolved, or formed part of even a loosely integrated empire or state of any remarkable size. Instead, each of these people were split into a large number of tiny political equivalent and autonomous units. Though none of these units was either isolated or self-sufficient, each had its own name, its own land, its own shrines and religious ceremonies, its own markets, warriors and political institutions".[132]

As the Intruders arrived in southern Nigeria, the Igbo people resisted them vehemently but this resistance was never a uniform phenomenon. Different societies – and individuals within societies – made different decisions at different times. Some did not resist when

---

[132] Anene, J. C., Southern Nigeria in Transition 1885-1906, Cambridge 1966, p.7

colonial rule was first imposed, but did so after a time, when its true significance was more apparent. Some wished to resist but were dissuaded by the fate of their neighbours. Others decided not to resist, after seeing the spectacular demonstration of British military technology. Others decided that their interests as individuals or as communities were best served, not by resisting the new power, but by co-operating with it. It was indeed a hard period for the people to accept the whiteman. This is because many of the communities were found to have known practically nothing about the newcomers. In many places there were people who had no doubt that the first Whiteman they saw was a ghost or a beast. Many people thought that the early Europeans were spirits since they "had no toes[133]" had four eyes and also riveted pieces of iron to their chest. One village still claims she killed a whiteman, because she did not know that he was a human being. This type of misunderstanding continued to exist between the Whiteman and the people. This means then that there existed a great problem between the two groups. The British did not speak Igbo, and had little knowledge of the society they intended to rule. They were, therefore, very dependent on those who gave them information. The Igbo people on the other hand, neither spoke nor understood English. Despite the barrier in communication, some people decided to co-operate with the whiteman. Who are those that decided to co-operate and give information to the British for effective administration?

4.4. The Native Council System.

In trying to make its administration very effective and unchallenged by the natives, the British administrators set up "The Native Council System" or the Native Court System". This is so called because it was vested both with the executive and legislative power. The extension of this 'Native Court' or 'Native Council' system to Igbo land was destined to prove the greatest blunder of the British agents charged with consolidating British rule in this part of the protectorate. Two contra-

---

[133] Achebe C., "They had no toes because they wore shoes, had four eyes because they wore goggles and the buttons on their clothes were generally regarded as pieces of iron riveted to their chests". in *Things Fall Apart,* London 1958, p.65.

dictory fallacies lay behind the British policy. The first was the assumption that the Igbos had no form of government and that anarchy was the order of the day in Igbo society.

The second concerned the efforts made in the early stages of penetration to find the chiefs through whom the British and their new order might be introduced to the people under the control of the chiefs. This erroneous attitude of the British must be corrected here. It must be made clear that before the whiteman came, the administration of the villages was in the hands of the elders. Most of them held titles. The administration and jurisdiction of the village were in the hands of these titled men. But when the white man set up his first "Native Court" in the town, these titled men were divested of their traditional authority. The jurisdiction of this court covered a wide area so that it was difficult for people to appreciate its significance. The court was presided over by the whiteman, with a number of native members as his associates. The appointment of these Native Court members led to great conflicts throughout Igbo land.

4.4.1. Members of the Native Council.

The British officials were all out to have full control of everything. In order to succeed, they first undermined whatever has been in existence. This is the primary reason why they suppressed all the existing traditional organs of government. It is not surprising then that the "native council" system provided an important means of undermining traditional authorities, and thus served the purposes of the consolidation of British rule throughout the protectorate. Under heavy penalties, the traditional organs of government and of the judiciary crumbled and progressively ceased to function. The native council became the sole link between the white man and the people. Semi-educated court clerks assisted by court messengers took control of them. The members of the 'Native' Councils who 'knew the whiteman's ways', began to acquire a new prestige and wealth, which the die-hards were slow to appreciate. A 'warrant chief' became a man of importance through whom the wishes of the new rulers were conveyed, and through whom severe punishments and other penalties could be obviated. The Court Clerks also acquired their own privileges. Many of them made their fortunes by virtue of their role as Court clerks and Court Messengers.

Election or selection of members of this council was left entirely in the hands of the administrators. They did not want the people to be involved in selecting those who will rule them rather they went and chose candidates randomly. In this way they deprived the local people the opportunity of selecting the rightful people. In certain towns, the story is that as the whiteman and his troops arrived, the elders, the women and the youngest age-groups fled to safety from the town or village. The most adventurous of the fighting age groups stayed behind to find out what the whiteman was all about. These young men therefore made the first contact with the political officers. The latter, understandably, assumed that the adventurers represented the vacated towns and it was from among them that the first members of the 'Native' Council were selected.

In towns where there was actual resistance to the British invasion by the elders, whoever was captured was considered *personae non-gratae* and therefore ignored for the purposes of the establishment of the 'Native' Council. Prominent among the members of this council were: "Warrant Chiefs", "the Court Clerks" or "the Interpreters" and the "Court Messengers". All these had various functions to perform.

4.4.2. The Warrant Chiefs.

The colonial administrators applied the indirect rule system in Nigeria. By this system, they made use of indigenous political agents for local government. This meant that indirect rule were a common feature of native administration in West Africa. For indirect rule, as understood by Michael Crowder implies the: "Government of the African peoples through their traditional political institutions, shorn of those features that conflicted with British concepts of civilised behaviour, the exaction of direct taxes and the establishment of regularised treasuries. In so far as this suit the colonial masters".[134]

Later the British government took a further step in abandoning the policy of laissez-faire which hitherto dominated British relations with

---

[134] Crowder Michael., West Africa Under Colonial Rule, London 1970, p.211

the Nigerian empires and kingdoms or communities. In this context the use of an indigenous agency for government was really advocated and encouraged. On the other hand was the practice of letting traditional chiefs govern their subjects as though they were under a protectorate in the nineteenth-century sense, so that having agreed to abolish certain customs they were internally autonomous, leaving to the British protector control of external relations and jurisdiction over its own subjects. At the other extreme, there was the attempt to discover chiefs where none existed, or to give executive functions to chiefs without traditional political authority. They damned the consequences by appointing whomever they want and at times to fill a particular post. Despite the fact that the administrators of the various territories received "General Instructions" on the extent of their responsibilities, with regard to local government, this document asked the administrators: "Not to interfere unduly with the "tribal government" of the protectorate, but to allow the local chiefs to continue to rule their peoples and to administer justice to them in traditional fashion. The new administration however, was to keep a vigilant watch over the chiefs and their functionaries in order to prevent injustice and check abuse".[135]

The administrators interpreted this Instruction to mean that they should get the people involved into the governing activities. This means that such a system was supposed to achieve the conversion of the indigenous political system of the peoples of the protectorate into an instrument with which the new rulers would govern, influence and civilise the natives. In seeking to apply this policy to the Igbos and their neighbours, the British selected certain natives whom they thought were traditional chiefs and gave them certificates of recognition and authority called *"Warrants"*. The Warrant entitled each of these men to sit in the Native court from time to time to judge cases. It also empowered him to assume within the community he represents, executive and judicial powers which were novel both in degree and territorial scope. Afigbo A.E. condemns this attitude of the British: "The decision to rule the Eastern provinces indirectly should not necessarily have led to the Warrant chief system, but that it did lead to this attempt to rule a chief-less society through chiefs is to be explained by a number of factors, which helped to determine official

---

[135] CSO 1/14 Despatch No. 2 of 18.04.1891 containing the General Instruction from Foreign Office.

policy. ... The early years of colonial rule which were taken up with the hurly-burly of military subjugation gave neither the administration the time to collect and collate nor the people the confidence and inclination to offer information on the indigenous political system. In this matter the British formed their opinion of the whole region from what they saw on the coast. Without proper investigation, they assumed first that the heads of houses and sections whom they saw along the coast were autocratic chiefs, and second that the house system was common to the whole region".[136]

Having been successful in the administration of the Northern Protectorate, Lord Lugard was very pleased and did not hesitate in introducing the same system of government in Southern Protectorate. However, the system of government, which the British introduced in northern Nigerian, and the system, which they introduced among the Igbo, differed in degree. The Emirates of the Northern Nigeria were more suited to the needs of a modern bureaucratic state mainly because of their centralisation and relatively large size. For this reason the British found them emotionally attractive. The British introduced then a system of warrant chiefs because they assumed that chiefs, if not kings ruled all Africans. Like all colonial governments in Africa, the British regime depended on the agency of Africans for the day to day running of their government.

We should also try to distinguish between the actual ruling of the people by their chiefs and using the so-called local chiefs as intermediaries by the British administration in order to achieve their objectives. This is what Crowder implies: "It is necessary to emphasise that indirect rule at least in theory, did not mean government of African peoples through their chiefs. In practice however indirect rule laid heavy emphasis on the role of the chief in the government of African peoples, even for those peoples who traditionally did not have political leaders as distinct from religious leaders".[137]

Initially the British administrators found themselves in a dilemma on the issue of who becomes a warrant chief. Should those local chiefs continue carrying out their duties or should there be a total overhauling? It was for the latter that the British administrators decided. This is of course without any consultation with the people.

---

[136] Afigbo, A.E., Op.cit, p.58
[137] Crowder M., West Africa Under Colonial Rule. London 1970 p.169

They started choosing randomly people whom they would work with, simply put, those who would be willing to carry out their orders. Many villages were not just reluctant, but uncompromisingly determined not to accede to the demand to give up their traditional leaders. It was believed that to sacrifice them to the unknown 'white creatures' was likely to provoke the anger of the gods and of the ancestors whose interests they were believed to represent among the living. Such oppositions not withstanding, the British administrators forced their wills on the people by choosing warrant chiefs randomly. Afigbo described how a "warrant chief" was chosen in a certain village: "This first Warrant chief was by then the "town-crier". Being an old man he was not fast in running into the bush when the British troops invaded their village. Consequently the soldiers caught him. When forced to rally his people, he beat his drum, as he would do to announce either a general meeting or communal work. On this occasion, some of the brave young men responded to his call. To the European officer who came with the soldiers this was positive proof of the town-criers authority over his people. When the time came to appoint chiefs, the town crier was called to take a warrant. But since he was very old, and felt incapable of carrying out satisfactorily the functions of a warrant chief, he pushed forward one of his slaves to take his place. No other person in the village was consulted when all this was taking place".[138]

In another village a man was caught on the road by the British military forces as he was taking a walk and was forced to lead the way to his village. Out of fear of the military might, he willingly obeyed without hesitation. After executing this duty to the satisfaction of the administration, he was subsequently made a warrant chief. The warrants were sometimes given to people in return for services rendered to the Government, and there was inevitably a tendency to appoint persons of intelligence with some understanding of European ways of life. This means as long as one agreed he would toe the line of the white man, he was sure of gaining warrant although they might have had no hereditary or customary status. In addition to this method Crowder Michael tells us: "Where the British could not find chiefs in a society, they tended to impose them. Clan elders whose authority was primarily religious were given executive powers alien to their societies. In Eastern Nigeria, with few exceptions, the establishment of

---

[138] Afigbo, A.E., The Warrant Chiefs London 1970, p.162.

chiefs was entirely foreign, for power in matters both religious and secular was shared in the community. In each case, the British did what they could to find someone with traditional authority of some kind to act as intermediary between their inadequately staffed administrative service and the people. In contrast to the French, they did take pains to discover people with some semblance of traditional authority to be chiefs. They rarely imposed chiefs of a different ethnic group on a people. That people without any real claim to traditional authority so often became chiefs was largely due to the ignorance of the administration about the nature of African society. So in Eastern Nigeria the British often acted in a very French manner in appointing warrant chiefs, as have been noted earlier".[139]

Isichei, Elizabeth tried to exonerate the administrators by seeing this imposition of the warrant chiefs positively thus: "The traditional elders were seldom chosen. They were too old for the mental adjustments which the new role acquired, they were often surrounded by religious taboos which would have made such participation difficult, they were physically too old for the frequent long journeys required of such duties".[140]

This means that the new system required young and energetic people to carry out the task involved. Nevertheless, the whiteman failed at this period to investigate so as to understand that there was already a existing democracy, which is different from the one he one wanted to introduce. This type of democracy is government by the people through congress of the elders selected on merits and age from each family and clan and not appointed at random as the white man had done. It is obvious that any building without solid foundation is bound to collapse. When the warrant chief system later collapsed, the administrators poured the blame on the natives. They claimed, the traditional leaders on arrival of the whiteman did not want to make any contact with them.

Further the administrators claimed, the traditional rulers waited for the white man to approach them. But other men who had no traditional authority did not hesitate to step forward.

It was these men whom the white man appointed as members of their administration. They started working hand in hand with the white

---

[139] Crowder, Michael., op. cit. P. 226
[140] Isichei, Elizabeth, The History of Igbo People, London 1976, p.144.

man. It was their duty to see that the orders of the white man were carried out in their respective village-groups. They became merely agents of the white man, and bore no resemblance to true African Chiefs, who were fathers or spiritual heads of their people, and whose absolute powers were kept in constant check by means of taboos and councils.

4.4.3. The Council Clerks / The Interpreters.

Giving a picture of communication handicap that existed between the Indigenous people and the Europeans, Isichei Elizabeth says at the time: "The Europeans officials did not speak Ibo, and the few Ibos who spoke English, controlled the channels of communication and came to wield great power. The most important agents of communication were the government interpreters, whose role was self-explanatory, and the court clerks. The power of the court clerks arose from the fact that they were usually the only members of a Native Court who spoke and wrote English, from being the servants of the courts and the recorder of their proceedings, they easily became their masters".[141]

At the heart of the colonial situation lay the problem of communication. This was a great handicap to the British officials. They never spoke Igbo. This made them to limit their contact with the people. They had no other alternative than to seek people who would act as interpreters or intermediaries. They were only the few educated people who understood and spoke the language of the whiteman. Only the clerk had the education to understand the esoteric mysteries of whiteman's language. The administrators had no choice than to elect or nominate these men into the native council. In most cases these men were foreigners who came with the whiteman. Frequently they were expatriates from Ghana, Sierra Leone, or natives of Onitsha or of the coastal areas, so they were not restrained by the fear of public opinion, in an area where they were strangers.

The clerk of the court was the "master" instead of the servant". His normal duties included the keeping of the court records. These comprised the cash books and judgement books. He took it upon himself

---

[141] Isichei Elizabeth, The Ibo People and the Europeans, London 1970, p.162.

to issue every summons without reference to the chiefs, gave orders for arrests, controlled the court messengers, took charge of prisoners and acted as intermediary between the District officer and the chiefs. Being the only official, apart from the Divisional officer who could read and write, he utilise the opportunity to enrich himself. The Natives could not challenge him directly to the Administrators because of the language barrier. Feeling so high in their posts, the court clerks became a terror to their people. They certainly misrepresented the intentions of the government, and by their actions contributed to the crisis in the society.

Whatever the whiteman knew about the Igbos was that created to them by the clerks and interpreters who normally worked in close contact. At times they misinterpreted the mind of the whiteman for their own selfish ends. In most cases they abused such office. They used the power and authority invested on them for their own private ends. At times they requested litigants to bring goats or fowls to them at home so as to favour such litigants in a case. When asked by the litigants why they should bring such items, they replied that the whiteman had said so, whereas the whiteman did not say so. This is because they knew that the whiteman did not understand Igbo and neither did the Litigants understand the whiteman's language.

The court clerks often attained power and wealth greater even than that of the warrants chiefs, especially after 1914 when European officers no longer sat as the court presidents. Like the warrant chiefs, they grew rich through corruption. On paper there were avenues through which the aggrieved could make their complaints reach the ears of the government. A litigant could ask for the review of his case by a political officer or the administrator. There was also chance that during his monthly tour the political officer could get round of local happenings and squabbles and perhaps probe them. But there is evidence that none of those channels was foolproof. If a review of a case was to be done, it would still be done through the interpretation of the council clerk or the court interpreter. The council clerks continued to grow rich in many ways. They grew rich through the sale of injustice in the courts. Frequently, they engaged in money-lending to needy litigants. All these abuses led to the downfall of this type of system.

4.4.4. The Court Messengers or the Police.

Another group of powerful intermediaries were the police and court messengers. They had the duty of serving court summonses. People described them as the British military police. Those who did not succeed in obtaining these privileged posts created one for themselves. In the early years of colonial rule, Igboland was overrun with importers, who claimed to be government officials and used their alleged authority as a basis for extortion. They acted therefore as the enforcement arm of the native council. It was their duty to compel the people to obey the laws passed by the council. The administrators knew that it was not easy to enforce some of the laws they passed in the council. They knew quite well that majority of the laws they passed were against the people way of life or against the peoples will. It is then the responsibility of the messengers to convey the whiteman's orders to the indigenous people.

This made his position very strong. There were many instances of court messengers issuing warrants of arrest against their personal enemies, and also took bribe to set some of the offenders free. They were trained specially for such functions. Nwabara S.N. describes them vividly: "The court messengers (kotoma) were able-bodied men whose primary jobs were to serve and execute court processed writs of summons and warrants, and to carry out all errand duties for the court. They were provided with white uniform – a pair of blue shorts, shirt and cap – and housed on the court premises in order to be handy for errands. But like the court clerks to whom they owed more allegiance than to the chiefs, the courts messengers became "demi-god" and became a law unto themselves as they went about serving writs of summonses and warrants. They demanded money under the false pretences from alleged offenders".[142]

The unpopularity of the court messengers derived not from its utter divergence from the indigenous political system but also from the fact that it was to many people a reign of terror. The people had little effective redress against this ill treatment. It embedded in many a sense of oppression, which alienated them from the regime.

---

[142] Nwabara S.N., Iboland: A Century of Contact with Britain 1860-1960, London 1977, p.171

4.4.5. The General Functions and Duties of the Native Council.

What were actually the functions and duties of this unwelcome native court? The Native Council was endowed with specific executive and legislative powers. Its power and functions were clearly stated in the Native Courts Proclamation. According to this Proclamation, the members of the Native Council had the power to make: "By-laws for the peace, good order and welfare of their areas of authority and to revoke or amend these as required. By-laws were to deal with matters like the construction and maintenance of roads, the establishment and preservation of landmarks, etc. This system of granting of power to make by-laws to minor courts was an innovation".[143]

This means the abolishment of all other organs that dealt with justice and peace in Igbo traditional society. In order to ensure that the Native Courts were patronised by the people, it was made illegal for any other person or body to exercise jurisdiction on any pretext whatsoever in any area under the jurisdiction of a court founded under the law. For Uchendu V.: "This was the origin of the policy and process by which the councils of village elders as well as the secret and title societies – some of the real indigenous political institutions of the people - were driven underground. However in many places, people continued to disregard this order. They continued to organise their affairs through their indigenous institutions, thus treating the Native courts with studded neglect".[144]

In the early years of British rule, this Native Court played an indispensable role as an outpost of the British Empire. It was the cheapest and most effective means of planting the British flag, wherever it became possible to do so after a military conquest.

---

[143] Native Courts Proclamation No.9 of 1900
[144] Uchendu V., Law of Southern Nigerian 1900, New York 1967, p.42.

4.4.6. The Demerits of Native Council.

4.4.6.1. The Warrant Chief.

Generally speaking, the Igbo communities were democratic since its inception as a community. This means that the government of the communities was the concern of all. It is very unfortunate then that the attempt by the British officials to elect "Warrant" chiefs as the principal authorities among the Igbo was bound to produce an air of artificiality, which contributed substantially to the disintegration of traditional Igbo society. The British officials failed to understand that any government without the support of the people is bound to fail.

It must be stated that some of the warrant chiefs were not expecting such a position. They were also men who, having found themselves in a new situation decided to make the best use of it. The people did not for once look upon them as performing traditional functions. The actual Obis and Chiefs complained openly. Some of the Chiefs and Obis were not members of the 'Native' Council. Members of the councils seemed to have more influence and respect than any other person in the society. They assumed air of superiority above every other person.

One should not forget that before the appointment of these Councils, there existed already council of elders which met from time to time. Crowder made this point clear by saying: "Before the white men came, the kings and chiefs had meeting in which they decided matters concerning the welfare of the country. The 'Native' Councils set up by the government had put a stop to such meetings."[145]

For E.G.Hawkesworth: "The warrant chiefs regarded their appointments as bestowing upon them executive authority of a new type which did not exist before the advent of the British. They regard such appointment not as recognition of their natural position but that they had received government office".[146]

Some of the warrant chiefs committed atrocities. They arrested people randomly. The villagers considered such arrests of titled and old men an insult and an abomination. Such forced arrests were humiliat-

---

[145] Crowder M., op.cit p.256
[146] Afigbo A.E., op.cit p.282

ing. This is because titled men were considered as worthy of the highest respect. Thus the warrant chiefs earned nothing but hatred and disaffection among the villagers. There were frequent clashes between them and the people. It was under this situation and as agents of a remote central government that the warrant chiefs performed their functions. In this new situation, traditional sanctions and their modes of execution were regarded as inapplicable. But under the traditional system these novel factors making for injustice did not exist. For Prof. Afigbo : "The supreme handicap or demerit of the warrant chief system was its lack of any real root in the political traditions of the people. The very idea of a man no matter what he was called, who had powers to issue orders to his village and or its neighbours or to a whole clan was a political novelty. Unfortunately for the administration, the very conferment of a judicial warrant on any body in this area no matter how the appointee was selected or his traditional position among his people, meant the creation of this hitherto unheard – of political prodigy".[147]

In spite of the drive to make the warrant chief system the sole agency of local government and in spite of the zeal with which warrant chiefs were said to have prosecuted non-warrant holders who attempted to try cases outside Native Courts, the indigenous system continued to function. This is not unexpected, since the political system of the old order was extricably embedded in the lineage system. The latter has continued to function to the present day as a base of social life and relationship within the village.

Furthermore the indigenous system was not designed solely for the settlement of cases. It was a full-fledged political organ and the attempt to deprive it of its judicial functions did not prove a fatal blow. Evidence that it continued to function actively is seen in the frequent clashes that occurred between it and the new system.

The second category of evidence for the continued existence of the indigenous system comes from the fact that the indigenous principle of decentralisation of authority triumphed over the opposite ideal represented by the warrant chief system.   Prof. Anene argues that any building without foundation is surely to collapse. For him: "The colonial government in carrying out its policy of indirect rule would have been better advised if it had sought out the elders in each village-

---

[147] Afigbo A.E., ibid. p .282

103

group as agencies of rule. Going further he said, among the Ibo and their neighbours the elders were not primarily political leaders but merely intermediaries between the dead ancestors and the living".[148] The whiteman did not want to know that in Igbo traditional society, duties and obligations were clearly defined. Decisions were made in the presence of the community according to universally acknowledged precedents and customs. But the warrant chiefs operated within the new and dimly comprehended system. There were no precedents to guide them, and they were less responsible to public opinion than to the white official who had the power to take away their warrants. They feared the government more than the people. The latter could not unseat a chief but the government could sack him at any time if he failed to dance to its tune.

With the successful establishment of the Warrant Chief system of administration, the white man then ganged up against the natives by using the warrant chiefs to subdue the people. Some of the warrant chiefs carried out their orders to the letter. They disregarded the feelings of the people and their masters. The communication gap between the people and their so-called warrant chiefs started to crack and eventually became sour. Despite all these, the warrant chiefs' did not want to know how their people are feeling about their new assignments. Once their masters were all right with their duties, there was no trouble. These warrant chiefs were not at all tactful, and when the villagers showed their resentments and annoyance, they made their orders more imperative and severe. This notwithstanding, the people did not listen to some of them. They forced people to obey. At times they fulfilled their threats by calling the standby-by-British soldiers, who usually arrested people including titled men.

However, the villagers could not do anything as they were fearful of the white man's war weapons. The history of the warrant chief system is a tale of wrong assumptions leading to wrong decisions and wrong remedies and finally to failure. In so far as the system was untraditional, it carried a fatal flaw from its inception.

---

[148] Anene J.C., op. cit p.258.

4.4.6.2. Other Organs of the Council and Abuse of Power.

The council interpreters and the court messengers were out of control because of lacuna in communication, so says Elizabeth Isichei: "The administrators knew it all but what could they do? The rulers of Southern Nigeria were well aware of the power in the hands of these intermediaries and their often-corrupt use of it... great injustice frequently occurs owing to the ignorance of 'European officers of the native languages and consequent blackmailing of natives by the official interpreters and police who are the sole medium of communication between European and native".[149]

The British agents who undertook the responsibility of administering the eastern protectorate began their assignment and their task on the basis of preconceptions that were both prejudiced and ignorant. They assumed that whatever system is applicable in one part of the land can equally be applicable in the other. The absence of extensive political integration was construed as evidence of anarchy. They believed that they had the best system of government, which every colony had to apply. Their basic task, as they saw it, was to establish order and stability where anarchy had hitherto prevailed. The complexity and subtlety which characterised the social and political institutions of the indigenous people were not their interest and therefore they did not appreciate it. They went ahead to impose their own system of government.

People often raise the question: Which of the two systems the indigenous or the British, administered justice more equitably and gave greater satisfaction than the other. To the people of the Eastern Province there was no doubt that the establishment of the warrant system marked the end of an era in their judicial history. As one of the chiefs put it: "Immediately whiteman came, justice vanished".

The indigenous people protested vehemently against such a system. Neither public opinion nor any other force put up by the people could have any effect against this new system. Since then no group of people ignore a warrant chief or set aside the orders of a native court without incurring the displeasure of the government. Asked whether the people ever thought they had any control over the Native Court and its members and staff, a former warrant chief replied: the Native

---

[149] Isichei E., op. cit p.257.

Court belonged to the government. The people did not establish it nor could they close it down, if they attempted to close it down they brought upon themselves a military patrol. Warrant chiefs feared the government more than the people. The latter could not unseat a chief but the government could. The interaction between the government and the governed continued to widen. The feelings of the people did not count any more. As for Afigbo, A.: "The fact that warrant chiefs were not accountable to their kith and kin was a proof to the people that the chiefs like the courts messengers, the police soldiers, court clerks and the like were civil servants. Revelling in their new position, the warrant chiefs exercised powers, which were unprecedented in scope in the political experience of the people. It was admitted that anybody who got the cap or a warrant or both became more powerful than he could ever have been under the indigenous system and for as long as he enjoyed the confidence of the government, was more powerful than all the people under him".[150]

The un-traditionalism and therefore the tragedy of the warrant chief system lay in the fact that it side-tracked the indigenous institutions of the communities of this region in favour of a handful of arbitrarily selected men.

The native council also contravened traditional practices and usage in all the vital aspects of its constitution and function. There is also evidence that warrant chiefs and clerks as instruments of oppression deliberately used Native Courts to perpetuate evil in the society. The chiefs in particular abused their office by prosecuting people for disobeying their orders. In the Native Court whatever orders the chief had issued were not generally probed. It was a vindictive order against an opponent. The trial of a defiant usually centred on whether he had disobeyed an order from his chief. The chiefs and clerks were also accused of being in league with disreputable men whom they used to bring rivals to courts for liquidation. On this point one chief R.J. Onyeneho says: "It was under the warrant chief system that the terrible thing called "*Akwukwo Nwanunu*" (This literally meant Bird's Summons. It was so described because it was summons from the air that is from fictitious enemies.) came into being. It was a system by which a chief could contrive to bring to court a man whose only offence was that he was forceful and progressive. Chiefs regarded such men as a

---

[150] Afigbo A.E., op. cit. p.257.

threat to their positions and used the court to liquidate them. Once such men were dragged to court the cased against them, which were often groundless ended only after they had spent in defending themselves all the wealth, which made them proud".[151]

The services which the Warrant chiefs and their Councils rendered were useful to the British administration, but a total failure to their people. If ever the courts accomplished much in the way of settling disputes, it was also true that before these courts came into being, the people had their own means of settling cases. Even the fairness of many of their decisions was often in doubt and put into question. Men operated a system whose purposes they did understand. They treated cases whose origin they had intimate knowledge of and dealt with litigants whose history and characters they knew very well. They gave each case the attention it deserved since there were not too many cases to deal with at a time. In traditional set up everybody who had anything to contribute was heard and not interrupted or hushed to save time or out of some ulterior motive as was the case in Native courts.

Another aspect of the warrant chief system which gave offence and which was connected with the size of Native Court's of jurisdiction areas was the greater distance, which some litigants had to travel in quest of justice. Furthermore the frequent adjournments, which caused much hardship and bred discontent – was also a direct result of the very large area that each court served. The Courts were usually congested with cases. The warrant chiefs found it difficult to cope successfully with the mass of litigation that came before them. Consequently cases were kept pending for months. The fact that the courts lacked an effective means of ensuring that litigants attended when wanted caused further confusion. The fact that every native court had jurisdiction over a wide area and the fact that each case was hastily treated were in part responsible for the unjust decisions, which the Warrant chiefs were notorious for. When a case eventually came up for hearing after series of adjournments, the time that could be spent on it was generally too limited to allow for a very careful investigation of the claims advanced by the parties. To make matters worse some of the chiefs who sat at the council came from different villages. They generally lacked deep knowledge of the local conditions, details of the custom and history of the village concerned, to be able to come to a

---

[151] Afigbo ibid. p.274

just decision quickly, especially as many of the cases were very complicated.

Furthermore, the traditional system did not take delight in the multiplication of litigation and therefore, always sought to give a final solution to each case, if need be by sending it to an oracle that would settle the case once and for all. But native court had an interest in the multiplication of cases for it meant more openings for bribes. It brought into being professional money lenders, petition writers and lawyers, touts, all of whom were interested in multiplying litigation.

4.5. Education: The Building of Schools.

The colonial masters had to think fast about the shortage of personnel in the administration of the colonies. They started building schools so as to train manpower for such posts. This incentive was for the indigenous people enormous. Affirming this Isichei comments: "The incentive which colonialism brought was twofold. On the one hand, the people needed to communicate with their new masters, especially since the channels of communication tended to fall into the hands of corrupt intermediaries. On the other hand, the government needed Africans who were educated – albeit to a low level- to fill the post in its lower echelons, which had otherwise to be filled by Africans, imported from elsewhere. The commercial firms similar needed clerks and artisans, and were prepared on occasion, to subsidise the schools, which would supply them".[152]

In trying to interpret the minds of the Europeans on the establishment of schools, Frank Okwu asserts: "In what amounted to an attempt to atone for the sins of Europe during the dark days of the slave trade, missionaries set out to Christianise the freed slaves. They also educated them so that they would not only be helpful in spreading the gospel among their kinsmen but also useful to the Europeans in their business".[153]

---

[152] Isichei E., op. cit. P.154
[153] Okwu Frank., Mass Communication in West Africa, op. cit. p.28

The missionary work helped to improve communications and create a context of "law and order". The spread of colonial rule gave missionaries a new prestige and authority. Towns invited them to establish schools. All the Mission groups in Southern Nigeria were interested in educating the common people, but none served this cause more energetically than the Roman Catholics of the Eastern Region. Many people wanted to attend the Roman Catholic schools because of the excellent education they were offering to the people. This is why Onwubuiko K.B.C asserted in his book that: "Indeed, any study of the development of Western Education in Eastern Nigeria which does not give the Catholic Church its proper place based on the role it played should of course be seen to be grossly incomplete and lacking the heart of the matter. This is because the Catholic Church was the foremost of the Christian missions to adopt the school system as its chief strategy of evangelising the people of Eastern Nigeria".[154]

Adigwe H. supports the above opinion by observing: "In 1894, the Missionary Fathers wrote the following progress report: The boys are making veritable progress; they all speak and write English satisfactorily, and some of them even very well. What most attract the children are the things we teach them. Many occupy themselves with joinery and too with shoe making".[155]

Due to this tremendous progress made by the missionaries in the area of education the colonial administrators in 1923 decided to set up an Advisory Board on "Native Education" which was to advise the Secretary of State. It provided a forum in which the process and content of education of the natives were discussed. This board later suggested that education should be adapted to the mentality, aptitudes, occupations and traditions of the various peoples, conserving, maintaining and preserving as far as possible all sound and healthy elements in the fabric of their social life. Education they went further to say, should promote, among other things, 'the training of the people in the management of their own affairs and the inculcation of true ideals of leadership and service'.

---

[154] Onwubiko, K.B.C., *The Catholic Church and The Development of Education in Eastern Nigeria (1885-1984)* in Obi. C.A., (ed.) A Hundred Years of the Catholic Church in Eastern Nigeria 1885-1985, Onitsha 1985, p.224.
[155] Adigwe H., The Beginnings of the Catholic Church Among the Igbos of South Eastern Nigeria, 1885-1930, Vienna 1966, p.91

Again it should help the educated ones to strengthen the feelings of responsibility to their various tribal communities.

As the argument on the curriculum and objectives of offering education to the natives was going on, some Europeans opposed this strongly by saying that there were certain areas which Africans should not be employed. This is in the area of administration. They knew quiet well the danger involved in setting up schools because it help to make the people to be aware of their rights nevertheless, they went ahead to allow the missionaries to set up schools. They had no option because they wanted a way of improving the communication gap between them and the indigenous people. They saw it also as a way of increasing the manpower they have in the mini administrative sections. This is what Gerard Wanjobi had in mind, when he says: "Both the colonial governments and the missionaries introduced schools to teach literacy to the Africans, but with rather different aims. The majority, by far, of the schools were in the hands of missionaries, but the colonial government dictated the curriculum in those schools. The colonialists favoured and implanted just a basic literacy, which, even at that level, was heavily practical. This literacy was for the purpose of serving the colonial masters in administration, business and other fields. Africans did not take well to this type of literacy (education). They clamoured for a more substantive literacy, one that would introduce them to the dialectic of ideas. Yet, each time the colonialists thought of reforming education, it was to make it more practical, more rural, and more community-based". [156]

Even some indigenous people started thinking on the basis of the gain that will accrue from the European form of education. Some people saw education as the gateway to economic opportunity. They realised, as they never did before, that knowledge is power and that it can command a good salary. They were unknowingly expressing the same feeling with people from other countries that were colonised by Britain. Radhika E. Parameswaran told a similar experience in his hometown Hyderabad, India. He narrated that one-day: "He manages to wriggle into a crowded bus loaded with people. Knowing my journey was going to be a long one, I stood with my back against a pole and optimistically opened an issue of India Today, an English-language magazine. I thought I would pass the time by browsing through it. A

---

[156] Wanjobi Gerard, op. cit., p. 44.

little boy, obviously poor, shyly smiled at me and said in Telugu, 'Are you reading in Englees, Akka (sister)?' I smiled back and said, 'Yes, do you want to look at this?' He eagerly took the magazine and replied, 'Yes, my father says rich people read Englees, so if I can read Englees I can be like you right?"[157]

This incident he says is only one among numerous painful encounters he had had in India, encounters that brought alive for him the realisation of his own privilege as an upper-caste, middle-class English-educated urban India. However, not everybody in Igboland accepted this type of mentality.

In some parts they did not accept the claim that economic salvation comes from European education. In these places, people were contented with what they had. The wealthy were also contented with their position in life. They were not enthusiastic in embracing western education. The response by the wealthy people among the Igbo people was very low. This may be what the British administrator, Lord Lugard, was referring to in his report on the Amalgamation of Northern and Southern Nigeria, 1912-1919. He pointed out that, "in southern Nigeria in 1913, only one in every 180 children of school age had any sort of education whatever. This meant that more than 99% of the children were receiving no instruction at all. This illustrates the degree of illiteracy of the population at the time"[158] So those who came forward were educated by the missionaries. For Anene .A: "The mission's greatest instrument, in what they regarded as the transformation of Southern Nigeria, was the school. The school not only provided the passport for employment but provided a fruitful field for indoctrination. With the opening of unsuspected opportunities for earning ready wages, in contrast with the financially unproductive drudgery of farming or collecting palm produce, far-sighted families were determined that their children (not slaves as in the nineteenth century) should go to school, government or mission. The results are too obvious to require elaboration. The only question is the profundity of the change the missions and their schools have effected in the peoples' mentality and belief in the ways of their forefathers".[159]

---

[157] Radhika E. Parameswaran, *Colonial Interventions and the Postcolonial Situation in India*, in Gazette vol.59(1), London 1997, p. 21.
[158] Lugard, F.D., Report on the Amalgamation of Northern and Southern Nigeria and Administration 1912-1919, London 1920, p.59
[159] Anene, J.C., op. cit. p.326

Some argued that the educational system, which the missionaries offered, consisted of a marriage of convenience. The government was eager to use the mission's personnel and expertise in running the schools and provided subsidies accordingly. To the missions, the new state of affairs offered a solution to their financial problems and the opportunity to exercise a real influence on Igbland, which they had sought in vain for so long. Both Christians and traditional religionists wanted some schools directed by the Holy Ghost Fathers. The missionaries were probably the only Europeans who came to Igboland with the primary intention of working for the good of the people. The religious instruction was made compulsory and was a means of acquiring English, the language of trade, the language of native court and the language of government administration. The indigenous people regarded any education that does not lead to getting the white man's collar job as baseless. The colonial administration was very happy that people were responding to the missionary offer of education. It continued to encourage the missionaries in their quest to provide education for the people. For the fact that English, by then became the passport for higher positions in the government and business circles, many indigenous people availed themselves of the opportunities of English education provided by missionaries.

4.5.1. The Aftermath of Western Education.

The impact of the western education was very tremendous. However for Margaret Read the adjustment and change from the traditional system into the western style was something gradual. She continued: "Between traditional African and Western-oriented societies there were no dichotomy but a continual process of re-adjustment.... The first stage is one of conservatism, even to the extent of resistance, with regard to the introduction of modern education. The second stage is a gradual acceptance of some of the new ideas and the new ways of living introduced through the schools. This is followed by a third stage, marked by the rejection of certain traditional values and customs. This stage gives way to a fourth in which there is a full acceptance of the opportunities given by the British educational system and the determination of educated Africans to show they are equal to Europeans in intellect and can assimilate their entire standard. It is significant, Read points out, that those Africans who led the way in this new process of selectiveness had for the most part achieved a high level of educational parity with Europeans. The sixth and final stage is the determined effort on the part of the elite to weld Western and African culture together".[160]

This intermarriage between the Western and African culture brought with it series of conflicts among the indigenous people. The fact that western education brought with it positive elements will not make us to forget its side effects on the indigenous Igbo society. Its first assaults were against native customs. Christianity, with the secular education, which was the missionaries' second and most eagerly accepted gift, was bound to shatter the fundamental beliefs upon which all-important native institutions rested. Evangelisation, moreover, did not gradually permeate the mind of all members of the community at the same pace. The Aged were seldom open to its influence.

Thus, what is to Africans a deep and unnatural rift has been introduced between old and young. The basis of authority is shaken. The young have lost much of their respect for the elders and sometimes refuse to take up their "ofos", attend services at the ancestral shrines, or perform the ceremonies obligatory upon members of the group. The societies have been badly hit by the falling off in the numbers of new entrants, since Christians are discouraged, if not forbidden,, by the missionaries from passing through the ceremonies which accompany the achievement of each new rank. Perham Margery put it clearly thus: "Missions have not been the only cause of the disturbance of the balance between young and old. The introduction of money as a of way of earning outside the cultivation of the family lands and beyond the control of the elders, have made it possible for the young to become independent of, and richer than their fathers and grandfathers. The young ones escape from the pressure of overpopulation by going to work in the towns, and on railway and road construction. The development of the trade in palm-products, with the greater ease of communications, has increased the freedom not only of

---

[160] Crowder Michael, West Africa under Colonial Rule, London 1970, p.388

the men but also of the women who are vigorous petty traders and carriers".[161]

Despite all the arguments against the western education, its positive effect remain a thing to be proud of even till today in the whole of African society. When one reflects on how some African countries gained their independence, one should accord a very important role to literacy. Eminent personalities like Nnamdi Azikiwe, Obafemi Awolowo, all from Nigeria, Kwame Nkrumah of Ghana, Julius Nyerere of Tanzanian, Milton Obote of Uganda, Jomo Kenyatta of Kenya, were able to fight for independence because of the higher education they had received or because they had been enlightened through their travels abroad. It was literacy, which opened their minds to appropriate their dignity as human beings who enjoy the gift of freedom. Literacy also helped them to argue with the white man on his own terms.

4.5.2. Disintegration of Traditional System.

The establishment of colonial rule in Nigeria produced what has been described as the colonial situation. The indigenous people who never experienced such administration were forced to adjust their way of life in all ramifications. This led to many problems, which the indigenous people did not anticipate. This is what Wallerstein portrays when he says that: "The colonial administrators imposes in a given area a new institution, the colonial administration, governed by outsiders who establish new rules, which they enforce with a reasonable degree of success".[162]

They enforced it at the detriment of the welfare of the people. This system brought about great disintegration in the united indigenous society. The impact of European administration led to change in all spheres of the people's life. This new administration brought about the grouping of peoples into new political units, and ignited free movement to wherever one will find peaceful life, and improvement of life. This movement was principally towards the new urban centres, which were the focus of colonial commerce and administration. This sort of

---

[161] Peerham M, op. cit. p.239
[162] Crowder, M. op. cit p.335

114

movement facilitated the day-to-day contact with the white man, and in the interaction of these two groups, things continue to fall apart. People started migrating from one end to the other. Resultantly, peasant farmers became increasingly involved in the cash crop economy in which the dominant element was no longer the African but the expatriate European traders.

Furthermore, indigenous African religions lost ground to the great monotheistic religions of Islam and Christianity, though they succeeded in imposing some of their characteristics on these alien religions. An important minority of the population acquired western education and therefore an understanding, however partial, of the way of life and thought of their colonial masters. Traditional political authority decline in the face of the changes brought about by colonial rule.

4.5.3. Migration.

The most conspicuous phenomena noted by observers during the colonial era were the large-scale seasonal migrations and the related growth of urban centres, although most of the immigrants always return to the rural tribal areas after a long time. This is a movement of people from the rural area to the urban cities or from one rural area to the other in search of greener pasture.

This movement during the colonial era made it possible for people to broaden their horizons. It also led to new economic possibilities and arrangements, and these in turn caused traditional systems of authority to be called into question. Migration was a phenomenon congruent with modernisation. Most of the migrants were young people. Few of them were over thirty-five years. They were mostly bachelors; if married, they usually left their wives and children in the villages. This means bringing about the separation of families. When they succeeded in getting jobs their length of stay in employment places varied widely from several months to several years.

4.5.4. Urbanisation.

Life was no longer as it was before the advent of the whiteman. People started moving to and fro their homes in search of greener pastures. Much of the movement was towards the urban or town areas. Louis Wirth a contemporary sociologist gave a minimum sociological definition of a city or urban area as "a relatively large, dense and permanent settlement of socially heterogeneous individuals."[163] Therefore the focal point for the changes brought about by the movements of peoples and the impact of the new commercial and administrative regimes was the town. The growth of these new towns was one of the most marked developments of the colonial period. From these prerequisites, Louis Wirth then deduced the major outlines of the urban way of life. These include: "Number, density, and heterogeneity created a social structure in which primary-group relationships were inevitably replaced by secondary contacts that were impersonal, segmental, superficial, transitory, and often predatory in nature. As a result, the city dweller became anonymous, isolated, secular, relativistic, rational and sophisticated. In order to function in the urban society, he was forced to combine with others to organise corporations, voluntary associations, representative forms of government, and the impersonal mass media of communications. These replaced the primary groups and the integrated way of life found in rural and other pre-industrial settlements".[164]

Wirth argued that number, density and heterogeneity had two social consequences which explain the major features of urban life. On the one hand, the crowding of diverse types of people into a small area led to the segregation of people into separate neighbourhood. The unique communication and unity that existed on the rural could not be found in the city life. Again the lack of physical distance between city dwellers resulted in social contact between themselves, which broke down existing social and cultural patterns and encouraged assimilation as well as acculturation.

---

[163]Gans Herbert, J., People and Plans, Essays on Urban Problems and Solutions, New York 1991, p.34
[164] ibid. p.35

116

4.6. The Effects of Migration and Urbanisation.

4.6.1. Detribalised Man.

As means of communication continued to improve and various cities offering better ways of life to develop many people decided to settle in the cities. These cities comprise of assortment and varieties of men. The urbanised individuals are described as "detribalised", or "marginal" because they are without "roots" (land, chief, or kin). Heterogeneity became the order of the day. Here, some could not be identified with any tribe, or ethnic origin instead they are recognised with their occupation, rank and their titles. In urban areas, these newcomers imbibe immediately stereotyped identities that may not correspond with their own traditional ones, which however may regulate their place of abode and the type of work they do. This means cut off from home, and in separate social boundaries, the migrants lose their connection or attachment to tradition. They seek to join or create associations in which they receive recognition through groupings.

4.6.2. Economic Implication.

The fact that many people could not earn enough money in the village they then decided to migrate into the urban cities. The establishment of alternative economic avenues, in which the significance of kinship is slight, and the concurrent establishment of norms more appropriate to changing economic motives, had additional repercussions on kinship relationships. Kuper says: "Young men who traditionally would have followed lineage occupations are now attracted to newer and more remunerative way of earning a living. Many of them have incomes that far surpass those of their elders, and have become financially independent of their lineage for economic status or financial aid. This situation has a number of implications".[165]

---

[165] Kuper Peter (ed.), Urbanisation in West Africa. p.100

Differential income and upwardly mobile elements within a lineage imply a potential, if not actual status separation of kinsmen on the basis of individually achieved qualities. The sanctions available to a lineage for reinforcing traditional patterns of behaviour have also been curtailed by the diversification of economic roles. If a man no longer needs his lineage for economic status or financial aid, he may no longer feel obliged to recognise other reciprocities; he may therefore resent or evade obligations and responsibilities that were previously regarded as imperatives which expression to fundamental notions of lineage solidarity and unity.

The increased economic and political diversification has led to a reduction in the importance of a lineage as a corporate social entity in structuring social relationships. This process is accompanied by a transfer of responsibility and obligation from lineage groups to individuals, and a shift from an emphasis on relationships between persons to interaction that might be very impersonal and specific. The reason for this movement from the village into the outside economy, therefore, is the quest for a higher income. However the inability of urban cities to absorb the continuous inflow of new comers has led in many cases to unemployment, destitution and crime.

Migrants are exposed to new ideas but they readjust as quickly as possible to their new environment. The real impact of this is to be measured through the increasing number of children born in the towns who return later to the villages with their migrant parents: Under present conditions, the participation of children in the phenomenon of migration can play an important role in the formation and transmission of a national culture presently being created, in the context of new contacts among ethnic groups and between emerging nations. These children become adults for whom values and use of the nation as a reference group is a childhood experience rather than one acquired in adult life. For them, a village frame of reference is the new phenomenon rather than the reverse. During the colonial era migration made possible the contacts through which horizons were broadened and administrations were subverted. It led to new economic possibilities and arrangements, and these in turn caused traditional systems of authority to be called into question. Migration was, in short, a phenomenon congruent with modernisation.

4.7. Political Implication of Urbanisation

4.7.1. Freedom from Traditional Authority.

In most cases individuals flee to urban areas to escape the eyes of traditional authorities who usually punish offenders for crimes committed. These individuals live in cities with greater measure of freedom. They can commit crimes without punishment from the traditional head or family head. They live anonymously. The reduction in solidarity of the "Umunna" or kin group   and of its authority and control over members is a clear characteristic of migration into the cities. In extreme cases, a segment comprising a man and his children may live off from a lineage and form a separate economic, social and residential unit. Such units are confined to the few who have achieved complete economic independence from their lineage and have accepted, at least in part, new values and norms so that they are able to tolerate more easily the psychosocial separation from their kinfolks. For most individuals, the break from traditional patterns is not so radical. Segments usually continue to live in their lineage compounds and remain within the jurisdiction of the wider group. The conflicts and separations are then expressed in terms of a sharper definition and assertion of individual and group rights within a lineage, and a corresponding decrease in the rights of the wider groups.

In the political field, too, kinship has lost some of its relevance. The differential ranking of lineages on the basis of hereditary office has been modified. The powers of the chiefs have been limited and redefined and their control of resources has been restricted; thus, indirectly, the privileges of the chieftaincy lineages have been curtailed. New and effective political groups which are not based on decendancy have been established, and through them, men can achieve status and power, which traditionally had not been accessible to them.

On another level of organisation, the political function and corporateness of a lineage have been affected. The kin group formerly had corporate responsibility and was the primary agency for social control. Now, legally, the individual is separated from his status as a member of a kin unit. This separation has two important implications. First, the individual is now, according to formal law, responsible for his own actions; should he commit a crime, the guilt is his alone in the eyes of the government. Secondly, the notion of individual responsibility provides a conceptual and moral basis for individual contractual relationships.

The increased economic and political diversification has led, to a reduction in the importance of a lineage as a corporate social entity in structuring social relationships. A transfer of responsibility and obligation accompanies this process from lineage groups to individuals and a shift from an emphasis on relationships between persons to inter action that might be very impersonal and specific.

4.7.2. Family Separation.

Another striking feature was the large number of young people living in the towns. As much as two-thirds of a city could be composed of people less than thirty years. The city attracted the youth in particular, for without wives and children it was easier for them to leave home to seek their fortune in the cities, where they could escape oppressive features of home life. But the town with its bars, its prostitutes, its crime, its delinquency, its dedication to the pursuit of personal gain, its over-crowding, its unemployment, fought a strong battle in favour of individualism against the traditional values of communal African society.

Nevertheless, most of the urban settlers tended to link up with fellow settlers from the same ethnic group, and in some towns one ethnic group inhabited particular sections. The traditional sanctions, particularly those of religion, were not applied here and the urban settlers formed themselves into voluntary associations. The towns were also the residences of the new African educated élite, who found it easier than their less educated brethren to cross the barriers of ethnicity. They formed debating and literary societies, where a person's ethnic origin did not matter and where political questions came increasingly to the fore.

4.8. Language Implication.

It is obvious that such large-scale movements of people will definitely have series of repercussions on the most basic aspects of the societies involved; among these is the communication system or language. Hence Joseph Greenberg is of the opinion that: "Elemental problem of communication, which arises for the migrant, is that of a 'common language' with his employer and others with whom he comes into contact, whether in an urban or a rural situation".[166]

The overriding socio-linguistic fact about Africa is simply its vast language diversity. The conventional number of 800 separate languages for the continent is certainly an underestimation. These languages are, for the most part the primary spoken languages in relatively restricted areas. Hence migrations of more than local scope are bound to bring populations with divergent native languages into the same urban or rural areas. Wherever the Europeans lived and worked in Africa, they superimposed their own language on the people. The indigenous language was suppressed. In other areas the existence of linguistic heterogeneity tended to be the rule. The usual solution to this problem is the so-called lingua franca. In the present context nothing was being asserted about the linguistic nature of this lingua franca. It may be a standard form of some existing language, or a "pidginise" form, or even, conceivably, a new creation. All that is meant here by a lingua franca is "a language used for purposes of communication between people; it is not the first language of both communicating parties, but on occasion may be the first language of one party or of neither party." A given area might thus have more than one lingua franca.

Most frequently, however, there is a single lingua franca which tends to be dominant over a substantial area. This solution is rational, in a sense, particularly if the lingua franca is the first language of the numerically largest group, it is the solution that requires the least amount of second language learning. There is a further psychological advantage, for a single lingua franca it is likely to be, in many instances, a language foreign to both speakers. Thus neither has to make

---

[166] GREENBERG, JOSEPH. H., *Urbanism, Migration and Language Problem* in   Peter(ed.). op. cit. p. 51.

the compromise of speaking the other's language. That this element is important in interpersonal and inter-group relations and communication may be seen from the fact that in most instances, Europeans who were in the dominant position, not in terms of number but in terms of claimed superiority, did not learn the African language.

It was the African who had to make the linguistic adjustment, a situation that sometimes produced resentment on the African side. On this basis asserts Joseph Greenberg: "The single lingua franca tends to become the dominant solution not because anyone plans it that way, but because, once a language has a head start by being the language of a numerically important group, particularly the locally dominant one, others discover the advantage or even the necessity of learning it. Once it becomes at all widespread, it has an advantage over other possible lingua franca also that its expansion continues. The only thing that is likely to arrest its spread is a rival lingua franca. A lingua franca, however, may spread very slowly when it encounters a language with a large number of speakers in a compact area".[167]

Several African languages thus became established as lingua franca through political and commercial factors in the interior of West Africa, in the centuries preceding the exploration and the colonial expansion of the nineteenth century quite different lingua franca developed on the coast. Here the contact of Europeans and Africans led to the development of "pidginise" forms of European languages, mainly English, French and Portuguese.

The spread of lingua franca has been so extensive under the impact of Westernisation that there is now hardly any area in Africa which does not have a dominant lingua franca. For example, the dominant lingua franca of both the Western and Eastern regions of Nigeria is English. At the same time, languages such as English and French were being taught in mission and government schools, and have been in undisputed use for university-level education. This form of European languages became associated with illiteracy and, above all, with the colonial master-servant relationship.

On the other hand, a command of Standard English, French or Portuguese is the sign of the African elite. The ability to speak a European tongue becomes a supra regional, supra tribal, even supranational mark of a new elite whose badge of membership is education.

---

[167] Ibid. p.52

4.8.1. Language and Socio-Political Groupings.

The Colonialists have considered language mainly from the utilitarian point of view, as a means of communication. It is, however, more than that, language is perhaps the most important single criterion of group identification. For example, in Africa "Tribe" is defined, with very few exceptions in terms of first, language. The Igbo people themselves are aware that the loss of their linguistic heritage would almost inevitably follow their loss of tribal identity.

It is not surprising that a lingua franca may be current in the group without producing any evident movement toward assimilation. Such a situation is called by linguist's "stable bi-lingualism". Tribal intermarriage on a wide scale of course, tends to undermine this continuity. The evidence seems to show that up to now tribal endogamy has prevailed markedly over tribal exogamy in the urban centres of Africa. Systematic data seem to be lacking in regard to the language or languages spoken by the offspring of intertribal marriages, and in regard to the relationship of this question to tribal identification. It should be noted that language might be the subject of conscious planning and policy. During the colonial era, colonial governments made decisions on matters of language in Africa. For instance, the British and French policy of using their languages exclusively in education and administration has tended both to facilitate the spread of their languages as a lingua franca and to bring loss of prestige to African languages.

The impact of colonial administration on Igboland is far-reaching. Colonialism was mainly for economic exploitation. Although it brought along with it some positive and creative aspects of life such as education and the construction of better means of communications, all were geared towards the political and economic needs of the colonial power. When the colonial masters had settled down, they employed yet another means of communication namely, the electronic media. This served their political propaganda effectively.

4.9. The Advent of Modern Media in Nigeria.

4.9.1. The Empire Service: The Propaganda Media.

In 1932 the British government fulfilled its dream of introducing electronic media in Nigeria. This is the year when it started her propaganda media. It all began on December 19, 1932, when the British Broadcasting Corporation (BBC) launched the world's first regularly scheduled short-wave programme service. This was called the Empire Service. This Empire Service was intended to develop political, cultural and economic links between the United Kingdom and English-speaking peoples. It also required a number of overseas monitoring stations. These stations, one of which was located at Lagos, were to become the ears and eyes of the BBC. They advised on suitable wavelengths and aerial design and, in some cases, provided valuable information on broadcast reception in tropical areas.

This BBC Empire Service quickly surprised the world and Nigerians in particular. From this time on, Nigerians and other British colonies began to realise the potentialities of broadcasting. Unfortunately, at this time the world was experiencing an in depth economic depression and only limited fund were available for broadcasting in colonial territories. However the colonial administrators did not give up because of limited resources. They provided a welcome alternative when it encouraged overseas stations to re-broadcast the Empire Service.

The offer was accepted by a number of countries including India, Australia, New Zealand and African countries of which Nigeria was one. These BBC rebroadcasts were to provide the backbone for many newly created broadcasting services in the colonies.

It was Lord Reith who was the Director General of the British Broadcasting Corporation that initiated in 1924 this Empire Broadcast. At first he could not secure the support of the home government for this project. This was because of the financial aspect involved in carrying such gigantic project like broadcasting. Despite all criticisms from the home government the station was finished in December 1932. At the inaugural transmission, Lord Reith expressed the objectives of the Empire Broadcasting by saying: "If we succeed in dispelling some of the isolation and loneliness which is the lot of so many of our kindred overseas: if we bring to them and to others some share of the amenities of the home country and of metropolitan interests and culture, which for one reason or another may not be fully available; if we can induce among the constituent parts of the Empire a greater understanding and a greater sympathy; if we can broadcast at home some programmes from overseas; if in general, as is our hope, the several far-scattered units of the Empire may be drawn closer together then our efforts will be amply rewarded".[168]

4.9.2. The Wired Wireless or Rediffusion Radio Service.

Lord Reith went further in making effort to see that everybody heard this Empire broadcasting. The Nigerian Posts and Telegraphs Department was then directed to evolve, not a broadcasting service as we understand the term today, but a method of distributing programmes to the main centres of population. This entails re-broadcasting of BBC programmes and services. The Posts and Telegraphs Department began to experiment with wired wireless and planned to offer the public subscription relays of BBC programmes through re-diffusion boxes. This method, called a Radio Distribution Service (RDS), was based on the radio relay exchanges which flourished in the United Kingdom in the 1920's. These exchanges did not rebroadcast the programmes of BBC immediately to everybody. The "RDS" was a radio service, which could only distribute or relay radio programmes through wires connected to loudspeakers installed privately in homes of subscribers or in public listening centres. Why did the British administration undertake all these pains to install such Radio Distribution Service to all corners of the country? Olu Ladele put it rightly when he asserts: "Due to the burning need during the Second World War, to disseminate accurate information and war propaganda to the masses in the colonies, the few newspapers that existed could not cope with this because of limited circulation and the fact that only literate people could read them. Therefore at certain times of the day the BBC broadcast news at dictation speed. These bulletins were copied at the RDS stations and translated into the main languages spoken in the area covered by the different RDS stations as well as into pidgin English for the benefit of those who did not speak the local indigenous language. In addition to translating the news into the local languages,

---

[168] British Broadcsting Empire London 1936, p.2

125

gramophone records of local music were also played, and the occasional indigenous artist was heard singing or telling folk stories from the RDs stations".[169]

Thanks to the Second World War otherwise the electronic media could have taken a slow-march into Nigeria. Germany under Adolph Hitler had already got six short-wave transmitters, which championed war propaganda in their colonies. This German strategy awakened series of transmission activities in the BBC's transmitting station at Daventry Empire Broadcasting Service. One should not confuse this radio distribution service with the wireless radio system which is received through the wavelength. Milton Edward gave us a vivid description of Radio Distribution thus: "The programs in this system [i.e. RDS] are distributed by land from the studio to the various listening boxes for which the subscribers pay a small fees. Amplification is needed at some locations and was provided by a makeshift and home-built apparatus. This system caught the interest of Nigeria and was expanded to include stations at Ibadan, Abeokuta, Ijebu-Ode, Calabar, port Harcourt, Enugu, Kano, Kaduna, Jos and Zaria".[170]

Giving further clarification on how "RDS" works, Olu Ladele says that it also: "Advertised the conditions under which a radio distribution line would be installed in private homes and public places to enable subscribers listen to BBC programmes. A distribution line was simply a loudspeaker with all the wires leading to it. The loudspeakers were connected by a network of land lines to a highly selective receiver which had a specially designed directional aerial. BBC's overseas programmes were piped through the landlines to the loudspeakers in subscribers' premises. Each subscriber was required to pay a fee of fifty kobo per month after an initial payment of three months rental in advance".[171]

It redistributed the programmes later by laying pipe into loudspeakers to various subscribers' homes. This has been described as an extension of the telephone service but with one-way, instead of two-way, telephoning. It is not exaggerating to say here that Nigeria may have been one of the first African countries to become broadcasting con-

---

[169] Olu Ladele, Nigerian Broadcasting Corporation Committee Report 1974 p.3f.

[170] Milton, E.C., A Survey of the Technical Development of the Nigerian Broadcasting Corporation, Lagos 1955, p.34.

[171] Olu, Ladele, History of the Nigerian Broadcasting Corporation, Ibandan 1964, p.8.

scious. Although nineteen years were to elapse before Nigeria was to have a broadcasting service of its own reflecting the day-to-day life of its people, their music and folklore. In December 1935, a radio distribution station was erected in Lagos that replaced the experimental station. The Lagos station and the other stations which followed were destined to make a unique contribution to Nigerian broadcasting and provided the only satisfactory service. Mackay Ian reveals: "Not all Nigerian listeners depended on the Lagos station. The more affluent listeners paid ten shillings a year licence fee while the wired box subscribers paid five shillings a month or £2.10 annually. In the first year Lagos reported 500 subscribers and there was a waiting list. Subscribers increased to 753 and 829 in the next two years but there were probably less than a thousand subscribers and 2,000 licensed receivers when the Second World War commenced in 1939".[172]

Years were to elapse before broadcasting was to become a mass medium in Nigeria, but the audience was greater than the mere number of actual subscribers because many receiving points served as community centres. The overall audience was quite substantial.

The Lagos short-wave station was the first to broadcast Nigerian programmes and artists. Operating on 300 watts, it was located at the Posts and Telegraphs Department depot on Ikoyi Island. This station, also the first to operate under the call sign RADIO NIGERIA often broke down, was frequently off the air, and with its low power, could only provide limited coverage. In 1948 the Secretary of State for the Colonies drew attention to the slow development of broadcasting in West Africa, and this preceded the enactment of the Colonial Development and Welfare Act 1948, which provided funds for many projects.

The Colonial Office, realising the important of communications media would play in the economic and social development of Africa, commissioned the BBC to conduct an extensive survey in the four West African countries of Gambia, Sierra Leone, Gold Coast (Ghana) and Nigeria. This commission is popularly known as the "Turner-Byron Report of 1949". On the 10th of January 1949 the Commission was sent out with these research objectives. The main purpose of this survey was to determine broadcasting needs, report on methods of development and whether the existing facilities should be incorporated

---

[172] Mackay, Ian.K., Broadcasting in Nigeria, Ibadan 1964, p.3.

in any proposed new scheme. The report recommended the following: "Future coverage in West Africa should be by both wired wireless and actual transmission, that the former was economically limited to the densely populated areas. To draw up a technical scheme and estimates of cost to give a broadcasting service primarily to the African population; and to include proposals for communal listening; To recommend what technical facilities should be provided for reception and local broadcasting for programmes transmitted by short-waves from Great Britain; and to prepare estimates of cost; and to recommend the general lines of the organisation required implementing, maintain and operate any technical scheme".[173]

This Turner and Byron Report brought enormous changes in the history and capacity of the existing RDS of Nigeria. According to this report Nigeria was in an urgent need of a wireless broadcasting machinery. After the survey, Turner and Byron made some suggestions in order to improve broadcasting on both federal and regional levels. Transmitters were to be installed in stages.

Location	Stage 1	Programmes
Lagos	20 Kw short wave	National Coverage and West Regional Programmes.
Kaduna	10 Kw short wave	10 kW short wave
Ibadan	5 Kw short wave	Local coverage
	Stage 2	
Lagos	5 Kw medium wave	Local coverage
Enugu	5 Kw short wave	Eastern coverage
	Stage 3	
Kano	5 Kw medium wave	Local coverage.[174]

The Nigerian Broadcasting Service commenced operations on April 1, 1951. At this time there was no difficulty in deciding the nature of the problems to be tackled. They were:-

---

[173] Turner, L.W., and Byron, F.A.W., *Broadcasting Survey of the British West African Colonies* in Mackay Ian, K. Broadcasting in Nigeria, p.6
[174] ibid. p.8

a). To secure suitable sites for proposed transmitting, receiving and studio centres.

b). To acquire the equipment necessary to provide the proposed service.

c). To recruit suitable technical staff to install, operate and maintain the service.

d). To plan such buildings and installations as would be necessary to implement the agreed plan.

The report gave rooms for broadcasting programmes in some Nigerian languages. These main languages include:–"Hausa, Fulani, Igbo and Yoruba. And the regional programmes were to operate with the local language e.g.-Lagos with Yoruba and Hausa for the whole of "Western Region", In the Eastern Region – Igbo, Ibibio and Efik should obtain. The Northern Region should have Hausa, Fulani, and Kanuri and the Kano local programmes should include Arabic language"[175]

It is necessary to mention that the main problem that preyed on the development of the early radio electronic medium in Nigeria was the colonial politics. It was often noticed that the colonial government did this for their own interest. Even the location of the transmitting stations was politicised rather than technically decisive. They located them in those cities they had developed for themselves. This information system was not necessarily built to serve the local need and interest but was on the service of imperial taste and task. Head Sydney W. expressed this situation in this fashion: "Colonial radiotelegraph and radiotelephone circuits tended to radiate outward from the urbanised fringe; linking colonial enters of administration with London, Paris, Brussels, Lisbon, and Madrid. In most cases there was no lateral interconnection from one African territory to the next; newly independent African states found themselves unable to communicate directly with each other. Messages had to be routed thousands of miles out of the way through Europe to reach an African capital only a few hundred miles away".[176]

The colonial radio inventory was all urban centred and its operation was almost urban or township-limited. This means that it could not

---

[175] ibid. p.18

[176] Heads S.W., *Trends in Tropical African Societies*, in Gerbner. G. (ed.) Mass Media Policies and Changing Cultures, London 1977, p.55.

cover the whole country. This restriction was as a result of colonial economic strategy. Another problem was that the colonial contractors perhaps out of financial difficulties were always installing second-hand transmitters for the new wireless broadcasting system. This led to frequent break down. They never gave up their best. They often had the mentality that anything goes for the Africans. Even the financial aids given by the British government for the purchase of this equipment was not utilised, instead second-hand ones were purchased. Olu Ladele did not waste time in putting such embarrassing situation in his report; it reads: "A second-hand 7 ½ kW short-wave mobile transmitter which had seen service in the Second World war in Normandy was bought from the BBC for the National programme. It had provided the means by which the BBC war correspondents sent their reports from war front during the Allied invasion of Europe. The transmitter was installed in a temporary site at Oshodi and linked with Tugwell house by over twenty kilometres of cables. It was not surprising that this piece of equipment... declined to co-operate after the installation".[177]

The British officials who were involved in this scandalous act would always defend themselves. That is why Mr. Milton E.C, one of the chief engineers came up with an unfounded explanation. He tried to exonerate not only the British government but also members of his engineering crews. He rather blamed the West African climate as the cause of it all. He says: "When I inspected the transmitter in 1951 at its temporary resting-place at Brookamn's Park (one of the important transmitting stations) it had been tested "on power" and all seemed to be satisfactory. Unfortunately the equipment was not designed to work in this sort of climate, which is normal in West Africa on the coast, and where the insides of the trailers had been comfortably warm in Britain at the tail-end of winter, we found that the temperature inside the transmitter section in Lagos was around 140 degrees Fahrenheit. Something drastic had to be done. We practically rebuilt it and thereafter it worked fairly well but it never produced anything like its full output of seven-and-a-half kilowatts, but it did fill a gap".[178]

Other problems associated with broadcasting include staff membership and training of Nigerian broadcasters. The BBC staff members were controlling the early broadcasting affairs in the country with a

---

[177] Olu, Ladaele., op. cit. p.25
[178] ibid. p.25

little working contact with on-the-job-trained Nigerians. Later there were offers of "Overseas-BBC-Training" programmes. The broadcast training in London was conceived to be the "ideal training". This "ideal training" was of an "ideological transfer", because candidates had difficulties on their return with the application of their overseas-knowledge.

This situation changed when broadcasters began training in Nigeria in addition to overseas training. This made researchers opt for a combination of forces whereby both overseas and locally trained candidates co-operate to a single end.

Programming was also problematic because it was an extension of the BBC's philosophy. The basic programming philosophy of the BBC to inform, educate and entertain the audience remains successful as long as they were able to propagate their own ideology. They continued to manipulate the minds of millions of Nigerians by way of giving them filtered and censored overseas programmes. The BBC station was an instrument of the coloniser, which served to propagate their culture, and assert their domination on the colonised people. The broadcasting method in Nigerian was a carbon copy of what obtained in Britain. Programme contents and ideas tended also in this direction without necessarily considering the local environment, peculiarities and the national objectives.

At this time, the percentage of foreign programmes aired by Radio stations in Nigeria was very high. Local programmes which could reflect and foster indigenous culture and serve as a catalyst towards national orientation were ignored. Foreign news was given priority over Nigerian news to the disadvantage of the average citizen who should have been given the opportunity of understanding their environment. The news items were structured to make Nigerians more knowledgeable about foreign affairs than about their own country. These were the greatest problems during this period. Later, the British government decided to hand over broadcasting to the Nigerian government paving way for independence. The next chapter will examine how the Nigerian government handled the media when they were handed over to her by the British administration.

5. THE POST INDEPENDENCE MEDIA IN NIGERIA.

5.1. Freedom of Speech: The Fundamental Human Rights.

It is a simple fact that freedom of the press is an aspect of the freedom of expression. This means, the liberty to voice out one's opinion, thought and ideas either in a spoken or written form. In a democratic society, the individual is entitled to express his opinion on all issues and more especially on public matters. Without communication, social life has no meaning. Society grows on ideas. This is exactly what is entrenched in section 25(1) of the 1963 Constitution of the Republic of Nigeria. In the 1989 constitution, the same idea is located in section 38. This entrenchment indicates that the framers of our constitution have always considered freedom of expression an important aspect of our national life.

In this chapter then, we shall examine the applicability of freedom of expression as contain in the constitution of the Federal Republic of Nigeria after independence. The previous chapter has discussed the Colonial Government and the use of mass media at that period. From all indication, the colonial press was primarily a vehicle for providing news and information to the European population of businessmen and civil servants. Perhaps Jawaharlal Nehru best conveys the imagery of the colonial press in Africa and elsewhere in the British Empire in re-calling his youth in India: "I remember that when 1 was a boy, the British-owned newspapers in India were full of official news and ut-terances; of service news, transfers, and promotions; of the doings of English society, of polo, races, dances and amateur theatricals. There was hardly a word about the people of India, about their political, cul-tural, social or economic life. Reading them, one would hardly suspect that they existed".[179]

At that time the British press was for the British and the French ra-dio was for the French. Both press and radio supported colonial rule and interests and were unsympathetic or outright hostile to African needs and development.

---

[179] Wilcox Dennis, Mass Media in Black Africa: Philosophy and Control, Cape Town 1977, p.2.

THE UNITED NATIONS DECLARATION ON HUMAN RIGHTS article 19 states that: *"everyone has the right to freedom of opinion and expression; this right includes freedom to hold opinions without interference and to seek, receive and impart information and ideas through any media regardless of frontiers."*

THE AFRICAN CHARTER ON HUMAN AND PEOPLE'S RIGHTS ARTICLE 9: says (1): *"every individual shall have the right to receive information. Every individual shall have the right to express and disseminate his opinions within the law."*

Also the Second Vatican Council did not hide its feelings on the importance of freedom of opinions and views. In the document *Inter Mirifica* it says: *"This freedom of communication also implies that individuals and groups must be free to seek out and spread information. It also means that they should have free access to the media. On the other hand, freedom of communication would benefit those who communicate news rather than those who receive it if this freedom existed without needs upon which the right to information is based".*[180] Going further it asserts: *"There exists therefore in human society a right to information on the subjects that are of concern to men either as individuals or as members of society, according to each man's circumstances. The proper exercise of this right demands that the content of the communication be true and - within the limits set by justice and charity. Furthermore, it should be communicated honestly and properly".*[181]

Did the indigenous government that took over from the Europeans after independence made a radical change to use the press to educate the people?

Did they also try to free the press from the censorship which it has suffered under the British administration? Did they continue to use the media like its predecessors for their own aggrandisement? However, there are certain major areas that people expected the press to play an active role in post independence Nigeria. These areas include:

a). Using the press as an instrument for nation building.

b). Using the press as an instrument of national unity.

c). Using the press as an agent of mass education.

---

[180] Vatican Council II, Decree on the Media of Social Communication, Inter Mirifica, n.45, 12th April 1963.
[181] Ibid. n .5.

In the past the colonial government operated and owned many of the communications media, the new Nigerian governments assumed the same policy. Making his observation Legum Colin says: "After independence, television was operated on the same basis as radio.

It was wholly owned and controlled by the government, usually under the direct authority of the ministry of information or a commission, under ministry supervision. In most countries, contracts have been entered into by the government with one more International agency for the local distribution of news by radio-television or the press. But the selection and distribution of items from these external services are controlled by government appointee".[182]

In fact no real effort was made to de-colonise the western model of communication or to integrate the traditional African media into more effective communications for the masses in Nigeria.

However what was apparent was a change of name and ownership in some of these media organs. The post-colonial newspapers, radio and televisions still talk with a minority in the same format, the same content, the same style as in the colonial era. Hence Wilcox says: "By examining the colonial antecedents of the press, it is hoped that one can better understand the forces that shaped the contemporary African press scene. It is only natural that African leaders, once they assumed political power, continued to follow many aspects of the colonial press since that was the only model they knew. Control of the press made sense, not only from the standpoint of its own security and utilisation.... But the question remains, whether the African nations, one or two decades into independence, will continue to fall back on colonial models".[183]

---

[182] Legum Colin, The Continuing Colonial Legacy: Post Independence Press, London 1994, p.12.
[183] Dennis Wilcox, op.cit. p.14.

5.2. The Federal Government and the Nigerian Broadcasting Corporation.

As Nigeria was preparing to take over the administration of the country from the hands of the colonial masters from 1st October 1960, she was equally preparing for the take-over of the broadcasting media built by the British government. These broadcasting houses were structured and administered in the ways that suited the colonial administrators. People looked up to the indigenous government for enormous reforms in the area of broadcasting as they took over. At that time there was no difficulty in identifying the nature of the problems to be tackled. They included according to Bako George the following:

i). The provision of efficient broadcasting services to the entire people of the country, based on national objectives and aspirations and to external audiences in accordance with Nigeria's foreign policy.

ii). The provision of a professional and comprehensive growth through research and to disseminate the results of such research works for the benefit of the public.

iii). The provision of positive contribution to the development of the Nigerian society and to promote National unity by ensuring a balanced presentation of views from all parts of the country.

iv). To ensure the prompt delivery of accurate information to the people.

v). To provide opportunity for the free enlightened and responsible discussion of important issues and to provide a useful two-way contact between the public and those in authority.

vi). The provision of special broadcasting services in the field of Education and in all other areas where the national policy calls for special attention.

vii). To promote orderly and meaningful development of Broadcasting in the country through:

viii).Technical improvements.

ix). The Training of appropriate professional staff and

x). Programme and staff exchanges.

xi). To promote research into various aspects of the communications media and their effects on the Nigerian society which will include:- audience research, the investigation of fresh methods of production and the true indigenasition of the broadcasting media.

xii). To make every Nigerian feel proud of being a Nigerian.[184]

After independence, the Nigerian media were popular especially newspaper industries. They won for themselves the admiration of the citizens who saw the press as champion of the oppressed, especially those in the minority groups. The people helped the Press to grow. Perhaps this popularity of the press and the mass support it was enjoying from the people was a source of concern to some politicians, mostly ministers in the government. The post-independent journalists were to pay for their popularity among the people. The government saw that the media were enjoying unlimited freedom. Coupled to this they were the darling of the people. This phenomenon upset the government. They started looking for means to curtailing press freedom. In the year 1964, only four years after independence, a debate began on an amendment of the constitution which led to the press law of 1964.

The Press Law states: *"Any person, who authorises for publication, publishes, reproduces or circulates for sale in a newspaper any statement, rumour or report knowing or having reason to believe that such statement rumour or report is false shall be guilty of an offence and liable on conviction to a fine of £200 or to imprisonment for a term of one year".*[185]

Its first reading saw a lot of heated arguments from members of opposition parties; the press buttoned its trousers and began a war through editorial comments, and features to demolish parliamentary arguments already advanced in favour of a necessity for the amendment by its sponsors. Even though some members of parliament promised to put up a fight on behalf of journalists who were already applying "lobby" as an additional instrument to stop the law from being passed, it was too late. The 1964 Press Law was born. These pernicious laws against the media gave government officials legal backing to persecute, fine, detain and imprison journalists, and to proscribe media houses.

The then Federal Government seemed to have borrowed the idea of the Russian politician on questions over the validity of press freedom. The famous Russian politician and philosopher, Nikolai Lenin, scared

---

[184] Bako George, "Re-organisation and Future Development of Radio Broadcasting in Nigeria" Paper presented at the Conference on National Symposium on Broadcasting in Nigeria held at the University of Ife, Ibadan 1982, p.3
[185] Dayo Duylie, Meida and Mass Communication, op.cit. p.8.

to death by press power, in his speech in Moscow in 1920 said: *"Why should a government, which is doing what it believes to be right, allow itself to be criticised? Why should any man be allowed to buy a printing press and disseminate pernicious (ideas) calculated to embarrass the government? He declared, 'Ideas are much more fatal things than guns".* [186]

However, ideas can be said to be more constructive than guns. It is correct to say that in Nigeria there is no other opposition against the government other than that offered by the independent media. In an attempt, therefore to stay in power, many African governments often pass laws restricting free flow of information, regardless of whether the flow concept is guaranteed in the nation's constitution or not. Many of them feel unsecured. This has been the fate of the Nigerian press since after independence. For Dennis Wilcox: "It is only natural that African leaders, once they assumed political power, continued to follow many aspects of the colonial press since that was the only model they knew. Control of the press made sense, not only from the standpoint of its own security but for utilisation in programs of national development. But the question remains, whether the African nations, one or two decades into independence, will continue to fall back on colonial models". [187]

However, mention should be made here that private newspapers were given a little breathing space to operate. It was not the case with the broadcasting media. They were unfortunate. The Government thus appears to have singled out broadcasting as the media, which need to be watched at close range. This is also because it sees that radio and television are the most popular of the all the media. According to Nyamnjoh the government assumed that: "Political fortunes depend very much on how well it has harnessed the broadcast media. Elections can be won or lost not by the power of the ballot, but by the power to have access to radio and television, while keeping the private press in check". [188].

Majority of African governments view the establishment of private radio and television stations as a taboo and a threat to their govern-

---

[186] Ibid., p.17f.

[187] Dennis Wilcox, op.cit. p.14.

[188] Francis Nyamnjoh, Media Ownership and Control in Cameroon, in Media Development: Journal of the World Association for Christian Communication, 4/1998, London, p.31

ment. To make matters worse, what filters through the government-controlled electronic media is highly censored so as to fit the ideology of the respective regimes, most of which lean on dictatorship. From the point of view of objectivity and democracy, this is not a healthy situation. The literate Africans are often infuriated at the way governments withhold important news from the masses or at the way the news is distorted or given a wrong emphasis. Till today, many of the African governments have refused to give up the sole ownership of electronic media. It is true says Affenyi Dadzé Gifty that African governments believe that: "State radio is one of the legacies inherited from the colonial masters. This legacy was centralised and closely controlled broadcasting system. One needs no elaboration to show that radio stations in West Africa have not departed very much from its historical mission to transmit government views to the people and to provide information as a public service organisation. Successive government held the view that their own organs were in a better position to carry out the function of information and dissemination better than private broadcasting organisation. Objectives of these radio stations which are therefore used at will, is to communicate political objectives to the people and to solicit their support. The main elements in such radio stations are surveillance, control and propaganda".[189]

The Nigerian government, with all these in mind, set out immediately to control the only broadcasting house at that time in the country, the "Nigerian Broadcasting Service" (NBS). The ruling government brought it under its communication department. Many people opposed this idea. They wanted the "NBC" to be impartial and to reflect divergent views and the cultural set-up of the nation. On the autonomy of Nigerian Broadcasting Service, the Northern region was indifferent to the idea, while the East was in favour of autonomous independence of the Broadcasting Service, but what of the West? After lengthy negotiations the Western Region Government agreed to support the idea of an independent broadcasting corporation. Later, it was a West Region member, Mr. D.S. Adegbenro, who rose in the Federal House of Representatives and addressed the house: "Mr President, Sir, I rise to move the motion in my name, that this House calls upon Government to consider the setting up of a Corporation to take over the activities

---

[189] Affenyi Dadzé Gifty, *State Radio / Public Radio stations or Public Service Radio Stations?* in PANOS, Paris 1970, p.169.

of the Nigerian Broadcasting Service in order to remove the press criticism that the *Nigerian Broadcasting Service* is an organ of the Nigerian Government. We in Nigeria do not want half measures. We would like to see our own broadcasting service growing from strength to strength so as to reach the very high standard that has already been attained by the British Broadcasting Corporation. That onward march, Sir, cannot be achieved excepting a corporation is set up to develop our Nigerian Broadcasting Service".[190]

This Speaker considered that "if broadcasting remained a government department it would be difficult for the people to believe that its programmes were not controlled and it was necessary to look up to the world-famous BBC for its freedom from political interference and control. Finally, the *"Nigerian Broadcasting Service"*, by an Act of Parliament, was converted into a statutory corporation to be thenceforth known as *Nigerian Broadcasting Corporation* (NBC)". The reason for this change was to shield it from government interference and the propaganda of the views of the ruling political party.

This resolution was greeted with "thunderous claps and cheers". There was a general agreement on both sides of the House that the Government should establish broadcasting on a firm foundation removed from political control because the Government has political leanings, and they should not interfere with freedom of information. So the intention of the parliamentarians was to create NBS on the BBC model to provide for an independent and impartial broadcasting. This was how the Nigerian government started to administer for the first time its own broadcasting service. The policies she used in administering it would be another thing altogether.

5.2.1. The First Year of Nigerian Broadcasting Corporation.

The Nigerian Broadcasting Corporation was the first public service broadcasting corporation of its kind in Africa. According to the original Government proposal: "The Corporation should be modelled on the British Broadcasting Corporation with a national and regional organisation and that so far as the regional organisation is concerned

---

[190] HOUSE OF REPRESENTATIVE DEBATES, The Third Session March 6-25, Lagos 1954, p.595.

there should, within the broad lines of the Corporation's policy, be a large share of regional autonomy in deciding the content of programmes. The detailed arrangements when they have been formulated will be subject to approval of the House of Representatives. Among other provisions there would be laid upon the Corporation the obligation of impartiality. Controversial broadcasts could be given by the Corporation provided that all reasonable points of view are represented. It should be the particular care of the Corporation to ensure that reasonable expression shall not be denied to minority groups, whether cultural, religious or political".[191]

The part 111 Section 10 of the law establishing the Corporation states some duties and powers of the Corporation thus, "It shall be the duty of the Corporation to provide, as a public service, independent and impartial broadcasting services by means of wireless telegraphy and by television for general reception within Nigerian.

The Corporation shall ensure that the services which it provides, when considered as a whole, reflect the unity of Nigeria as a Federation and at the same time give adequate expression to the culture, characteristics, affairs and opinions of the people of each Region or part of the Federation."[192]

The Government decided that the best interests of listeners could be served by some form of public ownership, operation and control, backed by the power and prestige of the Government and people of Nigeria. The NBC was not to be an arm of Government. The essential role of the Corporation was to reflect the strength and diversity of Nigerian thought. Armed with exclusive rights, the Corporation was expected to raise standards of understanding and appreciation, satisfy many differing interests and tastes, foster ethical value, provide the impetus and create the climate for any necessary change. When Parliament delegated authority to the NBC it stipulated that public service principle should predominate and the Corporation, free from any overriding political responsibilities, would ensure an even distribution of coverage throughout the country. Surprising to everybody, in August 1961, the Federal Minister of Information sought permission in the

---

[191] Proposals for the Establishment of a Nigerian Broadcasting Corporation together with an outline of the Projected Further Development of Broadcasting in Nigeria, Lagos 1954.
[192] Mackay Ian, op.cit., p.117.

parliament to: Amend the Nigerian Broadcasting Ordinance to enable the Minister responsible for Broadcasting to give general and specific directions to the Corporation on matters of policy or matters appearing to the Minister to be of public interest and also to enable him, after consultation with the appropriate regional government in the case of regional Boards, to make recommendations to the governor-general in Council as to the appointment of all members of the Corporation".[193]

This action silenced the 'thunderous claps and cheers' that welcomed the birth of the Corporation. The enthusiasm which modelled the Nigerian Broadcasting Corporation on 'the world famous BBC' had evaporated. The fear that broadcasting might become 'an organ of the Government of Nigeria loomed ahead. The Minister of Information proposed to amend the Ordinance and provide for the appointment of all members of the corporation on the recommendation of the Minister responsible for broadcasting. Regional Boards were also to be appointed on the recommendation of the minister, after due consultation with the appropriate Regional Governments. The Minister said the provision for Regional consolation was added in the hope that it would still be possible for the Federal and Regional broadcasting systems to 'work together in the best interests of one Nigeria.

The Minister however did make it clear that the NBC retained the responsibility for the day to day running of its affairs, for the recruitment of its staff and all allied matters; thus the amendment did not absolve the Corporation from the responsibility for what it broadcast. The Corporation was still required to provide as a public service, independent and impartial broadcasting services.

The Bill to amend the NBC Ordinance was passed late at night on Monday August 28, 1961 and according to the Daily Express, "out of a total membership of about 300, there were only 137 members in the House – 104 Government and 33 Opposition."[194] The then ruling government having taken control of the internal services of NBC, decided to go further by establishing an external broadcasting corporation.

---

[193] HOUSE OF REPRESENTATIVES DEBATES, Lagos August 1-5 1954.
[194] Daily Express, August 31, Lagos 1961, p.12.

5.2.2. External Broadcasting Service.

Broadcasting became also weapons of power politics in international affairs. It recognises no boundaries, ignores censorship, can foster amity, entertain and inform and has no equal as a means of international communication. It can however provide a means whereby people of goodwill exchange programmes or link facilities for reasons of common interest, maintain international friendships by developing cultural exchanges, and present honest, objective or colourful pictures of a country through talks, commentaries, news or entertainment. It can be a friendly voice, and if government must accept responsibility for the resources under its control, then that government responsibility should be confined to ensuring that its facilities are in good hands and that the nation's interests are being safeguarded.

In examining the systems of other countries in which the NBC should be a model, it was noted that 'the Voice of America' lacks the independence, which the BBC has and it seeks to achieve, by means of careful selection of news, a long-term climate of opinion favourable to the United States. However it was difficult to compare VOA with the BBC. The Nigeria Government decided that its external service should incline to the more moderate traditions associated with the BBC, while still recognising the need to support foreign policy when necessary. the Director-General for broadcasting, Richmond Postage, arguing for this external broadcasting in his report made it clear that: "How events in the next five years may go in Africa, no one has any idea. But it seems to me – and I write personally because in some circumstances a personal expression is the most modest way of expressing a view – that Nigeria may be cast for a role in African history in which, despite or even because of its internal tensions of race and interest, it may achieve a stability which will enable it, above all the nations of Africa, to take over in broadcasting the role which the united Kingdom has held over the last thirty years".[195]

However there were interminable delays between the decision to start a service and its operational date. Meanwhile, NBC mounted a temporary external service using a ten kilowatt short wave transmitter which operated for two hours daily with time equally divided between

---

[195] Mackay Ian, op.cit. p.88.

English and French languages broadcast. This service, which commenced on January 1, 1962, was aimed at adjoining West African countries and the Prime Minister, Alhaji the Rt. Hon. Sir Abubakar Tafawa Balewa, made the first broadcast: "On behalf of the Government and people of the Federation of Nigeria, I send you greeting wherever you may be listening to this new service of the 'Voice of Nigeria' broadcasting from Lagos. For the first few months this experimental service will be directed to our neighbours in West and Central Africa. We in Nigeria believe in good neighbourliness and respect for others. We also believe in following the path of truth wherever it may lead. These principles will guide our utterances and we hope that in the months and years ahead, the 'Voice of Nigeria' will earn a reputation for its friendship to all and for its objectivity.[196]

On February 1, 1963 the NBC commenced what could be described as the second phase of the interim service, when it increased hours from two to six and added Arabic to the English and French broadcasts. This phase provided a full dress rehearsal for the full service, and programmes now consisted of news, news-talks, commentaries, music of Nigeria and the target areas, informative talks on Nigeria and editorials from the Nigeria press.

The pattern was now emerging. In the planning and content of programmes the NBC tried to publicise the policies, development, culture and way of life in Nigeria. The external service was completely free and unfettered in its activities. It received no instructions on programme content and its news was compiled by the same staff who handled news for the domestic audience. Programmes such as "From the Editorials" were used to ensure that views, whether political or otherwise, held by a substantial element in Nigeria, were aired. In this way, the Nigerian Broadcasting Corporation was facing up its responsibilities. This External Service popularly known as "VOICE OF NIGERIA" (VON) was re-organised and structured on the basis of Regional Services with three services initially. These are:

a). The West African Service in English, French and Hausa.
b). The East/Southern African Service in Swahili and English; and
c). The North African / Overseas Service mainly in English, French and German with limited Arabic programmes. The programmes orien-

---

[196] Ibid., p.88f.

tation and contents of each service were designed to suit the listening populations within the regional coverage.

5.3. Regional Government Owned-Stations.

Radio broadcasting in Nigeria was solely provided by the Nigeria Broadcasting Corporation until 1959. It was also entirely financed through government grants. This monopoly was later broken by the Broadcasting law. The then Western Nigeria broadcasting corporation was set up to provide television and sound broadcasting services which included entertainment and educational programmes and was to be financed as much as possible by commercial advertising. According to Duyile D: "The first regional radio station was born on 1st May 1960. The arrival of this new station constituted a great challenge to the Nigerian Broadcasting Corporation, which for years had been alone in the scene".[197]

"Daily Times" Columnist, Peter Pan, described the situation in which the Nigerian Broadcasting Corporation found herself. He wrote that Nigerian Broadcasting Corporation was "fretting nervously like an elder sister fearing the arrival of the school report, because she knows secretly that her junior and brilliantly more aggressive sister would have a better report."[198]

A similar pattern for the introduction and initial management of Regional Government-owned broadcasting and television stations appeared in each of the three Regions. These stations were independent of any central authority and the only federal Government control, which could be exercised, was in respect of frequencies, power and location of stations. This was primarily with a view to avoiding confusion within Nigeria. Only the Federal Government could apply to the international bodies regulating the use of frequencies, but it was doubtful whether the Federal Government could use their powers to reserve frequencies for a future Federal need, if there was a genuine Regional proposal requiring the use of an unallocated frequency.

---

[197] Dayo Duyile, op.cit., p.310.
[198] Ibid., p.310.

5.3.1. The Western Region.

The Government of the Western Region was first in the field of regional broadcasting. The Western Regional Government Broadcasting Corporation was established in 1959 to provide television and sound broadcasting services. The initial emphasis was on television. Western Nigerian Television (WNTV) commenced operation in October 1959, and is now the oldest television service operating in Africa. It is rightly proud of its slogan, "FIRST IN AFRICA." Sound broadcasting through Western Nigerian Broadcasting Service (WNBS) commenced in May 1960. Mackay Ian levelled some criticisms on WNTV-BS when he remarks: "WNTV–BS concentrated on covering Ibadan, claimed to be the largest indigenous populated town in Africa. The commercial incentive, evident in all Regional Government planning, then became paramount, and management, instead of concentrating on extending facilities to the larger Western Region centres of population, cast covetous eyes on the potential commercial market in the Federal territory of Lagos".[199]

The Station has since embarked on the performance of the traditional role of the medium – to educate, inform and entertain, in order to "Uplift the People and Unite the Nation". This Western Nigerian Broadcasting Service (WNBS) Ibadan is a linguistic Zone broadcasting in English, Edo, Igala, Urhobo and Yoruba.

5.3.2. The Northern Region.

The Northern Government appeared to be in no hurry in establishing her own regional broadcasting. The Broadcasting Company of Northern Nigeria Ltd did not commence broadcasting telecasting until March 1962. Television progress was immediate in the North and it was not long before a service was available in Kaduna, Kano and Zaria. In sound broadcasting, the North Region produced the most powerful domestic medium wave transmitter in the whole of Africa – 250 kilowatts.

---

[199] Ibid., p.61f.

5.3.3. The Eastern Region.

The Eastern Regional Government was not left out in this venture. The former Eastern Nigerian Government established in 1960 her own radio transmission. It was called "Eastern Nigerian Broadcasting Corporation" (ENBC). As the Western Region slogan was "FIRST IN AFRICA", the Eastern Region was not to be outdone. The Region came up with its own motto:" SECOND TO NONE".[200] At the end of civil war in 1970, the station was renamed East Central Broadcasting Service (ECBS). However after the creation of the twelve States in Nigeria, in which Anambra State was divided into two, Anambra and Imo states respectively, the Corporation was re-named Anambra Broadcasting Service (ABS) in 1976. Later in 1977, the name was changed to Anambra Broadcasting Corporation (ABC). The Anambra Broadcasting Corporation was the baby of the Anambra State Government.

This station was commissioned in December 1977. Later as states continued to be created, this corporation was renamed Enugu State Broadcasting Service.

At that time, many people saw the establishment of various stations in various regions as a waste of not only money but also time. Some people advised that these resources could be pooled together for effective operation. Some expert in view of this multiplicity of broadcasting warned, that this duplication was a wasteful expenditure of technical resources, money and manpower. A united broadcasting and television authority in which the Federal could share control with Regional Governments would be a force of incalculable strength and would make for maximum stability of purpose.

5.3.3.1. Objectives of Enugu Broadcasting Service.

The OBJECTIVES of this corporation can be classified into many categories, these include:

---

[200] Mackay Ian, p.62.

a. Education Broadcasting.

i). To impact academic, political, scientific, social, religious and economic knowledge to students in particular and the public in general;
ii). To create a general desire for knowledge;
iii). To aid teachers in schools;
iv). To supplement the work of teachers in the class room through "University of the Air" Broadcasting;
v). To create an awareness of acceptable life goals and values;
vi). To provide extra opportunity for learning for the not so fortunate group;
vii). To explain national educational policies to people who might benefit from them;
viii). To provide a forum for educational planners to know what people think of their plans.[201]

b. Public Enlightenment.

i). To re-enforce the general knowledge of the citizenry through thought-provoking programmes in the realms of social and political development, and science and technology;
ii). To promote the creation of law abiding citizens;
iii). To inculcate in the citizens the importance of orderliness and respect for the rights of others and taking their turn in public places;
iv). To promote healthy mental attitudes;
v). To assist in the creation of a healthy environment.[202]

c. Entertainment Broadcasting.

i). To relieve the tedium and strains of daily life;
ii). To provide useful and necessary information through light-hearted entertainment;

---

[201] Anambra Broadcasting Corporation Handbook, Enugu 1980, p.26.
[202] Ibid., p.26.

iii). To help correct the ills of society by satirising unhealthy social situations;

iv). To uplift the taste of the general public;

v). To serve as a patron of popular artistes;

vi). To reflect the general trend in the evolution of popular musical culture;

vii). To promote healthy development of contemporary Nigerian and African popular culture.[203]

d. Folks Music.

i). To promote research into Nigerian musical heritage;

ii). To act as a patron to Nigerian composers and performers in the field of serious music;

iii). To build up within the limits of our resources a musical archives;

iv). To promote research into folk music and act as a patron of folk musicians.[204]

e. Family Programmes.

i). To promote the proper role of women in the society;

ii). To help provide guidance to parents in the proper upbringing of children;

iii). To provide a forum for the self expression and mental development of children;

iv). To guide children towards a healthy physical, emotional and spiritual development;

v). To promote the family as the starting point for the development of a disciplined society.[205]

f. Igbo Services.

i). To promote the development and enrichment of Igbo language;

ii). To promote the wider use of Igbo language;

---

[203] Ibid., p.26.
[204] Ibid., p 26.
[205] Ibid., p.28.

iii). In conjunction with other Igbo language organisations, to promote the development and use of the central Igbo dialect taught in schools;
iv). To use Igbo language as a vehicle for the wider dissemination of information to masses of people especially in the rural areas;
v). To promote and conduct research into Igbo culture and traditions and musical heritage and assist in their healthy development;
vi). Recognising culture as a dynamic concept to assist in the development of Igbo culture and contemporary music to meet the needs of the future.[206]

g. Religious Broadcasting.

i). To foster the development of a God-fearing society;
ii). To uplift the spiritual balance of the citizens;
iii). To encourage the harmonious co-existence of the various denominations;
iv). To promote respect for law and order.[207]

h. News and Current Affairs.

i). To ensure that a broad spectrum of major events, political, social and economic, in the state is fully covered and broadcast to the listeners.
ii). To ensure the dissemination of major news of national interest.
iii). To ensure that the listeners are adequately informed of major events in the struggle to uphold the dignity of the black man on the continent.
iv). To disseminate news about other parts of the world that should interest a Nigerian audience.
v). To ensure that news broadcasts are objective, accurate and in the public interest.
vi). To ensure immediacy in the dissemination of news.
vii). To provide a forum for the expression of a diversity of informed opinion in a constructive manner on major issues of the day.

---

[206] Ibid., p.28.
[207] Ibid., p.28.

viii). To ensure objectivity and accuracy in current affairs programmes.[208]

The three regional governments' broadcasting organisations were
wholly independent of the Federal Government control. The only
thing they had to do that required action on the part of the Federal
Government was to apply, through the Federal Ministry of Communications, for Frequency allocation. Frequency allocation was necessary
so as to avoid interference with the already assigned frequencies to
other stations.

The purpose of regionalisation of the broadcast media was used as
powerful political instruments for the integration of each region and
cultivation of regional awareness more than national consciousness
and integration. The emphasis was on the regional interest rather than
on the national. The politicians who established them greatly exploited
them for sectional politics. When political crises occurred, these regional media became more powerful than the NBC. They were used to
the fullest in protecting the political, economic, cultural and social interests of the various regions. The reason given for the emergence of
regional media that were independent of any Federal Government
control was dissatisfaction with the NBC. Each region felt that its own
views were not being properly represented by the NBC. Some accused
the NBC of partiality and partisanship. For the proliferation of the regional media Ian Mackay said: "It is the sole responsibility of regional
broadcasting to radiate a regional image and that cannot encourage the
artistic endeavours of Nigeria as a nation. The setting up of regional
corporations does not bring about true competition. This can only be
achieved by setting up a number of corporations having national coverage and offering a range of programmes, which would benefit the
whole country. There is no sign of that in Nigeria. Whatever the benefits – and there are benefits – the cost is too high and the danger exists
that divided control in a developing society may promote regional
feeling instead of encouraging the desire to live together and act together".[209]

Mackay Ian should know that there is no crime to have developed
highly competitive media network in Nigeria. The only objection is
how the media, both at the Federal and regional levels, were misman-

[208] Ibid., p.28f.
[209] Ibid., 41. cf. Mackay Ian, op.cit p.64

aged by the politicians who established them. Otherwise, competition was wholesome for the audience and for national interest and variety, if such competition would provide balanced and objective views of events in the nation.

5.4. Military Government and The Federal Radio Corporation of Nigeria.

Historically, the relationship between the Nigeria Press and the military government has not been wonderful. As a watch dog on government on behalf of the people, the press had always been in friction with the government, with the press always seeking to expose government failings and the government always striving to put a leash on the press. This cat and dog relationship between the military government and the press has done more harm than good. Under normal circumstances, the press should serve the public interest and the government performs as representative of the public. This means that both the press and the government are really partners in service to the public; only that they are serving in different capacities. This partnership does not in any way suggest that the press should team up with the government against the public; neither does the difference in their service obligations imply that they ought to be perpetual enemies. How was this relationship nurtured in radio broadcasting during the military regime?

During the thirteen to fifteen years of military interregnum in Nigeria, 1966-1979 and 1984-1999, the military dictators did not only take-over the management and control of the entire state government-owned broadcasting systems, but also centralised radio broadcasting to ensure effective control. Even though they might have publicly accepted fundamental human rights, they did not hesitate to use their power to abrogate those rights by issuing detention orders or by rigid censorship of the mass media, when they found it convenient to do so. It is not surprising then that the military governments in Nigeria had issued various decrees, which limit the free flow of information. Many decrees have been promulgated since 1966 when the military administration began in Nigeria. Famous among these is the famous Decree 4 promulgated in March 1984 and made retroactive to December 1983 by the military government of Major-Gerneral Muhammadu Buhari. It provided that: "Any person who publishes in any form, whether written or otherwise, any message, rumour, report or statement... which is false or which brings, or is calculated to bring the Federal Military Government or the Government of a State, or a Public Officer to ridicule or disrepute shall be guilty of an offence under this Decree. The decree provided for a prison term of two years without an option of a fine and for a fine of not less than N10, 000 (ten thousand naira) in the case of a corporate body violating its provisions".[210]

When the military decided to retire to their barracks and handed over power to a democratically elected National Assembly in accordance with the 1979 Constitution, "it promulgated the Federal Radio Corporation of Nigeria (FRCN) Decree No. 8 of April, 1978. The decree decentralised radio broadcasting and restructures the nation's broadcasting industry."[211]

The Federal Radio Corporation of Nigeria (FRCN) is undoubtedly one of the most powerful political and social institutions of the Nigeria society. It has played a role that was second to none in the political leadership power struggle in the country. The military has always used it as a means of out-manoeuvring their rivals in leadership struggles in the country. This has consequently led to low credibility image perception of the system by its national audience. For Uka Luka: "The FRCN is virtually viewed among the Nigerian public as a big "white horse" that is only answerable to any government of the day. A sort of "prostitute" whose boyfriends come and go and is ready to meet the demand of each and every one of them".[212]

Before the Federal Military Government handed to the civilian in 1979, they re-organised the Radio Broadcasting in Nigeria. They changed the name from *Nigerian Broadcasting Corporation* to *Federal Radio Corporation*. Perhaps they thought it wise to discard the earlier name borne by this corporation before and after independence. They thought that it had still some links with the past regime and colonialism. They believed in the adage that there is something in a name. It is because of this that: "On February 28, 1978, the Federal

---

[210] Edeani David, West African Mass Communication Research at Major Turning, in Gazette vol. 41, London 1998, p.175.
[211] Uka Luke, op.cit., 54.
[212] Ibid., 47.

Military Government promulgated a decree establishing the Federal Radio Corporation of Nigeria. It was to take effect from April 1, 1978. An official gazette published on March 8, 1979 stated that the Corporation shall be a body corporate with perpetual succession and a common seal, and may sue or be sued in its corporate name".[213]

5.4.1. Inauguration of Federal Radio Corporation of Nigeria.

The full text of Decree No.8 of 1979 is as follows: THE FEDERAL MILITARY GOVERNMENT hereby decrees as follows:
"(1) There is hereby established a body to be known as the Federal Radio Corporation of Nigeria (hereafter in this Decree referred to as "the Corporation") which under that name shall be a body corporate with perpetual succession and a common seal, and may sue and be sued in its corporate name".[214]

5.4.2. Objectives of the Radio Corporation.

The activities and policies of the Federal Radio Corporation of Nigeria are guided by the following objectives:
i). "To provide efficient broadcasting services to the entire people of the Federation of Nigeria, based on national objectives and aspirations and to external audiences in accordance with Nigeria's foreign policy;
ii). To provide a professional and comprehensive coverage of Nigerian culture, to promote cultural growth through broadcasting; to promote cultural growth through research into indigenous culture and to disseminate the results of such research works for the benefit of the public;
iii). To contribute to the development of Nigerian society, and to promote national unity by ensuring a balanced presentation of views from all parts of Nigeria.
iv). To ensure the prompt delivery of accurate information to the people.

---

[213] Bako George, op.cit p.7.
[214] ibid., p.7.

v). To provide opportunities for the free enlightened and responsible discussion of important issues and to provide a useful two-way contact between the public and those in authority;

vi). To provide special broadcasting services in the field of education, and in all other areas where the national policy calls for special action;

v). To promote the orderly and meaningful development of broadcasting in the country through:-

Technical Improvements

i). The training of appropriate professional staff.

ii). Programme and staff exchanges, with other Broadcasting organisations in the country, where possible.

iii). To promote research into various aspects of the communications media and their effects on the Nigerian society. (This includes: audience research, the investigation of fresh methods of production and the true indigenisation of the broadcasting media);

iv). To ensure that the facilities and techniques of broadcasting in Nigeria keep pace with developments in the world of communication."[215]

The new organisation now known as the Federal Radio Corporation of Nigeria has been constituted by the amalgamation of what was left of the former NBC, the Broadcasting Company of Northern Nigeria, and the powerful transmitting complex of the Broadcasting Corporation of Oyo State, the Anambra Broadcasting Corporation and the Imo Broadcasting Corporation. One of the objectives of this move is to reduce and prevent the unnecessary and wasteful installation of very powerful transmitters in the country considering the exorbitant capital vote, the expensive running costs and the drain on the foreign exchange of the nation. As for the Federal Radio Corporation of Nigeria, the Corporation has been constituted with four operationally autonomous zones as follows:

"Federal Radio Corporation of Nigeria- KADUNA, will broadcast in four Nigerian languages; that is in Hausa, Fulfulde, Kanuri and Nupe.

Federal Radio Corporation of Nigeria- EUNGU, will cater for Igbo, Tiv Izon and Efik.

Federal Radio Corporation of Nigeria- IBADAN will transmit in Yoruba, Edo, Igala and Urhobo.

---

[215] National Broadcasting Commission, Growing Up with the Nation: THE FIRST TWENTY YEARS 1957-1977, Lagos 1977, p.23.

Federal Radio Corporation of Nigeria-LAGOS will handle its main transmission in English.

Federal Radio Corporation – 2, which is a light entertainment programme transmission initially limited to Lagos Area and Educational Service which will be broadcast on a separate frequency receivable throughout the country."[216]

5.4.3. Functions of the Corporation.

i). To erect, maintain and operate radio transmitting and receiving stations.

ii). To install and operate wired radio distribution services.

iii). To enter into arrangements with the Federal or a State Government or any other public body for the purpose of obtaining licences, rights, privileges and concessions.

iv). To plan, regulate and co-ordinate the activities of the Zones and the entire Federal radio broadcasting system.

v).To ensure the establishment and maintenance of high standards and promote the efficient operation of the entire federal radio broadcasting system in accordance with national policy.

vi). To establish and operate a formula for sharing funds amongst zonal stations.

vii). To organise, provide and subsidise for the purpose of broadcasting educational activities and public entertainment.

viii). To collect from any part of the world and in any manner that may be thought fit news and information and, subject to the News Agency of Nigeria Decree 1976, to subscribe to news agencies.

Subject to the News Agency of Nigeria Decree 1976, to provide and to receive from other persons matter to be broadcast.

i). To acquire copyrights.

ii).To publish printed matter that may be conducive to the performance of any or all its functions.

iii). To produce, manufacture, purchase or otherwise acquire gramophone and other mechanical records, tapes, and materials and apparatus for use in connection with records and tapes and to use them in connection with the broadcasting services.

---

[216] Bako George, op.cit. p.5.

iv). To provide facilities for training and advancing the skill of persons employed in its services and for enhancing the efficiency of the equipment used in its services including provision by the Corporation or by others on its behalf of facilities for training, education and research.

v). To carry out such other activities as are necessary or expedient for the full discharge of all or any of the functions conferred on it under or pursuant to this Decree.[217]

5.4.4. Duties of the Corporation on Other Zonal Stations.

The Corporation shall satisfy itself that the programmes broadcast by the Corporation and the Zones comply with the following requirements, that is to say:-

i). that nothing is included in the programme which is likely to offend against good taste or decency or is likely to encourage or incite to crime or lead to disorder or to be offensive to public feeling, or to contain an offensive reference to any person, alive or dead.

ii). that the programmes maintain a proper balance in their subject matter and a generally high standard of quality.

iii). that any news given in the programmes is presented with accuracy, impartiality and objectivity.

iv). that due impartiality is preserved in respect of matters of political, or industrial controversy or relating to current public policy; and

v). the Corporation may set up a committee, which shall consist of the Director-General as the Chairman and all the Zonal Directors, to draw up guidelines and advise the Corporation on such other matters connected with the foregoing as the Corporation may from time to time refer to the committee.[218]

---

[217] Ibid., p.9f.
[218] ibid., p.10.

5.5. Federal Radio Corporation of Nigeria: ENUGU ZONE.

The Eastern Nigerian Broadcasting Service (ENBS) Enugu was later renamed The Federal Radio Corporation of Nigeria on October 1ˢᵗ 1978. Enugu Zone was then, made of five States. – Benue, Anambra, Imo, Rivers, Cross River. The Zonal objectives is not to broadcast individually to the component States but to make programmes available within the Zone in four Nigerian Languages – Efik, Igbo, Izon and Tiv.

5.5.1. Objectives of the Zonal Corporation.

The philosophy of Zonal operations is grounded on the concept of grass-roots broadcasting that is, getting the programmes to the people in the languages they understand. It is linked with the idea of constant interaction between the people and government, with radio bringing government literally to the doorstep of the rural communities. It is also geared towards the level of enlightenment in the zone.
The average daily output for Nigerian Languages was increased from 8% to 21% within three months of the zone's existence. The ultimate aim is to operate the languages as distinct services, each having an equal share of available airtime. In October, 1984, the nation's former Chief of Staff, Tunde Idiagbon, while inaugurating a committee on the rationalisation of television services of the Nigeria Television Authority (NTA) as specified in the decree of 1977 that established the NTA, announced that: "All the 'mushroom' radio stations that the FRCN established in various states of the federation during the Second Republic were to be closed down. He indicted the ousted elected civilian government of breaking the military covenant on broadcasting structure and condemned the proliferation of radio and television stations in the last civilian administration, to engage in and disseminate open character assassination, all sorts of profanity, slander, falsehood and even pure incitement bordering on treason".[219]

---

[219] Daily Times, *Mushroom Radio Stations to Go*, October 24, Lagos 1984, p.1.

On further reflection on the politics of the broadcast industry during the second Republic, he was credited to have observed: " in the prevailing madness, the basic patriotic objectives of setting up stations to inform, entertain and educate were lost as the various political parties ensured that the government under their control engaged in the proliferation of television and radio stations throughout the country. The stations, without exception, became megaphones of political parties in power, suppressing or grossly distorting information to suit the whims and caprices of politicians and consequently fanning the embers of disunity, disaffection and disorder. They succeeded to such an extent that law and order broke down in many states of the federation... The present administration owns it as a duty to provide a virile, functional and effective broadcasting system to the nation and could not sit idly and watch the sector decay".[220]

Two months after these pronouncements, the Federal Military Government closed down some of the FRCN state stations that were located in Owerri, Ilorin, Calabar, Akure, and Ibadan. This closure carried with it its own consequences. It led to loss of jobs. "About 2000 of their staff had their appointments terminated."[221] The establishment of many radio and television stations were for the military government a waste. They did not see any reason for such establishment. The military saw broadcasting media as instrument of their success or failure. According to Luke Uka: "The broadcasting media have become so endemic in Nigeria political set-up that without them, the political juggernauts are nobody. The result is that the affinity between broadcasting and politics is like the birth of Siamese twins, in which any surgical operation that is performed to separate them that is not carefully carried out, might lead to the death of either, if not both".[222]

They enacted every available decree to control it. In neighbouring Ghana, also under the then military government the tone was somewhat not different. Major A.H. Selormey Commissioner for Information has told the press to thread softly. He told the press categorically clear: "We (the military government) will allow the freedom of the press to operate in this country as far as it is consistent with a military government. Every newsman should be experienced enough to know

---

[220] Uka Luke, op.cit. p.58.
[221] ibid. p.58.
[222] Ibid., p.58.

that a military regime is not a regular or normal state of affairs and that there is a need for caution and circumspection in their work. A military government, by its very nature is certainly inconsistent with any pretentious to subscribing fully to the concept of freedom of the press in the normal acceptance of the expression".[223]

This make me to believe that when one tries to debate the issue of a free press in a military regime, one believes that there is no need to begin the discussion at all in the sense that a free press and a military regime are incompatible. For David Edeani: "This perception of government and press relations does not seem to reflect reality, and its perpetuation has done more harm than good to the press, to government, and to the general public alike, since it tends to condition the attitude of the journalist toward government and public officials. The press exists to serve the public interest and the government performs as representative of the public. So, both the press and the government are really partners in service to the public; it just happens that they serve in very different capacities. This partnership does not in any way suggest that the press should team up with the government against the public; neither does the difference in their service obligations imply that they ought to be perpetual enemies".[224]

However, instead of this adversary, the press might be more appropriately and fruitfully used as an intermediary between the government and the public. Based on this, the federal military government decided to show its good will by creating a body that in charge of broadcasting in the country.

5.6. Nigerian Government and Liberalisation of Broadcasting.

Since the late 1980s, a new wind of change that started from Eastern Europe has been blowing over Africa, assuming the proportions of a hurricane in some places and pulling down buccaneer of military dictators and other low-cost civilian despots. People have entered the phase of a new liberation and are clamouring for their rights of which they had been systematically deprived. The right for the privatisation

---

[223] Wilcox Dennis, Mass Media in Black Africa, New York 1995, p.21.
[224] David Edeani, op. cit., p.174.

of broadcasting media numbers among these rights. The question is whether privatisation of radio is feasible and desirable? Since it provides an opportunity for alternative voices to be heard, it will contribute to the democratisation process by enabling individuals and groups to make their point of view heard. Nigeria is not left out in this wind of change. According to the 1989 Draft Constitution states,

Section (1)

"Every person shall be entitled to freedom of expression, including freedom to hold opinions and to receive and impart ideas and information without interference.

(2) Without prejudice to the generality of subsection (1) of this section, every person shall be entitled to own, establish and operate any medium for the dissemination of information, ideas and opinions: Provided that no person, other than the Government of the Federation or of a State or any other person or body authorised by the President, shall own, establish or operate a television or wireless broadcasting station for any purpose whatsoever.

However, chapter IV of 1999 Constitution in section 39 states:- (1) Every person shall be entitled to freedom of expression, including freedom to hold opinions and to receive and impart ideas and information without interference.

(2) Without prejudice to the generality of subsection (1) of this section, every person shall be entitled to own, establish and operate any medium for the dissemination of information, ideas and opinions.

Is it not time the Nigerian government to emulate some of the good policies of some developed countries concerning broadcasting? Two examples are United States of America and Federal Republic of Germany. In America, for instance, says Jörg Koch in his book Die Vermarktung privater und lokaler Hörfunk- und TV-Sender in Deutschland und den USA that: *"Rundfunk hat sich in den USA von Anfang an unter anderen politischen und rechtlichen Bedingungen entwickelt. Im Gegensatz zu den staatlichen Monopolstruckturen der Postverwalten hat der Staat zu keiner Zeit einen unmittelbaren Einfluß auf das Rundfunksystem ausgeübt. Eine Staatliche Ausgestealtungs- verantwortung ist dort nicht gegeben. Die Regierungsgewalt beschränkt sich in den USA somit auf die Herstellung gewisser mindestbedingungen, die ein Funktionen des Rundfunksystems sicherstellen sollen. Soweit eine Aufsicht stattfindet, ist sie zentral geregelt und obliegt der FCC (Federal Communications Commission)* ".[225]

Going further he added: *"Die zentrale Aufgabe der FCC ist die Erteilung und Kontrolle von Lizenzen, die zum Betrieb von Lokalstationen notwendig sind. Die FCC hat die Kompetenz, die Bedingung für die Lizenzerteilung und –erneuerung festzulegen und die technische Reichweite des lizensierten Senders zu bestimmen* ".[226]

In Germany, the broadcasting laws are a little bit quite different from that of USA. In the Federal Republic of Germany, the basic Law provided for functional division of powers in the field of mass communications between the Federation (the 'Bund') and the constituent states *('Länder')* of the Federal Republic. The Constitution assigned responsibility for, and ownership and control of all telecommunications networks to the state at the federal level, more precisely to the Post and Telecommunications Ministry (*'Bundespost'*) (Article 73). On the other hand, the states are responsible for the culture and it was generally accepted that they had 'cultural' sovereignty' (*Kulturhoheit'*). It was immediately widely interpreted that the states therefore had jurisdiction over broadcasting *('Rundfunkhoheit'*). Accordingly, there was a fairly general feeling that the states had the constitutional right to frame their own broadcasting laws, so long as these laws respected the guidelines laid down by the Constitution itself'.[227]

---

[225] *The broadcasting system in the United State from the beginning was developed under different political and legal conditions. Contrary to the monopolised governmental structures in telecommunication system, the State has at no time any direct influence on the broadcasting system. Government control and censorship of programmes are not allowed. In the United State, government control in the area of broadcasting is limited to level of guarantying that certain minimum conditions for the functioning of broadcasting are maintained. As far as control und censorship in the area of broadcasting are concerned, its is within the responsibility of Federal Communications Commission (FCC).* Koch Jörg, Die Vermarktung privater und lokaler Hörfunk – und TV Sender in Deutschland und den USA, München / Nürnberg 1996, p.30

[226] ibid. p.30 Going further he added: *The main function of the FCC is that of issuance of licences for local radio stations and also controlling their usages. The FCC also establishes the conditions for extending or renewing of licences. It also stipulates the technical radio frequencies.*

[227] Humphreys Peter, Media and Media Policy in Germany, Oxford/Providence 1994, p.134.

Country	Population	Radio Sets	Per 1,000	Television Sets	Per 1,000
Germany	80,000,000	150,000,000	1,875	30,500,000	381
Nigeria	122,840,00	17,000,000	140	6,000,000	50

Source: David Bobbett (ed.), World Radio and TV Handbook, The Directory of International Broadcasting Vol. 53, United Kingdom 1999, pp 74, 156, 383 & 404.

So, should the government in Nigeria entirely monopolise the broadcasting industry? Why should the federal government not establish an independent broadcasting commission just like some of these developed countries did? The Nigerian government will like to appoint members to such board and at the same time dictate to them what they should do. Should government continue to monopolise broadcasting industry? Here are some of the opinions of the people. *Should broadcasting be left at the hands of the government?*

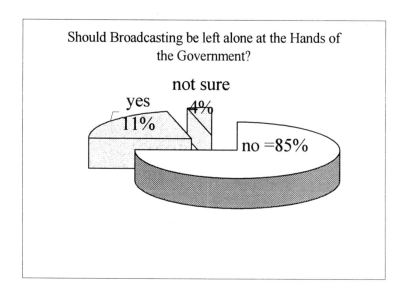

Should Broadcasting be left alone at the Hands of the Government?

not sure
yes
11%
4%
no =85%

Many people are of the opinion that broadcasting should not be left solely in the hands of the government either on the federal or states levels. The government should also not interfere in affairs of whatever board is set up to oversee the running of broadcasting in the country. This board should act like an impartial referee, who will act whenever any media house commits foul/offence in the field of broadcasting. The commission should not be seen as a government organ used for intimidation of other media organisations. Here are some of the arguments for and against government total involvement in the broadcasting media. As shown in the diagram above eighty-five percent (85%) of the populace are strongly against the Nigerian government's monopolistic tendency. They argue among other things that:

a). For years, most African governments have been known to monopolise broadcasting media especially radio broadcasting to their own aggrandisement. They have painted themselves good even when they are not performing. It is time they allowed individuals and Non-governmental organisations to participate in informing the public of the happenings in society.

b). The government should not in the first place involve itself in broadcasting business. There are other areas of life the government should begin to explore and invest their money in. The government's monopoly of the media will lead to the presentation of views favourable only to the government, thereby negating objectivity regarding press freedom.

c). Moreover, leaving government to monopolise broadcasting means allowing them to control the conscience of the masses as they like. Such a system can be possible in communist countries or in military rule; not in a democratic society.

d). Any available means should be used to stop this monopolistic tendency so as to guard against the public being indoctrinated and inundated with censored piece of information and also to create public and social awareness.

e). They argued also that one should remember that Nigeria is the giant of Africa. This should be reflected not in our population but also via true democracy. True democracy implies the freedom of the press. This means that the government and the governed should be heard. The government should not involve itself directly in broadcasting as a way of advertising its policy but indirectly by acting as a referee to the media organisations. This will allow for a balanced view so that the press can play its watchdog role fully.

The fourteen percent (14%) who supported the government sole involvement in broadcasting argues that the money used in setting up and running broadcasting house is enormous. They went further to say that the issue is not setting up a broadcasting house but maintaining them. Experience has shown that in Africa maintenance culture has always been a problem. Today a radio station goes on air and next time it is closed down due to one technical problem or another. At times they may close down because of financial constraints.

Five percent (4%) of the general public are indifferent as to who runs a broadcasting house. For them, let the best hand manage it. If possible, the government should recruit the best experts in broadcasting and team up with them to give society the best in broadcasting. From all indications, people are not satisfied with government performance in broadcasting media. This was made clear in the question: *Have governmental electronic media lived up to peoples' expectation in Nigeria?*

Peoples' Feelings-Expectations	Number Interviewed per 1,000	Percentage
No	**870**	**87%**
Yes	**40**	**4%**
Not Sure	**90**	**9%**

People are indeed disgusted with government media. Many people no longer listen or watch government broadcasting media. These media are known to be means of propaganda. People are indeed fed-up with them. However, is there any alternative to the government broadcasting media? In some parts of Nigeria, people have started making effort, searching for an alternative media, but in Enugu state this has not been possible. The only alternative broadcasting media that can challenge the federal and states radio stations in Enugu state is local or community radio. *"It is time to look for an alternative. I am really sick and fed up with the naked lies dished out by the government stations. I no longer have the appetite of listening to state radio,"* says one of the interviewed. The fact that Nigerian successive governments largely resisted private initiative in the area of broadcasting since independence shows the importance attached to media broadcasting. However, West Africa has experienced a boom in private, local and commercial radio. The military government had no alternative other than to set up the National Broadcasting Commission of Nigeria (NBC).

5.6.1. Inauguration of National Broadcasting Commission.

Since 1959 when Africa's first television broadcasting station commenced operations in Ibadan, radio and television broadcasting stations had been state-owned and state-regulated. Agitation for pluralism in electronic broadcasting in Nigeria has been going on for years. In August 24, 1992 approval was given to this agitation, when the then President of Nigeria signed into law the *National Broadcasting Commission* Decree No.38 of 1992. The decree established a commission whose responsibility it was to:

i). Advise the federal government generally on broadcasting matters;
ii). Receive, process and consider applications for ownership of radio and television stations including cable television services, direct satellite broadcasts and any other medium of broadcasting.
iii). Recommend application for granting of license by the President.
iv). Regulate and control the broadcasting industry.
v). Undertake research and development in the broadcasting industry and,
vi). Investigate complaints against broadcasting stations.[228]

The *Nigerian Broadcasting Commission*, known also as "Commission" or "NBC" is empowered to implement government policies as they concern broadcasting, is administering the 1992 Act.

In general, the Commission has powers to monitor public, private and commercial broadcast stations in Nigeria, to ensure fairness and balance. The President on the recommendation of the minister appoints the chairman and all the other members of the commission.

---

[228] Ogochukwu Basil, On Legal and Ethical Framework for the Pluralist Operation of Radio in PANOS, Paris 1980, p.158.

With the exception of the Director General, other members hold office for a three-year period renewable only for a second term. The Director General has a five-year renewable term. Applicants are to satisfy the Commission that they are not representing any foreign interests and must undertake to promote national interests, unity and cohesion, avoiding offending other religious sensibilities or creating ethnic or sectional hatred and disaffection among Nigerians.

5.6.2. Objectives of the Commission.

i). To increase number and variety of stations throughout the country with specific encouragement of rural and community radio and television;

ii). To increase ownership of radio and television sets by the average family or household;

iii). Encouragement of the establishment of more professional training institutions, research and rating companies, and local production agencies by both public and private entrepreneurs;

iv). Co-operation of the financial sector in accepting investment in broadcasting as profitable: from station ownership, equipment manufacture, programme production, to training, research and ratings, and marketing services.

v). Rationalisation of equipment sources to ensure compatibility and maintainability.

vi). Increased participation of the public in licence approvals, renewals and strategic programming decisions.

vii). More mileage from co-operation with foreign programme sources by way of co-productions, programme exchanges and local training agreements.

viii). Harnessing the benefits of the Internet, and the increasing convergence of broadcasting computers and telecommunication for the development of Nigerian broadcasting.

5.6.3. The National Broadcasting Commission Codes.

The National Broadcast Commission made a sustainable nation-wide enlightenment campaign and conducted also public opinion poll on all levels including: policy makers, scholars, professionals, station owners and ordinary citizens, young and old alike, on file profile and future of broadcasting in Nigeria. They held also workshops and seminars in different parts of the country on this issue. As a result of these, they came out with this code of conducts on National Broadcasting. The Code was launched in Abuja during the 1996 International Conference on Deregulation of Broadcasting in Africa. The National Broadcast Code include:

i). Only professionals can head professional departments and divisions of broadcasting stations;

ii). Self-correction: It is professionally mandatory to forth rightly admit a mistake once clearly established, and fully effect remedy as agreed with the aggrieved body;

iii). The portrayal of nudity and sexual scenes and expressions is justifiable only in context; however, it shall be presented with tact and discretion.

iii). Womanhood shall be presented with respect and dignity.

iv). Programme exclusivity shall be discouraged, but where exclusive rights have been acquired, such programmes shall be readily made available to other operators on mutually negotiated terms. The National Broadcasting Commission shall arbitrate when there is a fundamental disagreement in negotiation.

v). The National Broadcasting Commission shall regulate charges for foreign programmes where it is established that owners are charging either differentially, or unreasonably, compared with what obtains in other comparable parts of the world, or where one or a number of interested stations are being deliberately denied a right to participate. A similar regulatory process shall be applied in the case of local programmes. News is universally accepted as sacred. Sponsorship of news detracts from its integrity and predisposes a bias in favour of the sponsor. Therefore, newscasts shall not be sponsored whether by the use of commercial backdrops in televisions newscasts, or other device, either on radio or television.

vi). Equal opportunity and airtime shall be provided to all political parties or views, with particular regard to the amount of time.

vii). Coverage of public events of major national importance shall not be exclusive to any single broadcast organisation.

viii). The advertising of fortune telling or astrology is not permitted.

ix). An advertisement shall not contain a copy which is exaggerated by reason of the improper use of words, phrases or expressions, such as "magic", "magical", "miracle", "miraculous", etc.

x). An advertisement for all alcoholic beverage or tobacco product shall be aired only during adult listening/viewing periods. For television, advertisements for alcoholic beverages and tobacco products shall not be broadcast before 9.54 p.m.

xi). Advertisements by religious persuasions, including trade religious practice, shall not contain statements or visual presentations, which directly or indirectly, are likely to mislead the listener/viewer with regard to claims of miracles, hypnotism, palm reading, etc.

xii). Religious announcements that deceive people into believing that miracles are commonplace events shall not be accepted for broadcasting by any station.

5.6.4. Granting of Licences by the National Broadcasting Commission.

Is the power to grant broadcast licences the exclusive preserve of the Commission or that of the President? There is no doubt that the NBC has power to determine and apply sanctions (including the revocation of licences) for any act done in contravention of the Broadcasting Code, or acts which do not accord with public interest. Licences may also be revoked by the NBC if the holder defaults in paying prescribed fees or where the licence has not been exploited within a year of issue. However, it is not entirely clear who has the right to grant broadcast licences. Concerning this issue, Aida Opoku-Mensah says: "the allocation of licences is often based on the patronage of the Minister of Information, awarded in secrecy and therefore not determined by any guideline or framework. As a result, this process fails to guarantee a genuine plurality of the broadcast media, especially where it is becoming increasingly evident that those close to the political elite usually get to own such licences".[229]

Commenting on this apparent hidden agenda in the "Decree 38" that established the Commission Bankole Sodipo observed that Section 2(1) (c) of decree 38 provides that: "The Commission is to receive and process applications for ownership of radio and television stations, (including cable or satellite), and make recommendations through the Minister, about applicants to the President for the grant of radio and television licences. This suggests that the Commission cannot grant a broadcast licence. On the other hand, section 9(2) (3) (4), suggests that the NBC can grant licences. It must be noted that the 1992 Act did not state specifically "That grant of a licence by the Commission under this Decree shall be subject to availability of broadcast frequencies". This inconsistently calls for a review. It is arguable that if deregulation is the essence of the new policy for the broadcasting industry, the NBC should be able to grant licences and the President should have nothing to do with decisions taken".[230]

This means that the Commission only acts as an advisory board to the President. Licence is only issued to those whom they think are not a threat to the government. This is the reason why some individuals have decided to set up pirate radios outside the shores of the country.

5.6.5. Method of Applying for Broadcasting Licence.

The following steps should be taken when applying for a broadcasting licence:
Incorporate a limited liability company with Nigerians holding majority Shares.

Purchase all application form together with The National Broadcasting Code for the sum of N10, 000.00 (Ten thousand naira only) from the Finance Directorate of the Commission. Fill in and return the form to the office of the Secretary to the Commission, stating clearly how you intend to utilise the licence i.e. radio or television, open or scram-

---

[229] Aida Opoku – Mensah, *Deregulation of Radio in Africa-Political Expediency or Development Strategy* ? in Inter Media, 1982, p.39.
[230] Sodipo Bankole, Vanguard Newspaper, December 31, Lagos 1997, p.11.

bled broadcasting for cable/satellite retransmission: satellite television.

i). The application is processed by the Commission and then recommended to the Board:

ii). The Board sends it through the Honourable Minister of Information and Culture to the Head of State and Commander-in-Chief who give the final approval for radio and terrestrial television licences as well as satellite television.

iii). The NBC communicates this approval to the applying company, which is expected to pay for the licence before it is issued, and appropriate frequencies are allocated.

A licence is for five years. Currently, licence fees for key urban locations or category 1 markets are N1, 500,000.00 for television. N3, 000,000.000 for radio, N2,500,000.00 for cable/satellite retransmission; the fees for semi-urban and rural locations are correspondingly lower. For television, category 11 markets licences are N900, 000.00 and category 111 markets licences are N45,000.00. For radio, category 11 markets cost N2,250,000.00 and category 111 markets N1,500,000.00 for cable/satellite retransmission, category 11 markets are N1,800,000.00 and category 111 markets N1,350,000.00.

The fee for global satellite television is N12,000,000.00 for five years: The licence may be revoked, if it is not utilised within one year of issuance.

Every license is required to adhere to a minimum of 60% local broadcast content and a maximum of 40% foreign content for open broadcasts radio and television stations. The cable/satellite retransmission stations are expected to reflect a minimum of 20% local content in their programming.

5.6.6. Terms of Renewal of Broadcasting Licences.

Terms of a Licence stipulate that an application for file renewal of a licence shall be made to the Commission within a period of six months before the expiration of file licence. Consequently, the major criteria for the renewal of broadcasting licences shall include the following:

i). The applicant shall clear all outstanding financial and administrative obligations to the Commission.

ii). He shall submit to the Director-General, NBC through the Commission's Zonal Director in the area of operation, 15 copies of his application.

The application shall include: A report of its compliance with

1) The relevant provisions of the Third Schedule of the NBC Decree No.38 of 1992 such as: -

i). Submission of quarterly schedules accompanied by synopsis of programme listed.

ii). A local programme content not less than 60% for open broadcasts and 20% for satellite re-transmission stations.

iii). Keeping daily station logbooks of transmitted programmes, transmitter output power and radiating frequencies.

iv). Making available for inspection by the staff of the Commissions its broadcast facilities including equipment and station log books.

2) The National Broadcasting Code provisions comprise:

i). Emphasising national cohesion, national security, respect for human dignity and family values;

ii). Compelling Accuracy, Objectivity, and Fairness; Right of Reply:

iii). Integrity; Authenticity; Good Taste and Decency; Presentation of Womanhood with Respect and Dignity;

iv). Legal, Decent and Truthful Advertisement; Protection of children from X-rated programmes and harmful or deceitful adverts, etc.

v). Forbidding inciting broadcasts; advertisement of magical cures: exploitation of children: sponsorship of newscasts and monetisation of political coverage; etc.

5.6.7. Revocation of Licence by the National Broadcasting Commission.

The Commission may revoke a licence in the following cases:

i). Where the prescribed fee has not been paid as and when due;

ii). Where the licence has not been used within a period of one year after issuance;

iii). Where it is found that the licence was not obtained in compliance with the provisions of Section 13 of the Decree or where it is found that the provisions of this section are not being complied.

iv). Where in the opinion of the Commission, the station has been used in a manner detrimental to national interest or where a complaint from the public has been upheld after a hearing instituted by the Commission and whose decision is upheld by a majority of members of the commission.

Many thanks should go to the Federal Military government for establishing for the first time in Nigeria, the National Broadcasting Commission. We are not yet questioning the functionality of this organ. For instance how many private radio stations were they able to give licence to start operation? The military governments are also good in promises but the ability to keep those million promises is another thing altogether. We must remark here that this regulatory body set up by the government can be a source of positive and negative control of the media. Particularly worrying in the Nigerian context is the provision of sections of the National Broadcasting Commission Decree, according to: "Subject to the provisions of this Decree, the Minister may give the commission directives of a general character relating generally to particular matters with regard to the exercise by the Commission of its functions under this Decree and it shall be the duty of the Commission to comply with such directives."[231] For Basil Ogochukwu: "This is a rather curious insertion because the decree did not give the nature and limits of the directives which the Minister might give and which the Commission is under an obligation to comply with. It is therefore the belief in many quarters that this provision may lend itself to abuse since it gives ample ground for arbitrary interference by government in the work of the Commission".[232]

They can also be used for repressing freedom of expression. It is thought that government may intentionally leave loopholes to exploit silencing any opposition.

Luke Uka rightly asserts: "It is widely believed that one pitfall in the decree that set up the National Broadcasting Commission (NBC) is the power given to the commission to revoke the licences of station which do not operate in accordance with the code and in the public interest.

---

[231] Ogochukwu Basil, op.cit., p.159.
[232] Ibid., p.159.

The decree did not specify either how to seek redress or to what the public interests is, as in the America Federal Communication Commission. Thus the decree allows the NBC to provide licences in perpetuity only to withdraw them at whim".[233]

To avoid this absolute power as regards issuance and revocation of licence, such powers should be vested solely and fully in the National Broadcasting Commission but under the direction of the National Assembly. The National Broadcasting Commission refused to grant licence to groups and individuals, this led to introduction of some unauthorised radio stations.

5.6.8. Some Pirates Broadcasting Stations in Nigeria.

a). Radio "NEW NIGERIA".

It was machinery for the "Nigerian Advocacy Group for Democracy and Human Rights". A Boston based Pressure Group. It was inaugurated on June 12, 1997.

Transmissions are as follows: Nigeria – West Africa.: Every Saturday at 21.00 – 07.29 on 11.995 KHz on 25 Metre Band.

North America, the transmission was every Saturday at 21.00 – 21.29 GMT on 5.910 KHz on 31 Metre Band.

Central Europe: Every Sunday at 17.00 – 17.29 GMT on 6.175 KHz on 49 Metre Band.

Contact address: E-mail: RadioNNig@aol.com.[234]

b). Radio Nadeco or "THE VOICE OF FREE NIGERIA"

Internet address: http://www.nadeco.org.

RADIO NADECO – The VOICE OF NIGERIA is made possible by free Nigerians who wish to create an uncensored medium to remind the Nigerian people the values of democracy and human rights. This

---

[233] Uka Luke, *Mass Media, People and Politics in Nigeria, in Media Development*, World Association for Christian Communication, London 1983, p.47.
[234] http://www.radio-newnig.org.

173

voice shall be unequivocal in denouncing the evils of dictatorship, the brutality of military rule and the absence of the rule of law in Nigeria.
OBJECTIVE: The primary objective of RADIO NADECO will be to mobilise Nigerians to stop the military clique from ruling Nigeria by force. No armed power is greater than the sovereign will of people.
FREQUENCY: 5.07 MHz 60 – meter band short-wave tropical band
TIME OF TRANSMISSION: 6.00 AM Monday through Friday Nigerian Time.[235]
c). RADO KUDIRAT.

Internet address: http://www.udfn.com
FREQUENCY TRANSMISSION: 6205 KHz on 49 Metre Band and 1154 KHz on 25 Metre Band.
TIME OF TRANSMISSION: 19.00 – 20.00 daily.[236]

5.7. The Future of Nigeria in the Area of Broadcasting.

Since deregulation in broadcasting started, it has brought Nigeria greater freedom of expression, more employment opportunities, better entertainment and more education. The wind of freedom of expression is blowing in many concerns of the world. In all respects, the freedom to inform and be informed is the mother of all other freedoms. In many respects, then, radio appears to be a means of expression that is particularly well adapted to the cultural, social and economic realities of Africa

However, while newspapers and periodicals have been in the vanguard of struggle for democracy, radio as a segment of media can hardly be scored average in this historical endeavour to enhance free flow of information and promotion of democracy in Nigeria. The electronic media especially radio, had all along been monopolised, by the state to manipulate public opinion, contrary to the principles of professional ethics. Many groups engaged in the promotion of human and civil rights, but had to limit their various campaign channels to news-

---

[235] http://www.nadeco.org.
[236] http://www.udfn.com

papers and magazines because of the absolute control of radio by the state.

In 1998 more than 250 delegates from different parts of the African continent gathered in Abuja, the Nigeria capital for a conference to deliberate on the role of Broadcasting in development of the continent and its people. They urged each country to make maximum use of the opportunity of liberalisation of broadcasting media given by the various governments. They also pleaded with governments, who have not opened the liberalisation of broadcasting media to do the same. This conference was organised by the Nigerian Broadcast Commission with the theme: "Broadcasting and Human Development in Africa." At the end, they issued the following communiqué.

i). Excessive pursuit of commercialisation in broadcasting has tended to undermine the performance of its social responsibility functions.

ii). Preference for foreign channels and programmes by African elite and even children is a manifestation of low quality local programmes and is counter productive to the role of broadcasting in human development in Africa.

iii). The attitude of broadcasters to scientific and technical information has distracted from the function of broadcasting as a medium of information dissemination and thus its role in human development promotion.

5.7.1. Recommendations.

Participants who gathered in Abuja for a conference to deliberate on the role of broadcasting in development recommended that:

i). African governments, media regulatory bodies and Broadcasters should take necessary steps to make broadcasting meet Africa's urgent social-cultural, economic, political and other human development needs in the next millennium.

ii). The broadcast industry should strive to balance its freedom with responsibilities.

iii). Broadcasting should be sensitive to differences in language, culture, ethnicity, gender and religion in their role in human development promotion in Africa.

iv). Local origination of programme is imperative as it enhance constant focus on rural areas.

v). Continental and sub-regional co-production of radio and television programmes should be encouraged.

vi). Broadcasting should make conscious effort to promote the right of the child and women by packaging appropriate programmes that give voice to them; educational broadcasting should be revitalised.

vii). Media owners, especially in the private sector, should endeavour not to allow profit motive to override national interests.

viii). Environmental journalism as a method of propagating environment-friendly habits should be adopted and effectively used by broadcasters through research for the enhancement of environmental messages, in consultation with NGO's, involving communities in message creation.

ix). The media has a lot to do in protecting our environment. The media should not only be the watchdog of implementing the national policy on environment but also the mouthpiece of the grassroots who may be the worst victims of any environmental catastrophe.[237]

5.7.2. Conclusion.

In Nigeria, since the National Broadcasting Commission decree was enacted in 1992 and liberalisation of broadcasting media started booming, "114 licenses have been issued since As at May 1996, "31 of the 114 licensees had paid license fees, seven over-the air television stations had commenced transmissions, plus another 15 satellite re-transmission services. Two FM radio stations had also begun broadcasting. One of them- RAY POWER 100 FM is based in Nigeria's commercial capital, Lagos. The other Nigerian FM radio station is based in the eastern Niger River town of Obosi, Onitsha".[238]

When we talk of privatisation in this context, we are dealing primarily with a non-government system, which may or may not be commercial oriented. Private stations can be undertaken by individuals, reli-

---

[237] Okoh Aihe, The Vanguard Newspaper, Lagos November 4 1998.
[238] Ogundimu Folu Folarin, *Private Enterprise Broadcasting: Nigeria and Uganda,* in GAZETTE vol. 58 no. 1 Paris, 1996, p.161.

gious groups, benevolent societies, professional organisations, and other interest groups. Non-Governmental Organisations (NGOs) should be encouraged to set up private radio stations providing general service or specialised programmes. At this time, privatisation of broadcasting seemed to have attracted significant attention; partly on account of the profit potentials it holds for private entrepreneurs who see a window of opportunity for cashing in, on the global expansion of information and entertainment. So far, the emerging commercial private radio stations in the country have mostly confined themselves to only cities and major towns.

Can these types of radio stations help our rural people through the sharing of information and bring about people-centred development. The type of radio station people want is the one that can help the people to be actively involved in communal development. The failure of many government projects is often due to the lack of grass-roots participation. More often than not, flow of information is top to down. Unless radio decentralises and focuses on the specific needs of the grassroots community, people in rural areas will continue to be isolated, illiterate and poverty will continue to reign among them. Effective communication takes places in the situation where people have direct involvement in the information sharing process.

A radio station in which Igbo, Igala, Efik and other local languages are spoken, is what the people want; A radio that teaches people to take care of themselves, to know one another, to share with others. A radio that makes people dance, sing, play, a radio that is accessible to the people and with which a group of people is identified, a radio that provides an anchor for local democracy. Nigeria being the most Africa's populous country of some 120 million peoples has every reason to foster efforts in the area of radio broadcasting so that it can take root in the rural areas. There is no other radio that can fulfil such aspiration other than a "community radio station." The next section deals with and explains what community radio means.

6. COMMUNITY RADIO STATION: AN ALTERNATIVE VOICE: THE CASE OF ENUGU STATE.

In the pervious chapter we have seen that community radio station is necessary for the rural development. In 1999, according to *The Directory of International Broadcasting*, there were about 17,200,000 radio sets and 6,100,000 television sets among the 122,840,000 Nigerians.[239] This means that one out of every seven Nigerians has a radio set and one out of every twenty Nigerians has a television set. The percentage of radio and television sets in proportion of the population of the country is shown by the diagram below.

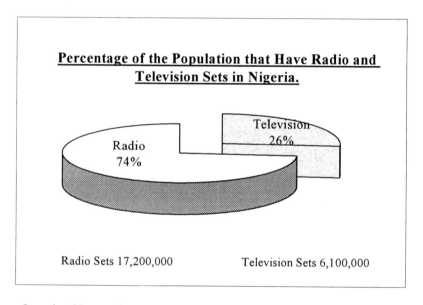

Percentage of the Population that Have Radio and Television Sets in Nigeria.

Radio 74%

Television 26%

Radio Sets 17,200,000   Television Sets 6,100,000

One should note that the use of radio sets in the economically developed world is quite different from the way this medium is used in developing countries, especially in Africa and Latin America. In the industrialised nations of the world, television, telephone and internet have assumed the role of principal source of information and entertainment, while in the non-industrialised countries; radio is still the

---

[239] Bobett David (ed.), World Radio and TV Handbook, The Directory of International Broadcasting Vol. 53 United Kingdom 1999, pp.156 & 404.

principal medium of communication and development. In Africa, the transistor radio is now standard in almost every household. For John Pungente: "In most (African) homes, a radio is on almost all day to provide a background for whatever activity that takes place in the house. From time to time, people stop and give their attention to news or information on the radio as they work around the house. Listeners use radio as a secondary activity to accompany work or play".[240]
The table below show the number of radio and television sets in ten selected African countries.

COUNTRY	POPULATION	RADIO SETS	Per 1,000	TV SETS	Per 1,000
Algeria	30,509,393	3,500,000	115	2,000,000	66
Cameroon	14,740,000	6,000,000	407	15,000	1
Congo (Rep. Of the)	2,525,000	2,400,000	950	22,000	9
Ivory Coast.	14,555,000	1,600,000	110	810,000	56
Ghana	19,444,200	12,500,000	643	800,000	41
Morocco	27,866,000	5,100,000	183	1,210,000	43
Nigeria	122,840,000	17,200,000	140	6,100,000	50
South Africa	44,000,000	7,500,000	170	3,485,000	79
Uganda	29,924,406	10,000,000	334	115,000	4
Zambia	10,231,670	1,300,000	127	200,000	20

Source: David Bobbett (ed.), World Radio TV Handbook Vol. 53, 1999 United Kingdom, p143-407.

---

[240] Pungente John, Getting Started on the Media Education, London 1985, p.12f.

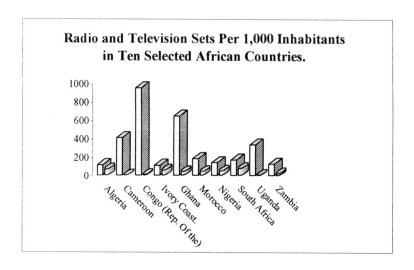

Radio and Television Sets Per 1,000 Inhabitants in Ten Selected African Countries.

The popularity of radio as a medium of communication in Africa is not disputable. In the introduction to his book, *A Passion For Radio* Bruce Girard writes: "Radio is undoubtedly the most important medium in Africa. Similarly, television is beyond the financial means of most people and national television service often does not extend to rural areas where much of the population lives. Radio, on the other hand, is available almost everywhere. Receivers are relatively inexpensive and programming is inexpensive to produce and distribute. In virtually all-African countries national radio services broadcasting from the capital and other major centres are the most important sources of information".[241]

Frank Daniela also affirm the popularity of radio thus, *"Ein einfaches Transistorgerät ist mittlerweile so billig geworden, daß potentiell jeder, auch die Ärmsten einer Gesellschaft, durch den Hörfunk erreicht werden kann, denn ein Radio ist fast überall der erst 'Luxus' den sich eine Familie zu leisten versucht".[242]*

---

[241] Girard Bruce (ed.), A Passion for Radio: Radio Waves and Community, Montréal/New York 1992, p.4.

[242]*(Meanwhile, a simple transistor radio is so cheap that everybody, including the poorest in the society can afford it. It is the first „luxury" which a family ties to have.)*

Radio as Head Sydney asserts has reached an apex to the extent that "no other medium can reach out to such a wide range of persons in varied environments under such diverse conditions in Africa continent. It can appeal to people of all ages in all places, to people of all classes, educated or not. And it achieves this coverage with remarkable economy if efficiently used."[243] Daniela also agrees with this affirmation of Sydney in her statement that: *"Hörfunk international zum populärsten Massenmedium geworden ist. Hörfunk ist (örtlich) direkt und (unter zeitlicher Rücksicht) potentiell immer verfügbar. Ist ein Empfangesgerät vorhanden und betriebsbereit, kommen die Signale direkt ins Haus, ohne daß aufwendig Vorbereitungen getroffen werden müßten.... Selbst die Fähigkeit zu lesen ist keine Bedingung, um das Medium nutzen zu können, was einer der wesentlichen Faktoren ist, weshalb Hörfunk auch in den Entwicklungsländern eine weite Verbreitung gefunden hat".[244]*

Although these authors may be writing in general about the importance of radio, their assertions are particularly the African environment. This is from the fact that developed world no longer consider radio broadcasting as the quickest medium of communication. They now rely more on the Internet and telecommunication. These media are not yet common to African people.

On their policy paper on "Community Radio in Africa", issued by Stem van Africa, they write, "in Africa today, aware of how radio can be used as a means of control and of propaganda, as well as a tool of hate and death, we however believe that radio is the most important and most appropriate means of communication. The reason for this observation is due to the fact that:

i). Radio is co-natural to the African oral culture and can be considered as a new way to develop this cultural value.

Daniela Frank, Dimensionen der Programmkonzeption entwicklungsorientierter Hörfunkarbeit, Konstanz 1994, p.23.

[243]Head Sydney, World Broadcasting Systems – A Comparative Analysis, Wadsworth 1985, p.4.

[244] *(Radio broadcasting has internationally become the most popular mass medium. However, radio is always locally and directly available? Wherever radio is available and in working condition, signals may be received directly in the house without a great amount of preparation. Not even the ability to read is required in order to use the medium. This is one of the most important factors why radio broadcasting has found such a wide acceptance especially in developing countries.)* Daniela Frank, op. cit. p.23.

ii). Radio is accessible to everyone, especially in a continent with the highest illiteracy rate and with so many local languages, where the majority of the population lives in rural areas where roads, telephone and telecommunication systems are not reliable, making access to newspapers, books and television difficult... radio can reach even the remotest areas.

iii). Radio is affected by the present political changes blowing over the whole of Africa.

iv). Radio has a central role to play in the process of democratisation in the continent, at least as contributing to a pluralist and participatory society."[245]

Franz-Josef commenting on the simplicity and importance of radio to African communities writes: "Radio does not require the ability to read, and even those who cannot write have full access to radio as long as they understand the language. This is an advantage in countries where the population is not used to reading or in a country with very few publications. Radio programs are easier to produce and they can reach the remotest listener. Production of items is more immediate. In fact, it is radio that launches the news, the television shows the images, and the newspapers give details and commentaries".[246] Every house in Eungu has a radio set. This helps them to know the happenings of the day. They can afford at least to buy battery for the radio set when there is no light. Unlike Television set which uses electricity. The importance of radio in society can be seen clearly from the interview conducted in and around Enugu.

People were asked: *"What is the quickest and widest means of communication especially in our society (Enugu-Nigeria) where roads, telephones and telecommunications systems are unreliable?*

---

[245] Unpublished Policy Paper on "Community Radio in Africa" issued by Stem van Afrika, Hilversum (The Netherlands) – October 1994, p. 1.

[246] Eiler Franz-Josef, Communicating in Community: An Introduction to Social Communication, Manila 1994, p.111.

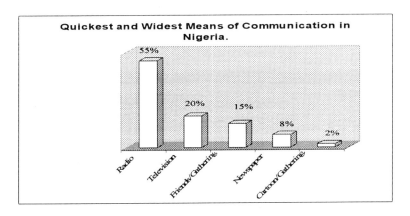

Quickest and Widest Means of Communication in Nigeria.

The statistic speaks for itself. It shows that fifty-five percent (55%) of the people acknowledged the popularity of radio sets as the quickest means of communication in our society. Every family has a radio set. They can afford to use it in listening to news and getting information on what is happening in society. On the other hand, many cannot yet afford television sets. Just twenty percent (20%) of the people living in Enugu get their daily information through television set. At times, it is not a question of having television sets in one's house that is determinant; one has to foresee the problem of unavailability of electricity. While fifteen (15%) get daily information from friends, gatherings, and market squares. Only eight percent depend on their daily information of happenings in the society on daily newspapers while two percent get their information from cartoon and theatre.

The importance of radio manifests itself even as a main source of information from different aspect of life. On *economic matters*, people's sources of information include the following:

Radio	47%
Television	23%
Newspapers	16%
Others	14%

47% People depend on radio to know the economic situation in the country. This is followed by newspaper reports of the market economy. While 14% of the population depend on "others" as means of gathering information about the market stand in the society.

As regard *religious matters*, people's major sources of information vary entirely from economic matters:

Sermons in the Church	56%
Diocesan / Parish Bulletins.	22%
Religious Seminar / Symposium	9%
Ecclesiastical Newspapers	5%
Pastoral Letters	5%
Encyclical letters from the pope	3%

In political matters, people's main sources of information are as follows:

Radio	41%
Television	36%
Newspapers	11%
Other/ people.	12%

From all indication, radio is indeed a major source of information to the people. For any development in the society especially in the rural areas to take place, the people's major source of information should be taken into consideration.

6.1. Community Radio vis-à-vis Development in Enugu State.

We shall focus our attention here on the major effects of broadcasting in rural development especially in Enugu State. The issue of rural development is one of the most formidable problems facing most of the less-developed countries today, including Nigeria. We must acknowledge that much progress and development have been made with community radios in Asian and Latin America. Regrettably however, the situation in Africa, especially in Nigeria, remains lamentable. Nigeria has about the most daunting task of rural development in the continent. At times, the policy makers forget that rural development holds the key to national development.

How do broadcasting and rural development relate? To a broadcaster in a developing society, one logical question is: to what extent are broadcasting and physical-human developments related? In an attempt to answer this question, Alhaji Kromah posited, "there is a consensus among international media scholars that the broadcast media can help develop and impart knowledge essential to economic and social progress in the developing nations of the world. Experts agree that community media can:

i). Teach new skills and new values to the people;

ii). Teach agricultural, health and literacy skills and thus bring about effective participation in the making of a nation;

Inspire the people to support government policy for national development;

iii). Open the flow of ideas across linguistic and social barriers so that people can learn from one another and begin the process of development;

iv). Mobilise the people and thus help to bring about unity in a nation.[247]

On the above views Peter Naigow says "broadcasting is an important element in the matrix of influences, which lead to innovation, and modernisation of a society. If used constructively, broadcasting can

---

[247] Kromah.G.V., *The Utilisation of Broadcasting for National Development in Liberia* in George Wedell ed. Making Broadcasting Useful: The African Experience, Manchester 1986, p.198.

help create an environment favourable for change and development."[248]

The relevance of community media for development depends upon an understanding of what development is. Development can easily come about through the community broadcasting. If people can be assisted in their quest for development, there is need to analyse their situation, and together with them, find strategies to improve their situation. According to John McNelly, there are four stages or points of view with regard to community broadcasting's role in rural development:

i). First is the Null Position: This position holds that mass communication has little or no role in national development and militates against the media's role in the drive for national integration and development. Rather, emphasis is placed on literacy, education or on economics.

ii). Second is the Enthusiastic Position: This is the position held by UNESCO and some academicians. This position assigns the mass media a decisive role not only in national development, but also in bringing about peace and stability.

iii). Third is the Cautious Position: It cautions that mass communication is not omnipotent and that a multitude of social and cultural factors serves to militate against or even nullify the impact of the mass media.

iv). The fourth position is the Pragmatic Positions: This is the "Try it and see if it works" position. Here the researcher seeks empirical evidence on the impact of mass communications in a culture, society or nation. He simply checks out the consequence case by case as they occur. This leaves open the possibility of no media impact, a limited impact, or a heavy impact, depending on the circumstances.[249]

Lateef Jakande agrees to the fact that community broadcasting has positive contributions to make in the society. He classified them into six distinct and crucial roles. They include:

i). Information role,
ii). The historian role,
iii). The educator role,
iv). The forum role,

---

[248] Naigow Peter, quoted in Joseph Wollie, The Role of Radio in National Development: A Case study of Liberia, Ghana 1983, p.3.

[249] McNelly John, *Perspectives on the Role of Mass Communication* in The Development Process, in Berlo D. (ed). Mass Communication and the Development of Nations. Michigan State 1968, p.48f.

v). The watchdog role,

vi). The leadership role

i). The first function is to inform its readers, listeners, or viewers. The flow of information is an instrument of unification without which nation-building would be an impossible task.

ii). The historian role of broadcasting arises from its function as a mirror of society. The state of the mass media of any country is a reflection of the political, economic and social structure of the society. As the media broadcast and publish all events in the country, they serve as recorders of history.

iii). The mass media provide forums where national issues are debated, thus stimulating political participation, when it is allowed by the leadership.

iv). The educator role arises out of the need to educate the citizens at a faster and quicker rate in all aspects of life.

v). In the watchdog role, the media serve "as crusaders for social justice, public morality, civil liberties and human progress. It keeps the nation's conscience."

vi). The leadership role comes from its duty not only to reflect public opinion, but also to guide and lead it.[250]

For Andrew Moemeka, rural development is very important and community radio should engage in this direction:

i). "because of the enormous size of the rural population as compared to the small percentage of people living in the cities.

ii). because of the very large share of the country's natural resources located in the rural areas.

iii). because of the big role the rural population plays in the economic, rural, and political life of the nation."[251]

It is now clear that rural broadcasting aids and inspires the citizens to work towards national development. What are those developments that community broadcasting can bring along with it? A UNESCO guidebook lists the following as important areas that should be emphasised by the community radio stations:

---

[250] Ndolo Ikechukwu, Radio Broadcasting and the Language Problems of Socio-Political Integration in Nigeria, Washington D.C. 1987, p.100f.

[251] Moemeka Andrew, Local Radio: Community Education for Development, Zaria 1981, p.iii.

General problems.	The role of agriculture in the overall economy of the country.
Community life.	Women's organisation.
Rural and agricultural economic.	Co-operative marketing.
Modern agriculture.	Crop storage.
Dealing with environmental conditions.	Floods.
Health and nutrition.	Maternal and child care.
Family life.	Premarital and marital care.
Family planning.	Contraception and physiology.
Home interests.	Home dressmaking.
Consumer's education.	Saving.
Education.	How does the school function?
Civics.	Administration of justice. [252]

We must acknowledge that successive governments in the country had for decades paid only lip service to the issue of rural development. It is a known fact that the bulk of development efforts and resources were geared towards the urban areas where only the very small minority of the population lives. The rural areas have always been neglected. This can be traceable to the time of colonial era, from the 1860's to the present day. Moemeka noted that: "Whatever coverage that occurred was carried out by urban-based newspapers which were later joined by urban-based radio and television, and the stories written pertained mainly to statements and activities of government officials, such as colonial Residents, colonial District Officers and Assistant District Officers, and other such colonial administrative functionaries. Other public figures who made news in the rural areas included tax collectors, mobile medical service staff, inspectors of education, and mobile cinema staffs of the ministries of information who moved

---

[252] Nwankwo Robert, *Educational Uses of Broadcasting*, in Sydney Head (ed.), Broadcasting in Africa: A Continental Survey of Radio and Television, Philadelphia 1974, p.294.

from one village to the other with their cinema vans showing public programme films of various kinds to rural audiences".[253]
He further asserts: "Nationalist politicians who fought for the country's independence also made news whenever they campaigned in the rural areas. News made by all these sources was of course, published in the city media for consumption by city people, and very rarely did ordinary events of everyday life in the rural area make news for the city media".[254]
What effect has all these for the then 70 per cent of the country's population living in the rural areas? They meant for the urban-based media of mass communication that the rural people are not worthy of receiving media coverage.
They were seen to be incapable, in their own rights, to make any news worth reporting. Occasionally, news filtered from the rural areas. But the unfortunate thing is that the reporters who cover this rural news all come from the cities, and promptly disappeared back to the cities with the stranger-officials who made the news. This meant that rural people had no hand in the reporting of development events occurring in the rural areas, neither did they exercise any control over how or whether those events were reported in the mass media. This was so because right from the inception of radio broadcasting, in the 1930's, and television transmission began in the late 1950's, radio and television broadcasting remained a government monopoly until 1992 when the federal government promulgated a decree permitting private interest in broadcasting. The result was that radio coverage of the rural areas was carried out from radio stations located in only the major cities across the country. Some radio stations have mounted special broadcast programmes devoted to coverage of the rural areas as a means of contributing to the solution of these serious problems; but this cannot be a substitute to rural-based broadcasting stations concentrating on rural coverage. According to the study conducted by Andrew Moemeka: "City news still dominated in the pages of newspapers as compared to rural news, for 75.5% of the total news stories published by the papers was city news while only 24.5% were rural news. But even this figure of 24.5% was a remarkable improvement on what the situation was in

---

[253] Ibid., p.127.
[254] Ibid., p.127.

the not very distant past when there was very little media coverage of the rural areas".[255]
But in recent times, some community groups in the rural areas now have their own community newspapers and magazines, while a number of daily and non-daily newspapers in the cities have introduced weekly supplements devoted to the coverage of rural news and other rural events. When will the rural people of Nigeria begin to enjoy their own local radio station that will be reporting their own activities?

Michel Philippart once narrated his journey to Ouagadougo, the capital of Burkina Faso. Describing his experience he said that, he was impressed to see so many things but the most impressive among them is the: "pylon of Radio Maria, the Catholic Radio station of the Archdiocese of Ouagadougou. Created in December 1993, Radio Maria is one of the five private FM radio stations on the air in Ouagadougou. Burkina Faso with (12 million people) is definitely a laboratory of the broadcasting pluralism in Africa. Actually 20 private FM radio stations exist in the country".[256]

It is unfortunate that rural or local radio broadcasting has not begun to penetrate Nigeria's countryside more than half a century after broadcasting was introduced in other countries. This situation is more painful when we consider that Nigeria is now blessed with numerous radio stations belonging to the federal and states governments respectively. The fundamental question still remains: To what extent have the citizens benefited from such media houses in the country. Many Nigerians are disgusted with the propaganda media mounted by the Federal and her Allies (the states) governments. In an interview with a Director General of one state radio station, he says: *"Look, we are here in radio house to obey the state governor. We broadcast his speeches and tours of the state without editing them; otherwise one will loose his job. We only transmit to the people what the government wants us to tell them. There is no avenue to know the people's reactions and feelings".*

---

[255] Ibid., p.129.
[256] Philippart Michel, *The Church and the New Broadcasting Pluralism in Africa*, in Information Bulletin CAMECO – 1/1995. Aachen, p.2.

This confirms the feelings of the common people as regards the question: *"To what extent are you informed about the happenings in society?"*

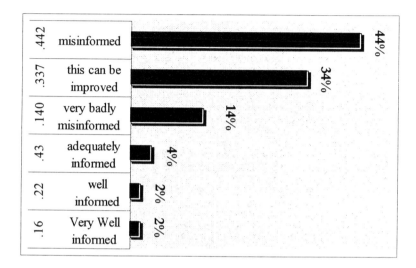

Forty-four percent (44%) of the interviewed believe that the government is not only misinforming the masses but at the same time not disclosing all the information necessary for the good of the society.

The government controls majority of media house. Government finds nothing wrong in telling liars through its media. What areas are government media found wanting? The next issue is to determine in what area of life, people are not getting enough information.

To this effect the masses were asked in a more precise way: *In what area of life are you not getting enough information?*

191

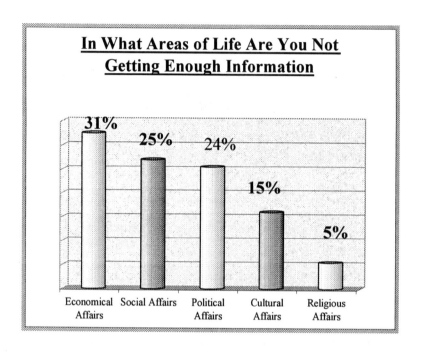

In What Areas of Life Are You Not Getting Enough Information

31%   25%   24%   15%   5%

| Economical Affairs | Social Affairs | Political Affairs | Cultural Affairs | Religious Affairs |

In Economic affairs, 31% say that things are getting bad daily due to lack of information on how to tackle these problems. There are astronomical increase in unemployment and inflation in the society. People are dying of hunger. The government media are not informing the masses on how to tackle such economic and social problems.

Politically, according to 24% interviewed, for a country to be a good society, the masses should be educated enough on political matters. It is unfortunate that in our country, this is lacking. The society is in a political mess. The media should make effort to expose some of the dishonest politicians. The masses should also be educated on their rights and duties in a democratic society.

On social level, 25% say the society is in a mess. The standard of living continues to fall. The situation is precarious. There is increase

192

of destitute all over. Enough information is not provided on how to tackle such societal problems. The 15% of those interviewed, believe that cultural values are no longer on the news. They are no more given priority by the government media. Even the few private media also do not consider it necessary. Cultural revival is necessary for the survival of any society.

While 5% believe that religious matters are longer given attention in the media, perhaps because there are little or no economic gains. Many of the media houses broadcast programmes that will yield them money. They relegate religious matters to the background.

Having seen the general features and importance of community radio, we are here going to see the opinion of the people as regards to ownership and management of community radio in Enugu State. They were asked? *"What do you understand by a Community Radio if such is to be establish in Enugu?*

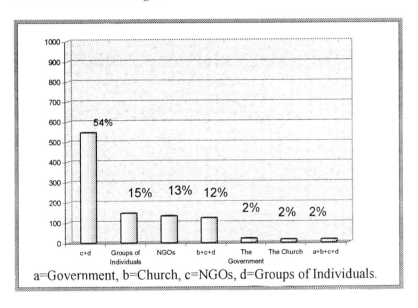

a=Government, b=Church, c=NGOs, d=Groups of Individuals.

From the above statistics majority of people believe that community broadcasting can best be run by non-governmental organisations and groups of individuals. This belief is supported by the fact that, the few

193

existing private/individual stations are doing very well. The fifty-four percent (54%) of the people in Enugu argue that the community radio that is established by non-governmental organisation and groups of individuals may perform better than others because:

a). Such a radio station will understand easily the problems of the masses and can enlighten the public on how to tackle such problems immediately.

b). Through such radio stations people will feel at home to air their views, unlike the ones established by the government which are only propaganda media and are subject of censorship by the government.

However fifteen percent (15%) believe that groups of individual may perform better than the government and the church. One remarkable thing here is that people opposed vehemently the establishment community radio that is managed either by the government or the church. Such mighty institutions may not give freedom of expression a chance in broadcasting media. If they want to establish a community radio station, they should do it in conjunction with other groups like the Non-governmental organisations or groups of individuals. People believe that community radio should be one established for the local community, run by the community and sponsored either by the government or the community or the Church or philanthropists. The people believe that they (government and church) can help or liaise with other non-governmental organisations to establish this broadcasting house. In effect, the people are saying that for broadcasting to be objective, it is supposed to be run only by groups of individuals or some non-governmental organisations. Are they saying that the church should not participate at all in mass media? Which media should the church use for her evangelisation? What type of mass media should the church then establish? Should the church participate at all in mass media in Enugu State?

Should the Church Participate in Mass Media?	
Yes	97%
No	1%
Not Sure	2%

The 97% argue that the presence of the church in mass media will help bring about sanity and moral discipline not only to the citizen but also in media broadcasting. While the dissenting voice of 1% argue that allowing the church(es) to come into media may lead to some of the fanatical sects setting up their own media house and start using it for "holy war" or "Jihad". It is better for the government not to grant licence at all to any religious body or organisation. The 2% of those interviewed believe that there are bound to be conflict between the government and the church. The church may be pursuing its own interest and thereby comes into conflict with the government. This may lead the government to close such media house thereby making the whole investment waste of resources. They also argue that Nigerians are not yet religiously matured enough to check abuses. Electronic media can have a very disastrous effect on the society if controlled by fanatics but can be good instrument for religious enrichment of the masses if well utilise. If the majority believe that church should play active role in mass media, the question remains with what organ should the church be presence in mass media?

How can the Church be Present in Mass Media?	
Printing media	38%
Electronic media	11%
All the above	51%

Some people (38%) believe that it is better that the church concentrates in printing media, leaving electronic media to private individuals. This is to avoid "religious war" or "Jihad". Electronic media can be an instrument of religious propaganda. On the other hand 11% of the population believe that church's presence in the media should be encouraged. This is irrespective of its abuse by any of the religious groups. The government can also continue to monitor them so as to act as check and balance. While 51% believe that the church be allowed go into any mass media she wants, for the propagation of faith, provided that she can afford the cost. Which organ do you think the church can use to effect her presence in mass media?

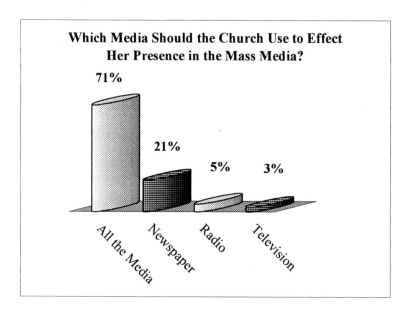

Which Media Should the Church Use to Effect Her Presence in the Mass Media?

71%

21%

5%   3%

All the Media   Newspaper   Radio   Television

Seventy-one percent (71%) of those interviewed are of the opinion that the church can establish any of the above mass media, provided that it can afford the cost. However, they should concentrate on printing media.

Twenty-one percent (21%) say that the church establish newspaper and then make use of the existing radio and television houses run either by private individuals or non-governmental organisations in their respective states. This will avoid duplication of media houses in the society.

On the other hand, 5% are of the view that the church should concentrate on radio broadcasting so as to reach wider audience and spread the gospel to the people.

While 3% of the people are of the opinion that television should be the best media to be used by the church to spread the gospel. Going further, they claim that in television media, the viewers see the presenters and can learn one thing or the other. Now it is clear that the people are clamouring for private media.

All these priorities cannot be achieved without the people having access to the radio stations in the state. If accessibility in government owned radio stations and some commercial radio stations is not possible, can it be possible in local or community radio? *"Is it possible that a community radio can ensure greater accessibility to the common people without being compelled purely by profit?*

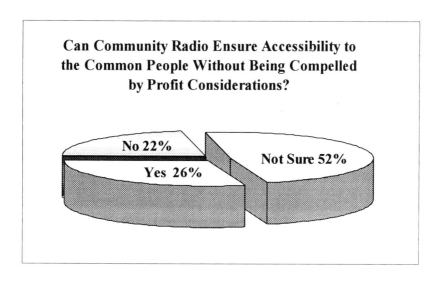

Can Community Radio Ensure Accessibility to the Common People Without Being Compelled by Profit Considerations?

No 22%

Not Sure 52%

Yes 26%

On community radio station and the issue of profit making, majority of the people (fifty-two percent) still doubt whether it is possible to separate the two affairs from each other. For broadcasting station to survive it needs money. Some say that for the station to survive, there should be at least a minimal profit making. Again it depends on who owns it and what the objectives are. If it is profit oriented, then profit making will be the compelling factor.

If it is meant to educate, inform and entertain and is well subsidised, then it can fulfil its objectives without being purely profit oriented. Profit making in broadcasting will help for more efficiency and better services to the public.

Twenty-two (22%) percent believe that community radio should not be established for profit making. They are meant for the common man to air his views. These common people cannot have access either to government media or to some of the private media that were established for profit making. For its sustenance the people can also contribute from time to time. While 26% are absolutely sure, that community radio give access to the common people to say their mind without calculating the cost.

In addition to the above criteria, the people of Enugu also listed area of interest, where they will like community radio to lay more emphasis so as to bring development to the door steps of the people: In the question, "what area of life would you like community radio to emphasis"? Here are their opinions.

Areas of Life to be Emphasis	Percentage.
News and information sharing on the happenings in the society.	21%
Human right of the people.	13%
Developmental education	10%
Political reporting on the government activities.	5%
Environment and social situation	4%
Information on the health situation in society	4%
All the above.	43%

Majority of those interviewed (43%) are of the opinion that community radios should emphasis all the areas listed above. This is because all round information leads to all round integral human development.

Ranking second (21%) on people's priority are "News and Information Sharing" on what is happening in society. Community radio should be geared towards collecting, processing and disseminating news, facts and opinions in a given community. It should be left for the people then to take appropriate decisions and then give their own feedback.

198

Thirteen percent (13%) of those interviewed say that community radio should ensure that human rights of the masses are protected by educating the people of their rights and as well as their responsibilities towards one another. Others, (10%) are convinced that community radio should engage itself more with developmental education of the people. Five percent say that community radio should occupy itself with political reporting on government activities. However, they advise that such radio should also be careful not to be biased or partisan while reporting the government's political activities. Finally, four percent respectively believe that community radio should emphasis environment and social situation or information on the health situation in society respectively.

People believe that, if community radio can take cognisance of the above observations in its broadcasting, it will lead to tremendous improvement in the quality of life, income, welfare and employment opportunities of the populace. Can community radio live up to the task of bringing development to the door-steps of the people? *"Do you think that a community radio station will contribute positively to the development of the society and Enugu state in particular?*

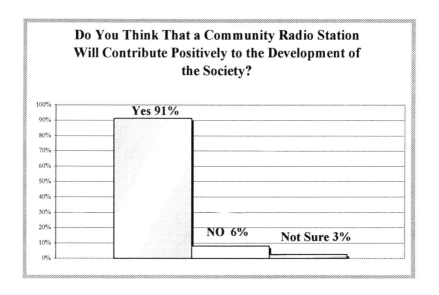

Do You Think That a Community Radio Station Will Contribute Positively to the Development of the Society?

Ninety-one percent (91%) are very optimistic that such radio station will bring about positive and tremendous development in society as long as there are no strangling laws and regulations from the government. It will help dispel the forces of ignorance and the level of education and awareness will improve tremendously in society.

The community will also use such medium to project its image norms and customs to other communities and foreigners. It will also create employment opportunities for individuals in the community and help them fulfil their fullest potentials. The establishment of such medium will help the society to become aware of its immediate environment, which will in turn bring about positive development of the society. The 3% and the 6% respectively said "no" and "not sure" that community radio will contribute to the development of the society argue that every thing will depend on the management of the station. The management may like to hijack the station and use it for its own selfish ends. People should not be too optimistic, they caution. The government may not allow it to function properly, by tying its hands and feet with draconian laws and regulations of broadcasting. Despite all odds, many believe that community radio will contribute tremendously to the development of the society. People are very optimistic that such radio station will definitely bring about development. For many, the existing radio stations in the state have made little or no impact on the people.

In Enugu state, especially in the city, one can receive some national and also international stations like "Enugu State Broadcasting Service" (ESBS) "Federal Radio Corporation of Nigeria" (FRCN), "British Broadcasting Corporation" (BBC), "Voice of America" (VOA). None of these are qualified to be called 'peoples radio'. The station will have the advantage of guarantee all political parties as well as individuals a genuine access to the media and will distinguish itself from the state owned stations. Community radio to be located in Eungu should be a grass-root one, for the people and should use the people's language, a language that is understood by the masses. The general public has already indicated the language with which they want the radio to operate. This they indicated when they answered the question:

In what language do you prefer to listen to radio?

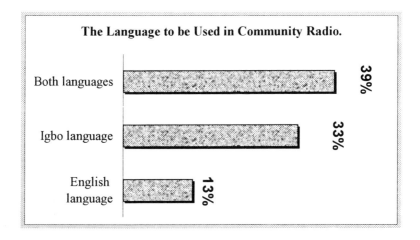

The Language to be Used in Community Radio.

Both languages — 39%

Igbo language — 33%

English language — 13%

6.2. Conclusion.

Radio, especially community media, is today as indispensable to the existence, cohesion and development of rural areas as oxygen is to the survival of living beings. A community radio station will help to enlighten and inform the rural people and make development faster. Therefore community radio station is inevitable for the development of rural areas in Eungu State.

7. OBSTACLES AND CHALLENGES TO BROADCASTING MEDIA IN NIGERIA FOR THE 21st CENTURY.

7.1. Obstacles Militating Against the Flow of Information in Nigeria.

In this chapter we are going to discuss the obstacles militating against broadcasting media in Nigeria. Broadcasting media have a special place in the life of Nigerians. In the developed world, people rely heavily on the different media (Telephone, Internet, Satellite, Newspaper etc.) for their daily information. In Nigeria however the case is different, many people cannot read the daily newspapers, magazines and journals. Even those who can read, cannot afford them. It becomes necessary to discuss in this chapter, those obstacles that can hinder adequate transmission of information through broadcasting to the common people. What are these major obstacles encountered by the broadcasting media in Nigeria in discharging their functions?

The range of obstacles to the free flow of information to the people in Nigeria varies, depending on the government in power. However, it is revealing that they abound in all societies without exception. In Western democracies, says Festus Eribo such obstacles limiting press freedom come under various laws enacted by government of the day: "such laws are generally limited to strictly and clearly defined matters, principally: liberal, slander and obscenity (to protect recognised private rights and vital social interests) as well as sedition, presenting a 'clear and present danger." Continuing he says: "wittingly or unwittingly, many of the Afro-Asian, South American as well as some European countries, have enacted extra legal measures to control and regulate in great detail the conditions under which newspapers, magazines, radio, television and other media of mass communication may be owned, established operated, published and distributed".[257]

However, in most developing countries especially in Africa, the issue of institutional control of the media is one that is of major concern to broadcasters, academicians and even to common man on the street. Chris Ogbondah remarks: "it is an issue that has generated fierce and

---

[257] Eribo Festus, Press Freedom and Communication in Africa, Trenton 1997, p. 2

vigorous discourse between the governed and governors for centuries"[258] He goes further to assert that: "Obstacles or restrictions on freedom of opinion started even centuries, within the church. For the church, the rationale to restrict expressions stems from the fact that the truth taught by the church is absolute. To protect this truth in its teachings as well as the purity of its doctrinal dogma from the inconsistencies of heretical opinions, the church has always sought to control expression and to punish deviant interpretations of its teachings and doctrines".[259] In any case, one should be able to distinguish between the dogmatic teaching of the church and the daily happening in the society. Street also observed that such practise of restriction of the press started "from the sixteenth century, with the English Crown assumed the prerogative power to grant printing privilege and thereafter treated this power as its monopoly."[260]

It should be noted that before the advent of the Europeans to the shore of country, the various ethnic communities, empires, kingdoms and emirates had already developed their own traditional means of public communication that is devoid of restriction of opinion, which we have already treated in the previous chapters. However, the Europeans brought with it new systems of communication and philosophies that were superimposed on the traditional means of communication. Therefore what we have today in the area of means of communication in Nigeria is "an offshoot more of foreign than indigenous means of communication.

In Nigeria, laws regulating the press were introduced for the first time by European colonial governments. Fred Omu notes: "colonialism was one of the factors that shaped the introduction of laws to regulate the African press."[261] Here in Nigeria for instance, the autocratic colonial administration did not grant the natives the same freedom of expression enjoyed by British citizens at home. The future indigenous leaders vehemently resented this policy. They mobilised the press and the masses in opposing the introduction of laws regulating the press.

---

[258] Ogbondah Chris, Military Regimes and the Press in Nigeria, Lanham/America 1994, p.1.
[259] ibid. p.1
[260] ibid. p.1
[261] Omu Fred, The dilemma of press freedom in colonial Africa: The West African example, in Journal of African History, vol. 9, London 1968, pp279-298.

Ironically, when Nigerian indigenous leaders took over the government of the country, after independence from Britain on October 1,
1960, they did not abrogate the colonial press laws that they so hated
and resented, rather, they adopted those laws to control the press.
"They turned to colonial statutory provisions to borrow the intent and
contents of the new press laws that they enacted."[262]

In an examination of the roots of post-independence Nigerian press
laws, Chris writes: "Almost three decades after the attainment of political independence, the spirit and contents of those colonial laws are
still found in the pages of law books. The roots of post-independence
laws are clearly found in colonial statute books, strongly suggesting
that the country's political leaders did not only inherit colonial statute
books after the attainment of independence but they review and adopt
those colonial statutory provisions when drafting today's laws regulating the press".[263] Obstacles to press freedom can be identified under
the following:

7.2. The Military.
7.3. Multilingualism and Cultural Pluralism.
7.4. Problem of NEPA.
7.5. Ethnicity and Religious Conflicts.

7.2. The Military Government and the Press in Nigeria.

In the forty-four years of her political independence, Nigeria has been
governed more of the time by military dictatorships. The relationship
between the dictatorships and the Nigerian press is worth giving a
consideration. Special emphasis is placed on the relationship between
the press and some selected military regimes in Nigeria. Here discussion will centre on some of the institutional measures utilised by each
military junta in attempt to suppress the dissemination of ideas and

---

[262] Ogbondah Chris, op.cit. p.2.
[263] Ogbondah Chris W., *Colonial laws: Model for contemporary African press laws?* in
International Third World Studies Journal and Review, vol. 1, no.1. London 1989,
pp191-192.

opinions in the media. It is generally belief that in the absence of elected Representatives, these media houses become organs through which the people could make their grievances known and seek redress for any wrong doings by government. During a military regime, the citizens saw the press as the "People's Parliament" – a parliament they believe should be free and unfettered. This means that the press of the nation must be free. It is the only way to safeguard the ultimate right of the people to know and to be informed. To victimise the nation's press unjustifiably is to erode the right and freedom of the citizens, especially their right to have a say, directly or indirectly in the way they are governed. In its role as watchdog over the government, the press is charged with investigating and reporting the truth to ensure effective governance. However, under military rule, the rule of law did not apply as the press often suffered at the hands of arbitrary exhibitions of power.

Nigerian's military government frowns at such sayings, "the press is the watchdog of the society". She contends that the western sense of press freedom is indeed a luxury for the African press. The explanation is that, given the conditions of scarce resources, a colonial legacy, a poorly educated population, tribal and ethnic rivalries, a free press can too easily lead to an inability of government to function, and to internal chaos. This may be the reason why Ike Nwosu, a colonel, the then military administrator of Oyo state says: "Private broadcasting would be more dangerous than privately owned newspapers and magazines, which, according to him do not take national interest into account in their activities".[264]

The military governments in Nigeria also believed that the press should show restraint in exercising its freedom. The reasons offered for this position include: "Events in the Third World countries are different from those in western societies. Most African (and other Third World) Journalists lack the experience and knowledge that would enable them to restrain themselves from destructive criticism. African countries (and other Third World countries) are politically too frail and fragile to withstand adverse press criticism. The leaders of Nigeria's military governments, like other Third World leaders, believed

---

[264] Nwocha Jossy, *The Ray Power Blast* in Newswatch vol. 21, no. 11, Lagos March 13, 1995, p.33

that the press should be somewhat restrained and rather harnessed to catalyse the process of social, economic and political development".[265] Now let us examine how the Nigerian media were treated under the various military governments in the country.

7.2.1. The Press under Muhammadu Buhari's Regime (1983-1984).

Muhammadu Buhari and his military juntas struck on December 31, 1983. They toppled the civilian government of Shehu Shagari. Their entry into Nigeria politics marked the beginning of another period in the relation between the government and the Nigerian media. It must be noted that during this regime obnoxious and draconian decrees were promulgated. Right from the time he seized power, Buhari made his impatience with the Nigerian media known and he did not hide his intentions to tamper with press freedom as enshrined in the 1979 Constitution. In the first two months in office, he unequivocally told some journalists that a decree to control the press was in the pipeline. He said that such a law was necessary to protect and shield government officials from slanderous and malicious accusations. Buhari said that discipline and responsibility were also necessary to the press just as freedom. In his first interview as the head of the military junta, Maj. Gen. Muhammadu Buhari said that press freedom provisions in the Constitution would be revised to check what he described as "excesses" that could endanger stability. Buhari said of the Nigerian press freedom: "I am going to tamper with that. It's because I know Nigerians very well"[266] The aftermath of Buhari's speech are the enactment of the following decrees:
Decree Nr. 1 of 1984: Suspension and Modification of the Constitution.
Decree Nr. 2 of 1984: State Security (Detention of Persons).
Decree Nr. 4 of 1984: Public Officers Protection Against False Accusation.

---

[265] Aggarwala N., *Press freedom: A Third World View*, in Development Communication Report, London July 1977, pp1-3.

[266] National Concord, Lagos Feb. 16 1984, p.1.

a). Decree Nr. 1 of 1984: Suspension and Modification of the Constitution.

To equip himself with the necessary institutional measures to control the press, Buhari's first promulgated Decree No.1, Constitution (Suspension and Modification) Decree of 1984 which did not only suspend sections of the 1979 Constitution but also empowered him and members of the federal military regime "to make laws for peace, order and good government of Nigeria or any part thereof with respect to any matter whatsoever."[267] Section 5 of the decree forbids the courts from adjudicating any questions about the validity of laws enacted by the junta.

b). Decree Nr. 2 of 1984: State Security (Detention of Persons).

On Feb. 9, 1984, he promulgated and signed "Decree No. 2", known as "State Security (detention of Person) Decree 1984", which retroactively commenced on December 31, 1983, the day that the regime came to power. The decree gave the Chief of Staff, Supreme Military Headquarters special power to detain anyone, including journalists and political commentators, for acts construed to be prejudicial to state security. It provided that: "If the Chief of staff, Supreme Headquarters is satisfied that any person is or recently has been concerned in acts prejudicial to state security or has contributed to the economic adversity of the nation, or in the preparation or instigation of such acts, and that by reason therefore it is necessary to exercise control over him, he may by order in writing direct that, that person be detained in a civil prison or police station or such other place specified by him; and it shall be the duty of the person or persons in charge of such place or places, if an order made in respect of any person is delivered to him, to keep that person in custody until the order is revoked".[268]

---

[267] Supplement to Official Gazette extraordinary, Federal Republic of Nigeria, Feb. 13, 1984, p.3.
[268] Ogbondah Chris W., op.cit. p.101

c). Decree Nr. 4 of 1984: Public Officers Protection Against False Accusation.

Decree No.2 appeared not to have given the Buhari regime enough grip on the Nigerian media. Hence, on March 29, 1984, Buhari promulgated Decree No. 4, otherwise known as "Public Officers (Protection Against False Accusation) Decree 1984". Its most formidable section provided that: "Any person who publishes in any form, whether written or otherwise, any message, rumour, report or statement, which is false in any material particular or which brings or is calculated to bring the Federal Military Government or the Government of a State or public officer to ridicule or disrepute, shall be guilty of an offence under this Decree".[269]

Going further the decree says: *"Any station or wireless telegraph which conveys or transmits any sound or visual massage, rumour, report or statement which is false in any particular time or which brings or is calculated to bring the Federal Military Government or the Government of a State or public officer to ridicule or disrepute, shall be guilty of an offence under this Decree".[270]* The law also conferred on the Head of State the power to ban newspaper circulation, and to revoke the license of a wireless telegraphy station in the federation or in any part of it. Section 2 of the law provided that: "Where the Head of the Federal Military Government is satisfied that the unrestricted circulation in Nigeria of a newspaper is or may be detrimental to the interest of the Federation or of any part thereof, he may by order published in the Gazette, prohibit the circulation in the Federation or in any part thereof, as the case may require, of that newspaper, and, unless any other period is prescribed in the order, the prohibition shall continue for a period of twelve months unless sooner revoked or extended, as the case may require".[271]

The Decree goes further to say: "Where the Head of the Federal Military Government is satisfied that the unrestricted existence in Nigeria of any wireless telegraphy station is detrimental to the interest of the Federation or any part thereof, he may by an order published in the

---

[269] Supplement to Official Gazette Extraordinary, Federal Republic of Nigeria, April 4, 1984, p.53.
[270] ibid. p.53
[271] ibid. p.53

Gazette- a) revoke the license to such wireless telegraphy station under the provisions of the Wireless Telegraphy Act 1961; or b) order the closure or forfeiture to the Federal Military government, as the case may be, of the wireless telegraphy station concerned"[272].

Journalists and publishers who contravened the law will be tried by a military tribunal composed of a High Court judges and three members of the armed forces, not below the rank of an army major. The tribunal's ruling could not be appealed in any court. Under Section 8 of the decree, which specified punishments for contravening the law, a journalist or publisher could be sentenced to as many as two years of imprisonment without the option of a fine and, in the case of business corporation, a fine of not less than N10, 000 (ten thousand naira) about ($13,000) at that time.[273]

Decree No. 4 was pregnant with ambiguities and therefore raises numerous questions. For example, Chris Ogbondah queries: "Was it lawful for a journalist or a press organisation to publish a true report or statement? Would the journalist or a newspaper organisation have contravened the law if the report or statement exposed the Federal Military Government, a state government or a public officer to ridicule or disrepute? Was it only when a published report or statement was false that a journalist or publisher contravened the law?"[274]

Again the draconian Decree No. 4, {Sections 2(1) & (2)}, *gave the head of the Federal Military Government the power to revoke the license of a wireless station as well as the power to order the closure or forfeiture to the Federal Military Government of such stations. It also empowered a military tribunal to order all or any of the printing equipment of a newspaper to be forfeited to the Federal Military Government.*

At the worst, past decrees gave the military the power to confiscate copies of newspapers or magazines already printed and circulating or about to be circulated in the country. Two journalists of The Guardian, Tunde Thompson, senior diplomatic correspondent and Nduka Irabor, assistant news editor and their newspaper were used by Buhari government as escape goats. The government accused them of publishing false statements in the Guardian issues of March 31, April 1 and April

---

[272] ibid. p.54
[273] Ogbondah Chris, op. cit. p.103
[274] Ogbondah Chris, op. cit. p.103

8, 1984, thereby committing an offence punishable under Section 1(1) of Decree No. 4.

On July 4, 1984, the two journalists and their newspapers were prosecuted under the provisions of Decree No. 4 "by a military tribunal, which held its hearings on the case at No.4 Queens Drive, Ikoyi, Lagos. The tribunal members were: "Mr. Justice Joshua Olalere Ayinde (chairman); Maj. Sanni Ahmed Fari(Army; Squadron Leader Clifford Maigani (Air Force) and Lieutenant Commander Joseph Ekeng-Ewa (Navy)"[275] Tunde Thompson faced a three-count charge and Nduka Irabor, a two-count charge which read thus: "That you, Tunde Thompson, being the Diplomatic Correspondent of the Guardian newspaper, Limited, being publishers of the Guardian newspapers on or about the 31st day of March 1984, at Rutam House, Isolo Lagos, Nigeria, published a statement which was false in every material with headline: "11 Foreign Missions to be Closed."[276]

That you, Tunde Thompson, being the Diplomatic Correspondent of the Guardian newspapers, Nduka Irabor being the Assistant News Editor of the Guardian newspapers on or about the 1st day of April 1984, at Rutam House, Isolo, Lagos, Nigeria, published a statement which was false in every particular: "Eight Military Chiefs Tipped Ambassadors" in the Guardian newspapers edition of April 1, 1984, published as Volume No. 289.[277]

That you, Tunde Thompson, "being the Diplomatic Correspondent of the Guardian newspapers, Nduka Irabor being the Assistant News Editor of the Guardian newspapers, Limited, publishers of the Guardian newspapers on or about the 8th day of April 1984, at Rutam House, Isolo, Lagos, Nigeria, published a statement which was false in every material particular: "Haruna Replaces Hannaniya as U.K. Envoy"[278]

Mr. Justice Ayinde, who read the military tribunal's judgement: "Acquitted the journalists on the first two counts, but sentenced them to one-year imprisonment each on the third count. Their newspapers, The Guardian, was fined fifty thousand naira (N50, 000) (about $67,000) at the time), N40, 000 over the minimum fine provided for in Decree No. 4 of 1984. In sentencing the editors, the military tribunal

---

[275] Ogbondah Chris, op. cit. p.127
[276] THE PUNCH, July 4, Lagos 1984, p.6
20 ibid. p.6
292 *The Guardian* Newspaper's Lagos April 8, vol. 296 1984, p.21

said: "however, the tribunal will be failing in its duty if it failed to impose a penalty that will serve as a deterrent to others".[279]
This and similar incidents widened the communication gap between the press and the government. Some government officials started committing atrocities under the disguise of Decree Nr. 4, which protects them from the eagle eyes of the journalists. One journalist in Imo State, Uwadiegwu Ogbonnaya, noted that threats of the enforcement of Decree No. 4 against journalists were frequently made by civil service officers in order to cover themselves from inquisitive newspersons. He said: "An attempt to...crosscheck from a commissioner an allegation that he personally supervised the distribution of essential commodities in his ministry was met with a stern warning by the commissioner that he would apply Decree No. 4 against the reporter if any nonsense should be published in their newspaper".[280] The media men continued to be in chains until Gen Muhammadus Buhari was over-thrown.

7.2.2. General Ibrahim Babangida and the Media.

The loss of individual freedom stemming from the enactment and enforcement of Decree No.4 of 1984, Public Officers (Protection Against False Accusation) Decree, created further despair and loss of faith in the Buhari regime. University students, the press, labour unions and political commentators were suppressed. Those who complained were labelled "unpatriotic citizens", and were jailed or punished in other ways. The denial of the right of political debate in a country that has always cherished its freedom to disagree on issues, further created loss of faith and despair in the regime. The regime that boasted of public accountability when it came to power on December 31, 1983, became unaccountable to the governed.

With the mountain of disgust and criticisms against the government of Buhari it was therefore a question of when rather than whether a coup would take place. The inevitable coup, Nigeria's sixth coup d'etat in twenty-five years, took place on August 27, 1985. Gen Ibra-

---

[279] The Punch Newspaper, Lagos July 8, 1984, p.5
[280] National Concord, July 3, Lagos 1984, p.15

him Babangida accused the Buhari government of "drifting" without improving the economy, oppression of the press and distancing itself from the aspirations and yearnings of the governed. And to drive the last nail into the coffin of the Buhari administration, Gen. Ibrahim Babangida made a welcome speech on freedom of expression – a speech that was antithetical in content from that made by Gen. Muhammadu Buhari in his own maiden speech.

While Gen. Buhari vowed to introduce a law to curb press freedom in his first speech as Head of State, Gen. Babangida abrogated this obnoxious press law, Decree No. 4 of 1984, (Public Offices Protection Against False Accusation) and pronounced an unconditional release of all journalists who had been in detention under the provisions of the decree. The pronouncements, according to Babangida, were made to encourage freedom of speech for the dissemination of diverse ideas and opinions in the mass media. He went further in maiden broadcast to the nation to assert that: "As we do not intend to lead a country where the individuals are under the fear of expressing themselves, the Public Officers Protection Against False Accusation Decree Number 4 of 1984 is hereby repealed with immediate effect. All journalists who have been in detention under this decree are hereby unconditionally released. The issue of this decree has generated a lot of controversy. It is the intention of this government to review all decrees. (Gen. Ibrahim Babangida's maiden speech to the nation on Nigerian radio network, Aug. 27, 1985)".[281]

In that broadcast, Babangida told Nigerians and the press to feel free to criticise the government policies because "criticisms of actions and decisions taken by us will be given necessary attention and, where necessary, changes made in accordance with what is expected of us. He assured the nation that his regime would not follow the brutality, iron-handedness and rule of force that characterised the Buhari government, Gen. Babandiga also promised to listen to public opinion because "we do not have a monopoly of wisdom."[282] Babangida's maiden response on the issue of press freedom was so antithetical to that of his predecessor that the West Africa News magazine pointed out that: "Where Buhari had sternly told Nigerians to shut up, Baban-

---

[281] Ogbondah Chris, op. cit. p.141
[282] ibid. p.141

212

gida is inviting them to resume what they enjoy doing most, that is criticizing their governments".[283]

Despite this wonderful speech coming from the head of state, the Nigerian people welcomed the government and its pronouncements with reservations. For the people, all the military men are the same. It did not last long before the regime of Babangida started bringing out its true colour.

The romance between Babangida and the Nigerian public continued for the next few years. While Babangida's approach to the media appeared more lenient, the honeymoon soon gave way to crackdowns and intimidations. For him the Nigeria media is too hot to handle. Something must be done about it before it is too late. Based on this prejudices, his administration rolled out many decrees all with the aim of caging the media.

The principal instruments that the Babandiga regime utilised in suppressing the dissemination of ideas and information in the mass media in Nigeria were:

a). Proscription and Prohibition From Circulation) Decree 48 of 1993;
b). The Nigerian Press Council Decree (No. 85) of 1992,
c). Offensive Publications (Proscription) Decree 35 of 1993.[284]

It is to be noted that some of these decrees used by Babangida were actually promulgated by his predecessors. However, when he came to power, he did not repeal all these draconian decrees rather, he retained some and invoked them from time to time when he deem it necessary.

a.) Proscription and Prohibition from Circulation (Decree 48) of 1993.

This was drafted on August 16, 1993; this decrees proscribed seventeen newspapers and magazines published by four of the nation's newspaper houses. The publications affected by the decree included: *African Concord magazine, Weekend Concord, Sunday Concord, National Concord, Business Punch, Saturday Punch, Sunday Punch, Daily Sketch, Sunday Sketch, the Nigerian Observer and Sunday Observer.*

---

[283] West Africa Magazine, September 23, Lagos 1985, p.1949.
[284] Ogbondah Chris, p.143

The closure of *The Observer Newspaper*, owned by the Edo state government, represented the first time in the thirty-three years of military dictatorship that a state government-owned newspaper was shut down by the federal government. The law took a retroactive effect from July 22, 1993 in order to legitimise the closure of four of the five media houses that the military junta had earlier shut down in the wake of media criticisms of the government's annulment of the June 12, 1993 presidential election.

The government said the decree was drafted to check the "excesses" of the press. However, it was press criticism of the military junta's inept handling of the transition to democracy and the annulment of the presidential elections in particular that pragmatically explains the rationale for the press decree. "The Sunday Concord of June 27 1993, four days after Ibrahim Babangida's nullification of the June 12 presidential election, for example, criticised the government for not honouring the wishes of Nigerians at the polls."[285]

The Concord editorial described the annulment of the election results as "a crude and unwarranted subversion of the Nigerian will. It said that Babangida's reasons for cancelling the results of the election was the "most repulsive insult on the intelligence of the average Nigerian." Subsequently, the quotes of every page three of the Sunday Concord was often from opponents of the military regime."[286] Against this background, the military junta continued to breed out decrees upon decrees. These decrees were aimed at curbing press criticisms of its vacillation to hand over power to a democratically elected government as well as its cancellations of the 1992 primary and 1993 presidential elections. The decree was aimed at in a special way, the proscription of Newswatch Magazine. According to an explanatory note that accompanied the decree, the law proscribes and prohibits from circulation in Nigeria or any part thereof the weekly news magazine known as "Newswatch" for the purpose of preventing it from publishing classified information which has not been lawfully released. Section 2 of the decree provided that the premises of the Newswatch Communications Limited, publishers of the magazine should be sealed up by the Inspector-General of Police or any authorized officer of the military junta.

---

[285] Sunday Concord Newspaper Lagos June 27, 1993 p.3
[286] ibid. p.3

Notwithstanding anything contained in the Constitution of the Federal Republic of Nigeria 1979 or in any other enactment or law, the weekly news magazine known as Newswatch and published by the Newswatch Communications Limited was proscribed from being published and prohibited from circulation in Nigeria or in any part thereof. The premises where the weekly news magazine referred to in Section 1 of this Decree was published was to be sealed up by the Inspector-General of Police or any officer of the Nigeria Police Force authorized in that behalf during the duration of this Decree.[287]

Section 3 of the press law gave validity and legality to actions taken by junta authorities to ban the circulation of copies of the magazine prior to the enactment of the decree. The section also ousted the courts from entertaining any suit brought by anyone challenging the constitutionality of the proscription of the magazine. It provides that: "Any person who on the direction of the appropriate authority has at any time before the commencement of this Decree dealt with or acted in compliance with this Decree or any order made there under or hereafter deals with any copies of the weekly news magazine proscribed or prohibited from circulation pursuant to this Decree, shall stand indemnified in respect therefore and no suit or other proceeding whatsoever shall lie at the instance of any person aggrieved in respect of any act, matter or thing done or purported to be done in respect of such direction or compliance; and where any such suit or other proceeding has been instituted in any court, it shall abate and be of no effect whatsoever".[288]

Newswatch was banned because it published what the Babangida government said was "classified information." The magazine published leaked information on the findings of the Political Bureau, a commission headed by Dr. A. Cookey that was set up by the military junta to look into issues concerning the Third Republic of Nigeria from 1992 when the military hoped it would have handed over the government to democratically elected governors. Newswatch obtained information on the commission's report to the government, and subsequently published it.[289]

---

[287] West Africa Magazine, Lagos April 20, 1987 p.749.
[288] ibid. p.732.
[289] Ogbondah Chris, p.145.

Among the things it published was "information on the philosophy of government in the Third Republic, the political system, political parties, the role of traditional rulers, states creation, office holding and transition to civilian rule. The junta claimed that these were "classified" documents, and that the publication by Newswatch was an "illegal and irresponsible action."[290] The government also said that the publication of the information could be explosive and pose a threat to the stability of the nation. The statement said: "Precipitate publication of far-reaching proposals on sensitive issues such as the political ideology for Nigeria, the creation of states, the role of traditional rulers, etc. can be explosive and pose a threat to the stability of the nation."[291]

The government statement further explained why the decree was enacted. It said that: "Government was convinced that (printing advance notice of the Cookey report's findings) would prejudice a balanced consideration of the recommendations in the report and could cause confusion and disaffection among the diverse groups in our society."[292] The government also said that it made attempts to stop Newswatch from publishing the Political Bureau's report once it learned that the report had been leaked. The statement said that: "Responsible government functionaries approached the management and advised them against premature publication. These approaches proved abortive. Government contacted relevant media professional bodies to use their good offices to dissuade the management from publication at this time. But Newswatch decided to break the law, defy the government, and ignore their professional bodies by publishing the report".[293]

The magazine's editor, however, denied that the government ever contacted them as it claimed. The editors said: "We wish to state, without fear of contradiction, that no responsible government functionaries or media professional bodies approached the management of Newswatch asking them to stop publishing the reported stories.[294] This he did in order to shut up other media houses. As this was not enough to terrorise the press, in 1992, he promulgated the Nigerian Press Council of 1992.

---

[290] Ogbondah Chris, p.146
[291] West Africa Magazine, ibid. p.701.
[292] ibid.
[293] ibid. p.732
[294] ibid. p.732

b). The Nigerian Press Council Decree (No. 85) of 1992.

Babangida later formally set up a council to regulate the press. The decree to this effect was signed in December 1992 but made public in 1993. The law provides that only those who have been trained at institutions recognized by the Nigerian Union of Journalists (NUJ) or have a certificate of experience acquired after five years will be eligible for registration as journalist. The law also provided that the council maintains a register of such accredited journalists for the benefit of the NUJ. The decree states: "The council will research into contemporary press development and press documentation, to foster the attainment and maintenance of high professional standards, and ensure the protection of the rights and privileges of journalist in the performance of their duties."[295] Into this council, the government will also appoint their own representatives, so also the Nigerian Press Organisation (NPO) of which the publishers' body is a member along with the Nigerian Guild of Editors (NGE) and the Nigeria Union of Journalists (NUJ). However the later bodies have through a special committee stressed the need for a press council "that is controlled only by professionals".

c). Offensive Publications and Proscription (Decree 35) of 1993.

Enacted in August 1993 but backdated to January 1, 1993, the decree empowered the head of the military government to seize or proscribe any publication or closedown any broadcasting stations deemed offensive to state security or public order. It was under the provisions of this law that the government seized copies of the July 1993 edition of Tell magazine.[296]

This law prescribed new registration guidelines for all newspapers in the country. It was made public in Abuja, the new federal capital, on August 16, 1993, the decree took a retroactive effect from June 22, 1993. According to the decree, the military government would appoint a board whose responsibility would be to register all existing newspapers in circulation. It required newspaper publishers to pay pre-

---

[295] Ogbondah Chris, op. cit. p.143.
[296] ibid. p.147

registration deposits of two hundred and fifty thousand naira (N250, 000) and a non-refundable deposit of hundred thousand naira (N100, 000), section 2 of the decree provided that:
"Notwithstanding the provisions of subsection (1) of this section, where, on the commencement of this Decree, a person carrying on business as the owner or publisher of a newspaper, should within 3 weeks where he desired to continue that business, apply to register the newspaper under provisions of this Decree but should therefore cease to carry on that business after the expiration of 3 weeks unless he complied with paragraphs (a) and (b) of this section.
Paragraph (a) and (b) required all Newspapers to carry, on their first or last pages, the true names and addresses of their proprietors and editors. The law stipulated that a copy of each newspaper should be signed by its editor and delivered to the secretary for information. According to the decree, "anyone who publishes a newspaper which is not registered, will on conviction go to jail for seven years or pay a fine of N250, 000 (two hundred and fifty thousand naira) or both, while registered newspapers may face a similar fine or a 10-year jail term for publishing false report or rumour."[297]

Section 5 "granted the board discretionary powers to register or renew the registration of newspapers on the basis of public interest and performance during the pervious year. It also required that the secretary of information – as the information minister was then called- must be informed of appointments of editors in all the newspapers."[298]
The decree met with stiff opposition by the media. Sani Zorro, the then national president of the Nigeria Union of Journalist, NUJ, described it as "a very tragic development." Lateef Jakande, former president of the Newspapers Proprietors Association of Nigeria, NPAN, said it was unconstitutional because the federal government could only legislate on matters on the exclusive legislative list, adding: "Legislation of newspapers and magazines is not on that list."[299]

Various institutions dragged the Federal Government to court because of this draconian decree. The Guardian Newspapers Limited "challenged the decree in court of law. On November 18, 1993, a judge of an Ikeja high court ruled that the decree was unconstitutional,

---

[297] ibid. p.148
[298] Newswatch August 14, Lagos 1995, p. 14
[299] ibid. p. 15

null and void. It was a major victory for the Nigerian press. Government did not appeal the judgement or enforce the registration."[300]

Olu Onagoruwa, the then Federal Attorney General and minister of justice, subsequently pronounced the decree dead. He said that government would not appeal the judgement. While Jerry Gana, minister of information, also said the decree was dead. It was a serious battle won by the Nigerian Press Media. However more battles were yet to come between the Babangida administration and the media.

7.2.2.1. General Ibrahim Babangida and the Saga of Dele Giwa's Death.

It was the murder of Dele Giwa, the editor-in-chief of Newswatch, one of Nigeria's most successful media businesses that marked a major watershed in government – press relations during the Babangida regime. Giwa was murdered on October 19, 1986 on his breakfast table with a parcel bomb delivered to him at his 25 Talabi Street residence in Ikeja, Lagos, by alleged agents of the military government. The persons who delivered the parcel bomb to Giwa claimed that the parcel was a Christmas gift from the Head of State, Ibrahim Babangida. There are, however, other complex speculations about the mystery of Giwa's death.[301]

The London bureau chief of the magazine, Kayode Soyinka who was with the editor that fateful morning barely escaped death, but not without problems caused by the bomb blast. The military government promised to clear its hand in the murder. But a lame-duck panel set up since then to investigate the murder did not produce anything to write home about. This incidence continued to follow Babangida until he left office. He stepped aside when public pressure was too much on him. He had to constitute a transitional government led by Chief Ernest Shonekan. The administration of Shonekan only lasted for months before the military led by Sani Abacha struck again.

---

[300] ibid. p.14
[301] Newswatch Magazine, Lagos November 1986, pp15-22

7.2.3. Abacha and the Freedom of the Press. (Nov. 17 1993- May 1998.)

The unceremonious exit of the former head of state Gen. Ibrahim Babangia was widely welcomed by the populace and the media. The battle had been raging when on August 27, 1993, the administration of General Ibrahim Babangida stepped aside without having resolved the problem of *June 12*. This problem revolved on the annulment of the 1992 election, which every Nigerian believed was won by Mushood Abiola. Instead of announcing the winner of the election, the then president Gen. Babangida annulled the election. The masses opposed this unpopular decision of the head of state. He was so handicapped, and appointed a Transitional Government of Chief Shonekan, an Interim National Government with, a life span of six months at the end of which a civilian president would be elected. But because of the debate over the constitution under which the government was installed, the masses and the press had decided that Abiola the winner of the election should be declared the President of the country without delay. The legitimacy of Shonekan government was challenged in the court. The court declared the interim government illegal. With the government being declared illegal, it was a question of time before the inevitable would happen. By November 17, General Sani Abacha, the most senior serving minister in the Interim Government, took the mantle of leadership. He was welcome because the country and the media wanted the problems that were sorely testing the nation's very foundation resolved.[302]

As often happened when a new regime emerges on the scene, there was relief on the arrival of Abacha, and of course great expectations. Although the country could be said to have been on the brink of collapse, and many had openly called for intervention of the military, it was expected that the root cause of the problems would be resolved by the new regime.

Did Abacha live up to the expectation of the media when he ascended the theatre of power? The answer is yes and no. Immediately he took the mantle of leadership, he waved an olive branch to the press. To

---

[302] Newswatch Magazine, Lagos Nov. 24 1997 p.35

concretise this, he lifted the ban on the Punch, Concord and Abuja Newsday Newspapers, which the former president, Ibrahim Babangida proscribed. In his maiden broadcast, he said: "On the closed media houses, government is hereby lifting the order of pro-scription with immediate effect. We however appeal to the media houses that in the spirit of national reconciliation we should show more restraint and build a united and peaceful Nigeria".[303]

Many thought that with the good gesture, a foundation of good rela-tion between the government and the press had been laid. It was not to be so forever. Before the press could know it, 13 publications had been barred from production and circulation. They belonged mainly to the Guardian, Punch and Concord groups. And at the end of Abacha's first year in office, the press and the government were back to the cat and mouse relationship. The honeymoon was over in a matter of months[304].

On Monday 15 August 1994 till 14 August 1995 the government sealed the premises of "The Guardian". This move sent panic through the industry as many editors regarded it as a prelude to a general clampdown on the pres. Editors in some media houses not only moved materials necessary for their operations out of their premises, they abandoned their offices in anticipation of raids by security men. An editor said: "We have been told to expect an invasion of our premises. So we are not going to be sitting ducks for them this time. And we must find ways of publishing even if they raid us".[305] The raid never materialised. Abacha wielded the big stick. He banned The Punch, National Concord and The Guardian for six months. He late extended the proscription of the Guardian newspaper for another six months.

It was titled: The Guardian Newspapers and African Guardian Weekly Magazine (Proscription and Prohibition from Circulation) (extension of Time) Order 1995. This means all these newspapers were forced out of the newsstands. The Civil liberties Organisation shaded the situation at that time thus: "Armed ant-riot policemen at the gates of these newspapers' premise were a constant reminder of the state of siege under which the press has had to operate in Nigeria

---

[303] Usen Anietie, *Pen Against The Gun* in Newswatch Magazine, Lagos Nov. 24 1997, p.40.
[304] ibid. p.36.
[305] Newswatch Magazine, Lagos August 29, 1994, p. 37.

in the pas few years. It was a testimony to the shackles gleefully imposed on freedom of expression, a necessary medium of which newspapers are. The government disobeyed several court orders made in respect of suits instituted by the management of The Guardian to challenge the closure. Even an order that employees of the several other independent businesses that shared premises with The Guardian be allowed access to their work places was also disregarded".[306]

7.2.3.1. Abacha's New Strategies: Arrest and Detention of Journalists.

When Abacha saw that the closures of Media houses were not helping matters, he then resorted to the strategies of arresting and detention of journalists. This he did from the belief that the closure of media houses amounted only to the scourging of the snake and not killing it. When a newspaper was proscribed, it emerged with a new name. Periodic shut downs of magazines and newspapers were common. Only those controlled by or which did not rock the ship of state remained untouched. The majority of the press, however, sought middle ground, reporting only hard news void of editorial perspective. Those that did step out of line felt the crack of the whip. Under this new scheme, many journalists were arrested and none of the media houses were shut down. Even his worst critics would give him credit for his tolerance of many adversarial publications against his person and government. However, left for some of his officials in the ministry of information, in addition to the arrest of journalists, nearly half a dozen newspapers should have been proscribed.

As the new strategy came into full swing, security operatives were on the heels of many journalists. As a result of this system, there were more journalists in detention, than at any other time in the history of Nigeria. Some who were not in detention went underground and those who were not underground were not sure when they will take their turn in detention. Those who do not want anything to do with deten-

---

[306] Annual Report, 1995, A Civil Liberty Organisation Report on the State of Human Rights in Nigeria, Lagos 1990.

tion and underground trooped out of the profession in search of greener and less turbulent pastures.[307]

Sensing danger, wives of journalists started dragging their husbands' ears every morning about what they write. According one reporter, "if his wife says strike out this sentence, he does not hesitate because he understood that to mean: she will not follow him to Kirikiri prison."[308] Under the Abacha government, many journalists had various detention and prison sentences.

In March 1995, four journalists were framed-up and arrested in connection with an alleged plot by some military officers to overthrow the regime of General Sani Abacha. On 10 March, the chief of defence staff, Major-General Abdulsalam Abubakar, said "the government had established that the 29 officers and civilians already arrested by then had formed the intention of "disturbing the peace of the nation" Curiously, when the press first reported that there had been a coup, the government vehemently denied it. Speaking through the director of defence information, Brigadier Fred Chijuka, the journalists who reported the story were described as rumour-.mongers. The press was castigated for reporting rumours, and that was fastened on to as further evidence of its irresponsibility."[309] It was, thus, quite a surprise when the army later claimed that there had been a coup after all, and proceeded to arrest both officers alleged to have been involved in the plot and civilians, including, strangely, journalist whose papers had reported what was earlier described as rumours. The four were tried in secret by the Brigadier Patrick Aziza special military tribunal appointed to try all the suspects for being accessories before the fact of treason. They were convicted and sentenced to life imprisonment. As a result of the very loud protests, both local, and especially international, the sentences were on 31 October 1995 commuted to 15 years each".[310]

The Civil Liberty Organisation says, "The secret trial and conviction of the journalists marks a very dangerous turn in the government's seeming determination to use all means, fair or foul to undermine the

---

[307] Usen Anietie, op. cit. p.38
[308] ibid. p. 39.
[309] Civil Liberty Organisation, op. cit. p.38
[310] ibid. p.39

freedom of the press. The following Journalists were arrested and sentenced to various imprisonments:

i. **Kundle Ajibade; "THE NEWS". Imprisoned: May 5, 1995.**

Police arrested Ajibade, an editor of the daily TheNEWS, and demanded to know the source of the article "No One Guilty: The Commission of Inquiry Presents an Empty File Regarding Suspects in the Coup d'Etat." They held him because he refused to divulge the whereabouts of his colleague Dapo Olorunyomi, who went underground. In July, a special military tribunal held a secret trial for Ajibade and George Mbah of Tell magazine, charging them as accessories to treasonable felony and sentencing them to prison terms of undisclosed length of time. On Oct. 1, 1995 Nigeria's Independence remembrance day, the Provisional Ruling Council amended their sentences to 15 years in prison.[311]

ii. **Christine Anyanwu; "THE SUNDAY MAGAZINE" (TSM) Imprisoned: May 1995.**

Anyanwu, publisher and editor in chief of The Sunday Magazine, was arrested for her reports on an alleged coup plot in March. In July, a special military tribunal secretly tried Anyanwu, along with Ben Charles Obi, editor of Weekend Classique. [See below] Both got life sentences. On Oct. 1, 1995 Nigeria's Independence remembrance day, the Provisional Ruling Council commuted their sentences to 15 years in prison.[312]

iii. **George Mbah; "TELL": Imprisoned May 5, 1995.**

Soldiers arrested Mbah, assistant editor of Tell magazine, for contributing to a report about a military officer who died during interrogation about his involvement in an alleged coup plot. In July, a special mili-

---

[311] ibid p.40
[312] ibid. p.41

tary tribunal secretly tried Mbah and Kunle Ajibade of TheNEWS, charging them with being accessories to treasonable felony. They were sentenced to life in prison. On Oct. 1, Nigeria's Independence Day, the Provisional Ruling Council amended their sentences to 15 years in prison.[313]

iv. Ben Charles Obi; "WEEKEND CLASSIQUE": Imprisoned May 1, 1995.

Obi, the editor of the weekly newsmagazine Weekend Classique, was arrested for his reports on an alleged coup plot in March. In July, a special military tribunal tried Obi and Christine Anyanwu of The Sunday Magazine. [See above] Both received life sentences. On Oct. 1, Nigeria's Independence Day, the Provisional Ruling Council commuted their sentences to 15 years in prison.[314]
Others who suffered similar fate include:

v. Nosa Igiebor;

On 17 December 1995, the security operatives raided the premises of academy Press, printers for "Tell", and seized 55,000 copies of the week's edition with the cover title: "Abiola's Freedom: The World Watch for Abacha." As if to say that this move did not have any effect on the magazine, then on 23. December 1995, Nosa Igiebor, editor-in-chief of "Tell" magazine was arrested and detained by the State Security Service (SSS). Although no reason was given for his arrest, it was generally believed that it was for the radical position of his magazine on most of the activities of the military-in-power, especially on the question of military rule and the violation of human rights. Consequently, Tell has been a prime target of the repressive machine of the Abacha regime as it had been of his predecessor, General Ibrahim Babangida.[315]

---

[313] ibid. p.42.
[314] ibid. p.41
[315] ibid. pp40-43

vi. Okina Deesor; RADIO RIVERS. Imprisoned: July 31, 1996.

Deesor, a producer with Radio Rivers in the state of Rivers, was arrested and detained at the Government House Cell prison, reportedly without food or water. On Aug. 3, he was transferred to the Mobile Police Headquarters in Port Harcourt. According to Maj. Obi Umabi, Deesor's detention was in connection with the July 18 Radio Rivers broadcast of the national anthem of the Ogoni people. In a letter to President Sani Abacha, CPJ denounced Deesor's continued detention and asked for his immediate and unconditional release.[316]

During those five years of Abacha's regime, newspapers were commonly seized, vendors jailed and journalists either fled or disappeared. During this period, the Nigerian press, which had enjoyed manys years, as the most "prolific and vociferous" in sub-Sahara Africa, suffered stunning blows. Because of this repression, the growth of what has been called "guerrilla journalism" became extremely popular in Nigeria. Journalists viewed this style of journalistic practice as the most effective weapon against their persecution under Abacha's government.

There were many cases of indiscriminate arrest and detention of journalists that many started posing the question: Did Abacha actually order the closure of all these media houses and the arrest of these journalists? In the closure of some newspapers, the ministry of information, which oversees government media relations, obviously knew nothing about it, according to Jerry Gana, the then minister of information and culture, says "at times the security agents took the action in the interest of national security, he added that the situation would have been averted had journalists heeded the call to exercise their freedom with utmost reasonability."[317]

---

[316] The Committee to Protect Journalists is an Independent, Non-Profit Organisation (NGO) that works to safeguard around the world. It is based in New York, U.S.A.
[317] Newswatch Magazine, Lagos August 29, p. 37-38.

7.2.3.2. Abacha Associates and the Media.

Following the footsteps of Gen. Abacha, other agents of the federal military government (the military governors or the administrators) tried to exercise their own powers. They exercised their own might in their various states. There were instances where they also became tyrannical.

i. For instance Newswatch in one of her write-ups "JUSTICE AT LAST" describe an incident, where the then former military governor of Anambra state, Mike Attah sacked six journalists wrongfully during the reign of Sani Abacha. The journalists, who were posted to the government house from the state-owned media organisations namely the Anambra Broadcasting Service, ABS (radio and TV stations), *National Light* newspaper and the state ministry of information were sacked by Mike Attah, retired colonel and former military administrator, in 1994. He reportedly sacked them because they could not join his entourage to an official function in Onitsha. It was learnt that the vehicle that was to carry them had no fuel.

The journalists did not obtain reprieve in spite of several petitions they wrote to Attah and his two successors, Rufai Garba, a group captain and Emmanuel Ukaegbu a wing commander. "Garba failed to act on the recommendations of a panel set up by him. The Panel exonerated the journalists but Garba was said to have queried the report instead of re-instating them."[318]

On December 6, 1999, Chinwoke Mbadinuju, the governor of the state, gave an approval for the reinstatement of the dismissed journalists. A letter dated December 7, and signed by the commissioner of information, conveyed the good news to the affected journalists.

The Anambra state governor, Chinwoke Mbadinuju stating his reason for restating them says according to the report of the panel that investigated the matter "the journalists did not make the governor's entourage because their vehicle had no fuel. If it was because of their negligence to duty, they deserved what they got, but they made a case. And with a story like that, it was not difficult for me to restore them, he said, adding, we have come in this administration to correct the

---

[318] Chigbo Maureen, *Justice at Last* in Newswatch Magazine, vol. 31, no.3, Lagos February 2000. p.38

anomalies of the past. Journalists do a very difficult job and we granted them reprieve."[319]

In Imo State, Oby Agbai, the chairperson of the state council of the Nigerian Union of Journalist, NUJ, was on September 3, 1997, thoroughly flogged by security men in Government House Owerri and later hospitalised for multiple injuries. Agbai who works for the state-owned tabloid *The Statesman* had a few days earlier criticise the state government for poor funding of *The Statesman* Newspaper at a luncheon organised by government for media executives. That seems to be her offence.[320]

In Yobe State, John Ben Kalio, the then military administrator of the state in September 1997 "ordered the *Yobe State Television*, (YTV) station to be shut down and the staff on duty flogged mercilessly by his aides. Eight members of staff of YTV were arrested and taken to Government House where Ben-Kaliom a wind commander, allegedly supervised their caning. What was their crime? They had aired a documentary on the tenure of Dabo Aliyu, former governor of the state."[321]

On 8 February 1995 the then military administrator of Oyo State, Col. Ike Nwosu, ordered the *Broadcasting Corporation of Oyo State* (BCOS) to be closed down. He also ordered the suspension of the entire workforce of the corporation. Col. Nwosu's action followed a strike embarked upon by the workers of "BCOS" over management problems, part of which was the non-payment of their January salaries.[322] These actions of the military administrators show how well the continued closure of press houses by the federal military government without cause has come to be emulated at the state level.

On 3 February, Mr. Fidel Egwuche, editor of the Kogi State-owned newspaper, The Graphic, was placed on indefinite suspension by the state military administrator, Colonel Paul Omeruo. Egwuche's offence was that he published an editorial, which called for the disbandment of the *National Constitutional Conference*. He was also accused of publishing negative reports on the state government. The state government had dissociated itself from the editorial and restated its support

---

[319] ibid. p.40
[320] Usen Anitie, *Pen Against the Gun* in Newswatch Magazine , Lagos Nov. 24, 1997, p.39
[321] ibid. p.39.
[322] Daily Times Newspaper, Lagos February 9, 1995, p.1

for the federal military government. However, later the state government rescinded the decision.[323]

We must here admit that the *Nigerian Independent Journalists* met their waterloo during the reign of Abacha. The Military junta, during his rule from 1993 to 1998 scored a "string of straight As" in his repression of Nigerian media. The Committee to Protect Journalists named him the "world's foremost enemy of the press" in 1998. On 30 April 1998, Committee to Protect Journalist (CPJ)[324], released the following statement in recognition of World Press Freedom Day, 3 May 1998. Among other things they said:

"The leaders of Nigeria, Burma, Belarus, Cuba and Indonesia are among the world's 10 Enemies of the Press named today by the Committee to Protect Journalist. Selected for their relentless campaigns of suppression of journalist as documented by CPJ world-wide, they were identified in connection with World Press Freedom Day, 3 May 1998. Gen. Sani Abacha of Nigeria was named the press worst enemy. Other enemies include Meles Zenawi of Ethiopia and Jiang Zemin of China. Leaders of Jordan, Tunisia, and Turkmenistan were cited CPJ's annual ranking for the first time. Going further the report says: All of these ten individuals are intent upon suppressing any independent media voice, through whatever means necessary.

They are collectively responsible for unabating press freedom abuse that has penalised hundreds of journalists through physical attack, imprisonment, censorship, harassment and even murder."[325]

On the person of Abacha the report says: Five years into his dictatorship, Abacha has escalated his outrageous assault on the country's once-thriving independent press and reneged on his promise to return the country to democracy. His brutal tactics kept 21 Nigerian journalists behind bars: Nigeria then held more journalists in prison than any other African nations.[326]

---

[323] Civil Liberty Organisation, op. cit. p.34.

[324] The Committee to Protect Journalists is an Independent, Non-Profit Organisation (NGO) that works to safeguard around the world. It is based in New York, U.S.A.

[325] Report by the "The Committee to Protect Journalists. At the occasion of World Press Freedom Day May 3, 1998.

[326] Ibid.

7.2.3.3. The Saintly Side of Gen. Sani Abacha.

The Nigerian media remain surprisingly ebullient and vibrant, despite intimidation and outright physical brutality and some sections of the independent press have continued to thrive. They remained at the forefront of civil society's search for and determination to entrench, a new Nigerian tradition of transparency, good governance, accountability and morality. To the credit of the press, Nigerian journalism remains surprisingly ebullient. Under the Abacha administration several new titles such as *This Day, Post Express, The Diet, The Source* and *National Post* joined the newsstands. Under his regime that some of the private radio and television stations, which now include African Independent Television (AIT), Ray Power radio, Independent Television, Channels Television, Minaji International Television (MIT) emerged. They have the aim of reaching out to the whole world, hopefully reflecting an African perspective in the reporting and analysis of the world events.

If the period of Abacha's administration has been a tale of woes for the press, pressmen cannot escape blame. The state of the media and the practice of the profession have left most professionals gasping for breath. At the biennial convention of the Nigerian Guild of Editors in 1996, Abacha summed up his impression of the press in a speech many regarded as "acerbic." He said: "The rational dimension of the practice was jettisoned for the more salacious variety that came dripping with the sectional and unprofessional and gutter practice. These days Journalists have forgotten the underlying demands of objectivity, respect for facts and existence of different viewpoints".[327]

After Abacha, the Nigeria government and the media have learnt their lessons. Now they agreed to march forward with the sole aim of serving the masses. In the face of democracy what will be the relationship between the government and the press? Apart from the military regimes in the country, another cankerworm eating deep into the broadcasting arena is the ethnic multiplicities and languages in the country.

---

[327] Usen Anietie, op. cit. p.39

7.3. Broadcasting and Multilingualism in Nigeria.

In many contexts the words "language" and "communication" imply each other to such an extent that they are interchangeable. Language is actually the mirror of any given society. It crystallises the thought of a people. The language of the people does reflect their dominant concerns and interests. Language makes communication between individuals, groups and nations possible. It makes possible also the continuity of societies, and the effective functioning and control of social groups. "There are about 3,500 languages used in verbal communication in the world. Out of this number about 1,250 languages are spoken on the African continent."[328] This multilingualism is a phenomenon that is common to most African countries south of the Sahara. There are just about half a dozen countries in which an indigenous language is spoken as a lingua franca, and still fewer in which a local language is used as a medium of instruction within official and administrative purposes. In fact "this is the case only in Ethiopia, Somalia and Tanzania, which use *Amharic, Somali* and *Swahili* respectively. In the vast majority of countries, the language used for government business is the language of the colonial power, and even in the exceptional cases where a local language is used as the official national language, a foreign language is still resorted to for all forms of international communication."[329]

One of the major problems therefore facing Nigeria as a country since her independence till date is how to weld together the various ethnic groups living within the national boundaries with different languages and culture. Brann, C.M.B observes: "The making of modern Nigeria is one of the greatest problems... A state of such ethnic and religious diversity containing dozens of ancient cultures and hundreds of living languages is indeed more difficult to centralise than was any nation of Europe. Here we have representatives of all the known African language families".[330]

Admitting the problem of language in Nigeria, Paul Ansah concurs "whereas regional disparities can be overcome by a conscious effort to

---

[328] Macbride Sean, Paris 1980, p.49.
[329] Ansah Paul: *Broadcasting and Multilingualism* in George Wendell (ed.) Making Broadcasting Useful, Manchester 1986, p.47.
[330] Brann C.M.B, Language in Education and Society in Nigeria: A Comparative Bibliography and Research Guide, Quebec 1975, p.2

reallocate resources in such a way as to reduce the differences, the existence of a plurality of language is a fact that cannot be wished away without provoking deep resentment and arousing the suspicious of one ethnic group wanting to establish some hegemony or condemning others to cultural extinction. The language factors become a sensitive issue because it is one of the most evident characteristics that define a given ethnic group and gives it identity and character as a distinct, homogeneous body."[331]

Nigeria is called the giant of Africa. It has played and should continue to play a vital role not only in Africa, but how can she play such a role adequately, when the diverse language situation reveals diversity of people? The number of languages almost corresponds to the number of ethnic groups. Thus, Nigeria is simply a politico-geographical mass of land that contains, within her borders, a large lump of diverse cultures, languages, religions, and other social forms. For her to be able to function strongly, she needs all the unity and goodwill of her people. There is a dire need for mutual understanding among the various ethnic groups, and one of the major means of achieving that is through inter-ethnic communication.

The major instruments for diffusing these values and symbols are the mass media, especially radio, which has the advantage of covering extensive areas and overcoming the barrier of illiteracy.

The messages should be able to reach the people and facilitates the task of unity. In this regard, it is necessary to recall the following observation by Cantrill and Allport: "When a million or more people hear the same subject matter, the same arguments and appeals, the same music and humour, when their attention is held in the same way and at the same time to the same stimuli, it is psychologically inevitable that they should acquire in some degree common interests, common tastes and common attitudes. In short, it seems to be the nature of radio to encourage people to think and feel alike".[332]

Accepting the validity of this observation, it is obvious that it is based on the assumption that a common language is being used to reach the audience simultaneously. *This is where the operations of broadcasting in multilingual societies pose peculiar problems.* One indicator therefore, how much of the broadcasting is able to reach the

---

[331] Ansah Paul: op cit. p.47.
[332] Ansah Paul: op.cit. p.47

villages is the languages used for transmission. A 1975 study by Connolly of language use in the Nigerian mass media revealed that "the majority of the 178 Nigerian languages are un-represented in any media, with only 27 receiving any mention. He concluded that for people who do not understand English, Hausa, Igbo or Yoruba, Nigerian media consist of little more than music broadcasts."[333]

As already said in the earlier chapters, this tower of Babel in the country today is man made. The British colonialists kicked the ball rolling when they arrived in the country. They saw that the various people of their new territory, each inhabiting mainly a particular geographical area, did not have a common administration and spoke different languages. For administrative convenient and commercial purposes, they decided to merge all the people with divergent languages into one administration.

This problem of multi-lingualism in Africa and especially in Nigeria has given some experts concern and sleepless nights. The Intergovernmental Conference on Communication Policies in Africa (AFRICOM), which met from 22-31st July 1980, expressed also their concern about the problem of poly-lingualism and culture in reference to national integration. According to them: "The success of a national integrative broadcasting policy in Nigeria for example depends on the achievement of a harmonious balance between the particular needs of an ethnic or linguistic group and the "Nigeria national interest" and between the ethnic or lingua-cultural identity and the Nigerian 'collective' identity if any. The elements of such a policy must therefore be a communication process, which serves a national and regional integration on social, cultural and ethnic harmonic playgrounds".[334]

Efforts must be made by the Nigerian government and also other Non-Governmental Organisation to unite all these factions of ethnicities in the country.

---

[333] Connolly Patrick, Language Use in the Nigeria Mass Media, Unpublished Survey, Yaba, Lagos, 1975, p23
[334] UNESCO: Intergovernmental Conference on Communication Policies in Africa, Paris 1980, p.16.

7.3.1. Local Languages in the Nigerian Broadcasting Corporation.

The 1999 Constitution chapter V, Part 1, Section 55 gives approval to three major local languages. It states: "The business of the National Assembly shall be conducted in English and Hausa, Ibo and Yoruba when adequate arrangements have been made therefore." Due to the sensitive nature of the language issue, Nigerian government has retained the use of English as the official language for national administration while allowing the local languages as and when necessary. The three major languages of Nigeria are: *Hausa, Igbo* and *Yoruba*. They have been used as official media of communication right from colonial days. This implies a long-standing recognition by Government of the special status of these languages vis-à-vis other Nigerian languages. Public notices such as "Warning", "Notices" are written in English and where necessary in one or all these recognised languages.

The use of 'English as official language, should start from the highest levels (the executive and legislative arms of the government) down to the schools. Since the acquisition of proficiency in English is a good springboard for social and economic mobility, many parents want their children to learn English at the earliest stages of their education so as to facilitate their social advancement. English also has the advantage of providing a vehicle for international communication in a way that no local language has. Again, despite the fact that English is a foreign language, even the most ardent nationalists encourage its use and study because of its 'neutrality' and its ability to promote communication. Many have argued that too much emphasis on the various local languages will provoke divisiveness and parochialism and make the question of national integration more difficult.

Apart from the fact that English has been recognised as national official language, there is often the problem of choice of language to be used at broadcasting. This is because not all the languages could conveniently be accommodated. Perhaps some criteria can be adapted in choosing the languages to be used in broadcasting. For instance, the major criterion could be the number of people speaking a particular language as a first or second language. Added to this criterion, are also the availability of trained personnel and the adequacy of technical resources to be used in conveying the language in the locality. On the basis of these criteria, Radio Nigeria has tried to reach a compromise by selecting twelve out of 250 spoken Nigerian languages to be used in her broadcasting. Each of these three Zonal Divisions is assigned responsibility to broadcasts in a number of languages as follows:

IBADAN ZONE :	Yoruba, Edo, Urhobo
KADUNA ZONE :	Hausa, Fulfulde, Kanuri, Nupe
ENUGU ZONE :	Igbo, Izon, Efik, Tiv, Igala.

Based on this, the media in Nigeria in order to qualify as community media must be made to give priority to the local and not foreign languages. Neglecting the local languages, spoken by the majority of the people means a "cultural genocide". A serious problem envisaged by the use of these selected languages for broadcasting is the scheduling of programmes. There should not be too much airtime to one at the detriment of the other. In order not to appear to be devoting peak listening hours to a particular language, the schedule should be worked out in such a way that each language gets a fair distribution of programming in the early morning, noon, afternoon and evening transmissions.

In addition to the above-mentioned problem of time allocation to the local languages, there are several other inconveniences. For instance, when there is a national event being covered on radio, there cannot be a running commentary because of the need to switch over from one language to another to give all the various languages the benefit of the commentary. This can be very disconcerting and irritating in the case of soccer, for example, where the commentator will have to hand over the microphone to a colleague operating in a different language at a time when the game has become very exciting. This local program that is running at that time suffers, because its allocated airtime is used for national program.

7.3.2. Suggestions for Better Local Language Coverage.

It is obvious from what has been said so far, that the "Illiterate-Masses" or those who cannot understand English language well (most often the majority) are not adequately served by broadcasting in terms of time allocation. Many of the broadcasting houses allot more airtime to English programmes than to programmes in local languages.

Experts have suggested that the only way out of this problem is the establishment of other channels that should take care of other neglected local languages. However, this may entail expenditure, which the national economy may not be able to sustain.

Another possibility is the decentralisation of broadcasting on a geographical, linguistic or administrative basis or the establishment of community radios. The advantage of such arrangement is that it will bring broadcasting nearer to the people and enable it to be used more effectively as a tool for national development. It will also mean that since the various stations will cater for communities which are linguistically or culturally more homogeneous than the national community, they can devote more time to programmes in the local language or languages and address themselves to the local problems that more directly affect their audience. However, some experts argued that decentralisation if not properly supervised and regularly monitored, can engender parochialism and divisiveness, which can threaten national unity. However, some advise that if these regional stations or community radios should be made part of a national network so that they will carry local as well as national programmes on a daily basis, the danger that they may promote apartness rather than togetherness can be considerably reduced, if not eliminated altogether.

7.3.2. Enugu State: The Dilemma for Vernacular or Foreign Languages.

Enugu state is located in the South-Eastern Nigeria. "Igbo" is the spoken language in this state. According to the Federal Republic of Nigeria 1991 population census, *it has a population of 3,161,295 million people. Among this number, 1,482,245 are males and 1,679,050 are females.*[335]

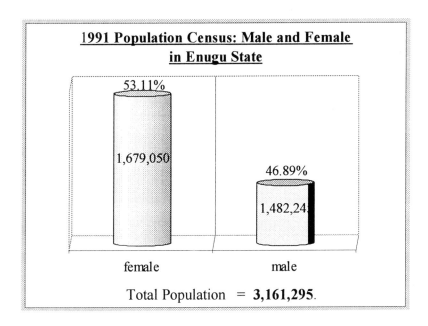

1991 Population Census: Male and Female in Enugu State

53.11%

1,679,050

46.89%

1,482,24

female   male

Total Population = **3,161,295**.

The state, Enugu, is not free from this syndrome of multilingualism. Before the creation of sister states namely Imo, Anambra, Abia and Ebonyi states, there was also the problem of which dialect to be used for broadcasting. The dialects of Anambra, Enugu and Ebonyi differ sharply from one another. It was very difficult to give special airtime to any of them. Yet after the creation of these sister states, the problem

---

[335] Census News: A house Magazine of the National Population Commission, Nigeria September 1992, vol. 3 No. 1. p.14

still persists but not in a large scale. For instance the Nsukka people have a different culture from those of Udi and Awgu.

The various communities will like the media house to use their own dialect for broadcasting. The existence of these different communities in Enugu state does not imply that the state consists of isolated communities among whom there is little or no interaction. There has been always a considerable amount of bilingualism or multi-lingualism that facilitates intra-community communication. The broadcasting houses however, have not helped solving this great difference by way of giving more airtime to these various dialects instead; they worsen the matter by allotting 70% of their airtime for English programs. English, they say is the language of the "educated" within the state and Nigeria as a whole. This breeds a social rift between the minority- English-speaking citizens- and the majority who speak only the Igbo indigenous language. It gives the minority which speaks English an edge over the others. During the writer's interview of people living in Enugu, as to which programme (local or foreign) they prefer listening to, the following results were obtained.

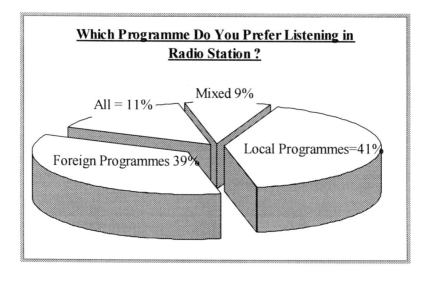

As the diagram indicates, it is unfortunate that the percentages of people who prefer local programmes and those who prefer foreign ones are almost on the same level. The reason for this is the negation of Igbo traditional socio-political, socio-cultural and socio-economic ontology by the youths in the name of modernity. On account of this, the Enugu state government should enforce it as law that all the media houses in the state should devote 75% of their airtime to Igbo programmes instead of English programs. This will go a long way in the preservation of the people's culture. It is unfortunate that things are moving the wrong direction. The people were further asked: *What radio station do you receive and listen often in your area?*

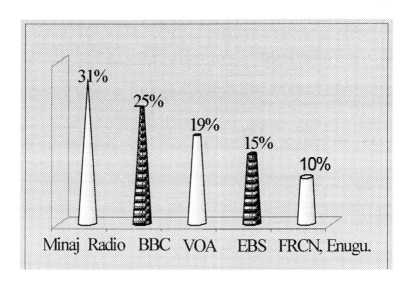

It is sad to note that for the three million living in Enugu state, only two radio stations are available, all belonging to the Federal and state governments respectively. It is not surprising that people tune in private stations like Minaj Radio located in Obosi, Anambra state, British Broadcasting Corporation, or Voice of America to get their daily news and information.

The people were further asked: *Which programme do you listen to most in the above stations?*

Name of the Station	News	Music	Good Wishes	Entertai-ment	Anounce-ment
Minaj	14%	74%	14%	12%	10%
British Broadcasting Corporation	35%	4%	--	--	--
Voice of America	33%	2%	--	--	--
Enugu Broadcasting Service	11%	13%	67%	77%	57%
Federal Radio Corp. of Nigeria	7%	7%	19%	11%	33%

It is necessary to mobilise the people of Enugu state to transform their lives and develop their state, they need more relevant information and programmes at the appropriate times presented to them in their own language. The broadcasting house should know when best to present the people with different programmes. When do they have time to listen to the above programmes? This answer was given when they were asked: When do you have time to listen to the above programmes? Some of this vital information will help the planners of radio programmes to know when to air some important programmes.

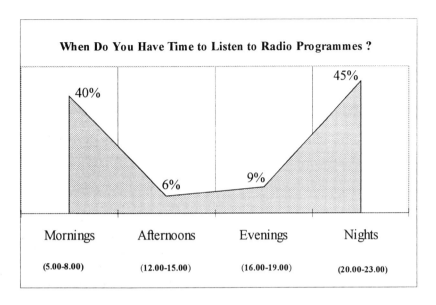

When Do You Have Time to Listen to Radio Programmes ?

45%

40%

6%   9%

Mornings   Afternoons   Evenings   Nights

(5.00-8.00)   (12.00-15.00)   (16.00-19.00)   (20.00-23.00)

In the above diagram, people listen to radios especially in the nights and early mornings. Apart from language, another barrier to broadcasting media in Nigeria is Ethnic conflict besieging not only Nigeria, but also the whole of Africa. How has radio broadcasting played vital roles in ethnic conflict in Nigeria?

7.4. Ethnic Conflict: The Role of Broadcasting Media in Nigeria.

As we noted earlier, radio broadcasting in the country was solely at the hands of federal government until the year 1959. Later, the regional governments set up their broadcasting media, which were independent of the federal government. Through such regional radios, each government of the day took steps to ensure that its activity was aired, as they wanted. The need, therefore, to present attractive, competitive and quality information became available. They were able to put their messages across to their various constituencies. What roles have these regional and private broadcasting played in the life of the Enugu state?

241

7.4.1. Broadcasting and Ethnic Conflict: The Case of Nigeria / Biafra War.

In an atmosphere of war, where the print media became more limited in circulation than they were at peace times, during the civil war in Nigeria, the Biafran authorities resorted to the use of their regional radio. This was in response to the campaigns initiated by the federally owned broadcasting outlets. Here Olorunnisola Anthony gave a vivid picture of the main weapons used by the warring sides during the Nigeria/Biafran civil war. The Eastern radio broadcast was very useful for the people of Eastern Nigeria throughout the duration of the Nigeria-Biafra war. It all started with atrocities and injustices committed against the Igbo people, among which are the premeditated murder of over 30,000 of their innocent men, women and children by Northern Nigerians and the calculated destruction of their properties. Based on this injustice, the Consultative Assembly and the Advisory Committee of Chiefs and Elders of South-East Nigeria, went into joint session on the evening of Saturday, May 27 1967 and came up with the following resolutions:

"We, the Chiefs, Elders and Representatives of all the Twenty Provinces of Eastern Nigeria, assembled in this Joint Meeting of the Advisory Committee of Chiefs and Elders and the Consultative Assembly, at Enugu this 27th day of May, 1967, hereby solemnly:

MANDATE HIS Excellency Lt. Col. Chukwuemeka Odumegwu Ojukwu, Military Governor of Eastern Nigeria, to declare at the earliest practicable date Eastern Nigeria a free, sovereign and independent state by the name and title of the REPUBLIC OF BIAFRA.

RESOLVE that the new REPUBLIC OF BIAFRA shall have the full and absolute powers of a sovereign state, and shall establish commerce, levy war, conclude peace, enter into diplomatic relations, and carry out, as of right, other sovereign responsibilities.

DIRECT that the REPUBLIC OF BIAFRA may enter into arrangement with any sovereign unit or units in what remains of Nigeria or in any part of Africa desirous of association with us for the purpose of running a common services organisation and for the establishment of economic ties.

RECOMMEND that the REPUBLIC OF BIAFRA should become a member of the Commonwealth of Nations, the Organisation of African Unity and the United Nations Organisation.

RECOMMEND the adoption of a Federal Constitution based on the new provincial units.

REAFFIRM His Excellence's assurance of protection for the persons, properties and businesses of foreign nationals in our territory.

DECLARE our unqualified confidence in the Military Governor of Eastern Nigeria, Lt.-Col. Chukwuemeka Odumegwu Ojukwu, and assure him of our unreserved support for the way and manner he has handled the crisis in the country."[336]

This declaration was made available to the people thanks to the *Eastern Regional Radio Station*. Thus at the dawn of that momentous Tuesday, May 30, 1967, the firm, slow and articulate voice of Lt.-Col. Chukwuemeka Odumegwu Ojukwu brought the good tidings to the 14 million anxious Eastern Nigerians. *In a radio broadcast*, he declared:

"Fellow countrymen and women, You, the people of Eastern Nigeria:

CONSCIOUS of the supreme authority of almighty God over all mankind, of your duty to yourselves and posterity;

AWARE that you can longer be protected in your lives and in your property by any Government based outside Eastern Nigeria;

BELIEVING that you are born free and have certain inalienable rights, which to be un-free partners in any association of a political or economic nature;

REJECTING the authority of any person or persons other than the Military Government of Eastern Nigeria to make any imposition of whatever kind or nature upon you;

DETERMINED to dissolve all political and other ties between you and the former Federal Republic of Nigeria;

PREPARED to enter into such association, treaty or alliance with any sovereign state within the former Federal Republic of Nigeria and elsewhere on such terms and conditions as best to sub-serve your common good;

AFFIRMING your trust and confidence in ME;

Having mandated ME to proclaim on your behalf, and in your name, that Eastern Nigeria be a sovereign independent Republic, Now, therefore, I, Lieutenant-Colonel Chukwuemeka Odumegwu Ojukwu, Military Governor of Eastern Nigeria, by virtue of the authority, and

---

[336] Nwankwo Arthur and Ifejika Samuel, The Making of a Nation: Biafra. London, 1969, p.348

pursuant to the principles, recited above, do hereby solemnly proclaim that the territory and region known as and called Eastern Nigeria, together with her continental shelf and territorial waters, shall henceforth be an independent sovereign state of the name and title of The Republic of Biafra. "³³⁷

Going further Lieutenant-Colonel Chukwuemeka odumegwu Ojukwu, Military Governor of Eastern Nigeria said: AND I DO DECLARE THAT:

"all political ties between us and the Federal Republic of Nigeria are hereby totally dissolved;

all subsisting contractual obligations entered into by the Government of the Federal Republic of Nigeria or by any person, authority, organisation or government acting on its behalf, with any person, authority or organisation operating, or relating to any matter or thing, within the Republic of Biafra, shall henceforth be deemed to be entered into with the Military Governor of the Republic of Biafra for and on behalf of the Government and people of the Republic of Biafra, and the covenants thereof shall, subject to their tenor; all subsisting international treaties and obligations made on behalf of Eastern Nigerian by the Government of the Federal Republic of Nigeria shall be honoured and respected;

Eastern Nigeria's due share of all subsisting international debts and obligations entered into by the Government of the Federal Republic of Nigeria on behalf of the Federation of Nigeria shall be honoured and respected;

steps will be taken to open discussions on the question of Eastern Nigeria's due share of the assets of the Federation of Nigeria and personal properties of the citizens of Biafra throughout the Federation of Nigeria;

the rights, privileges, pensions, etc., of all personnel of the Public Services, the Armed Forces and the Police now serving in any capacity within the Republic of Biafra are hereby guaranteed;

we shall keep the door open for association with, and would welcome, any sovereign unit or units in the former Federation of Nigeria or in any other parts of Africa desirous of association with us for the purposes of running a common services organisation and for the establishment of economic ties;

---

³³⁷ ibid. p.349

we shall protect the lives and properties of all foreigners residing in Biafra, we shall extend the hand of friendship to those nations who respect our sovereignty, and shall repel any interference in our internal affairs;

we shall faithfully adhere to the charter of the Organisation of African Unity and of the United Nations Organisation;

it is our intention to remain a member of the British Commonwealth of Nations in our right as a sovereign, independent nation.

LONG LIIVE THE REPUBLIC OF BIAFRA !

AND MAY GOD PROTECT ALL WHO LIVE IN HER!"[338]

Joyous crowds who thronged the streets shouting "Hail Biafra" greeted this broadcast and proclamation with wild and unrestrained jubilation all over Eastern Nigeria. Schools and shops were closed. Offices were deserted. Men, women and children, old and young – everybody joined in the jubilation. Both sides (the Nigerian and the Biafran governments) started preparing for the civil war through propaganda in their respective radio stations.

Eventually, the „Nigerian-Biafran War, otherwise known also as „the Civil War", began after Gowon (the former Military Supreme Commander of the Nigerian Armed Forces) declared a state of emergency on the 27th of May 1967. The Civil War officially began on the 6th of July between the Federal and Biafra forces. After the declaration of Biafra as a Republic, the *Eastern Nigerian Broadcasting Corporation* (ENBC) was automatically acquired by the Biafran side. It came to be their mouthpiece as "Radio Biafra" popularly known as *Broadcasting Corporation of Biafra* (BCB). The BCB was one of the strongest arms of the Biafrans. In addition to Biafran Broadcasting Corporation, the Biafran government carved out also the external service known as "Voice of Biafra" (VOB). The greatest impact of the BCB was on war propaganda. The BCB succeeded in influencing its audience both external and internal. Within Biafra the BCB boosted the morale, convincing the people of the "Republic" that their cause was worth dying for. The popular slogan was: "Morale is high". The VOB raised an air of wonderment in the world's war communication strategy.

---

[338] ibid. pp.349 – 350.

7.4.2. Radio Biafra and Propaganda War.

The function of Radio Biafra (VOB) from the inception of the war was clear and laud: to boost internal morale of the people. It also played a clever game of disseminating misinformation. Hale J. affirms this in his book, *Radio Power: Propaganda and International Broadcasting* when he asserts: "While morale-boosting at home and misinformation to the enemy remained the first preoccupations of the radio station ... there is no question that its PR (Public Relations) role added a powerful dimension. The main criticism of Radio Biafra was that it over did its propaganda ... whether it can be counted a success depends on one's viewpoints: as an example of effective use of radio it was frequently brilliant".[339]

In his own description of Broadcasting Corporation of Biafra John De St. Jorre put it this way: "In Biafra, the critical issue {of the BCB} was to boost morale and convince the masses that their terrible sacrifices were worthwhile because victory would ultimately be theirs."[340] The civil war continued to rage on without either side looking sideways or backwards. They continued their propaganda through their various media. Lt. Col. Odimegwu Ojukwu continue to broadcast through BCB trying to raise the morale of his people. In his broadcast on the 20th of July 1967 as the war raged on, he exhorted the people of Biafra as follows: *"Fellow countrymen, all of us know what Biafra means to us. It means the rejection of all that was bad, obnoxious and repugnant in the old Federation of Nigeria. Our young nation stands for the restoration and preservation of the dignity of the individual, for the protection of personal liberty, life and property, and for the guarantee of social equality and justice – particularly, equality of opportunity. Brave and valiant Biafrans, we are fighting for our survival as a nation, and for the preservation of these fundamental values ... I am obliged to warn that any Biafran who, by his misguided conduct or attitude, one toward the other, does anything likely to cause suspicion, disaffection and fear among any group, or behaves in any way to cause embarrassment and division among our people, will be regarded as much a saboteur and an enemy... Such people will be dealt*

---

[339] Hale J.: Radio Power: Propaganda and International Broadcasting, London 1975, p.118f.
[340] De St. Jorre J., The Nigerian Civil War, London 1972, p.346.

with in the severest possible way. In this regard, I must warn against over enthusiasm on the part of the civil defence organizations. They must bear in mind that theirs is to guard, not to molest the citizens. Brave and proud Biafrans, our commitment to this war is total and irrevocable. The general response has been most overwhelming and made a mockery of Gowon's boast to overrun Biafra in 48 hours. It must be clearer by now to him that the war has only just started and that he has taken up a little more than he can chew. Fellow citizens, I am proud of you and I have confidence in your ability to carry this war through to victory. Our cause is just and God is on our side. We shall vanquish".[341]

This propaganda helped greatly to boast the moral of the soldiers and the people. So many people worked day and night behind the curtains in order to see that this propaganda succeeded. They were specially drawn from the; "Universities, civil services and other professions. They were among the hardest workers, were very dedicated and derived much satisfaction from their work. They had about fifty specialist groups all concerned with different fields and aspects of propaganda. Even more effective than the literary output and programmes were the emotional songs composed by the many talented musicians discovered in the country since the war began. There were dramatists; artists, actors and actresses devoted to touring the fronts, towns and villages, nooks and corners, to inspire the people".[342]

The Broadcasting Corporation of Biafra was the greatest source of political education for the people during the time of war. It succeeded in its mission through massive use of slogans, fiery speeches, war chants, dramatic presentations and commentaries. This activity was championed by a popular genius of the then BCB, *Mr. Okonkon Ndem*. The Broadcasting Corporation of Biafra, especially through its propaganda became the most remarkable last resort and a resourceful armoury for the Biafran survival. John De St. Jorre describe it classically with these words: "It (BCB) was a key factor in preparing the general mood for secession and equally crucial in maintaining an appropriately bellicose fervour during the war, especially in the later

---

[341] Broadcasting Corporation of Biafra, 20th July 1967, cited by Kirk-Greene A.H. : Crisis and Conflict in Nigeria: A Documentary Source Book 1966-1970, vol. 11, July 1967- January 1970. London 1971, p.146f.
[342] Akpan, N.U., The Struggle for Secession, 1966-1970: A Personal Account of the Nigerian Civil War, London 1972, p.109

desperate stages. The beauty of the genocide consent for the propagandists was that it left no loophole. It ensured that the masses, which firmly believed it, would support the leadership's decision to fight on to very last – even beyond the point where all reasonable hope of victory had faded – because they were convinced that there was no alternative".[343]

The Radio Biafra and its sister station, "Voice of Biafra" were heard throughout the duration of the Civil war. The dynamism of the BCB surprised everybody including the officials of the Biafra Republic and operators of the stations. The only incident that brought down the "High Morale" of the people was the sudden exit of General Ojukwu to Ivory Coast in search of peace, which eventually led to his exile till 1983. This sad news of Ojukwu's departure to Ivory Coast came on air on 11th January 1970 at 6.00 a.m. Thanking his people for their bravery throughout the civil war and in seeking peace for his people, he said: "... once more, to show our honesty, and in accord with my own frequent affirmations that I would personally go anywhere to secure peace and security for my people, I am now travelling out of Biafra to explore with our friends all these proposals further and fully and to be at hand to settle these issues to the best of my ability, always serving the interests of my people. Our detractors may see this move as a sign of collapse of our struggle, or an escape from my responsibilities ... In my short absence, (this foreseen short absence was to last for an unforeseeable period of thirteen years) I have arranged for the chief of General Staff, Maj. Gen. Philip Effiong, to administer the Government with the rest of the Cabinet to run the affairs of this Republic while I go on this mission, accompanied by my political advisor and my chief Secretary. I once more pay my tribute to the Biafra Armed Forces, and urge all ranks to maintain their positions while I seek a early and honourable end to this struggle and all the suffering it has brought on our people. Proud and courageous Biafrans, Biafra shall live. God bless you all".[344]

On account of Ojukwu's exit, "the mantle of leadership fell on Lt. Col. Philip Effiong, who immediately gave a broadcast through Radio Biafra at 4.40p.m on Monday 12th January 1970 of the surrender of

---

[343] De St. Jorre J. op. cit. p.351.
[344] Kirk-Greene A.H., Crisis and Conflict in Nigeria: A Documentary Sourcebook 1966-1970, Vol. 11, July 1967-January 1970, London 1971, p.450.

Biafra. In his announcement he congratulated the officers and men of the Biafran Armed Forces for their gallantry and bravery, which have earned them the admiration of the whole world. In his radio broadcast, Lt. Col. Effiong disengaged the Biafran Army and dispatched emissaries to Nigerian government for peace talk."[345] It was indeed back to square one, the war was fought and lost. At the end both sides declared "NO VICTOR, NO VANQUISH". Indeed, without Broadcasting Corporation of Biafra, the war could have ended within the shortest time. So it was, the war that was started through radio propaganda ended through a radio broadcast calling for peace and reconciliation."[346]

In more recent history, the entire world was caught by surprise when two Rwandan tribes went after each other in an open armed conflict, which many have described as ethnic cleansing. The tribal war says Olorunnisola, was fought almost equally on land as well as through the airwaves with the active participation of extremely partisan radio network. The Hutu-operated Radio Mille Collines incited racial hatred, instigated half a million murders, and sang the death march of more than two million Tutsi on Rwandan airwaves. The routine became a ceaseless twenty-four hour a day assignment, on 94 and 106 MHz, of messages such as the following: "In truth, all Tutsis will perish. They will vanish from this country. They believe they will rise from the dead, but they are disappearing little by little thanks to the weapons hitting them, but also because they are being killed like rats... The graves are only half full, fill up the graves... The Tutsi children too must be killed... their home is in Ethiopia and we will send them back through the Nyaborongo River as a shortcut...."[347]

From the other side, Radio Muhubura, which served as the voice of the Tutsi-led Rwandan Patriotic Front (RPF), also carried similar war of propaganda President Habyrimana and the Hutu opposition.

It is now almost thirty years since the end of this civil war; it was speculated that the core North was planning to launch their own broadcasting station, "Jihad Radio". The pirate radio they claim was conceived to protect the interest of the core northern Nigeria which

---

[345] Okonkwo Jerome, op. cit. p.105.
[346] Uka, U.L., The Mass Media System in Nigeria: A Study in Structure, Management and Functional Roles in Crisis Situations. Ohio State University: 1977 (Diss.) p.448.
[347] BBC Transcript of Broadcasting, February 8, 1995. in Gazette vol.56 No.2, 1995, p.129.

was reportedly being marginalised by President Olusegung Obasanjo. However, many have seen the pirate station, like Sharia, as a smoke-screen under which some forces from the northern part of the country were working to destabilise the newly elected democratic government. Apart from the above-mentioned problems, another factor plaguing the broadcasting media in the country is the irregular supply of electricity.

7.5. National Electric Power Authority (NEPA).

In Nigeria, the organ solely responsible for supply of electricity to the citizens is called *National Electric Power Authority* (NEPA). One of the greatest radio broadcasting handicaps in all parts of Nigeria is the perpetual inefficiency of this organ. Due to its inefficiency many of her critics have nickname it:

Never Expect Power Always	NEPA
No Electric Power Available	NEPA
Never Except Power Anytime	NEPA

This organ, National Electric Power Authority" (NEPA), is one of the greatest internal problems of mass communication in Nigeria society. It has not dawned on this organ that one of the essentials of life is light and electricity. It is an obvious fact that, one of the essential parts of life if not the first is light. Many have argued that where there is no light, there is no life.

This is why God began his works of creation by first creating "LIGHT." According to the book of Genesis: he said: "Let there be light and there was light." (Gen.1.3) This was the first thing he created on the first day. This is because of its importance to man, who will be the beneficiary.

In developed and indeed most developing world, this same concept informed the decision of leaders to establish reliable and enduring power generation, transmission and distribution facilities to guarantee uninterrupted energy supply which they know will form the bedrock of their advancement technologically, economically, socially and even politically.

Having achieved that primary objective, it is believed that a firm foundation has been laid for other forms of developments. Almost all the activities of these nations, ranging from communications, construction, manufacturing, social and domestic works are anchored to constant power supply. It is not surprising then that the developed world has taken over the leadership of the world in various spheres of life due to the foresightedness and dynamic leadership. Today, the USA, most of European countries, Asia, South America and part of the Middle East no more thinking of how they will provide their populace with light. Provision of electricity no longer features in their electoral manifesto and campaign. In Nigeria, the reverse is the case. Here the politicians promise the masses uninterrupted power supply and to those villages which have no power supply, provision of electricity for all. This promise they have never kept.

The reverse is the case in developed countries. The populace does not have to go on its knees before electricity is provided for it by the government. It is given as of right, not as a favour granted in order to score a political point. A solid foundation had already been laid from the onset. What these countries are thinking of now, is how they can make the world a true global village and engage themselves in more challenging tasks like the exploration of outer space. A look at the wonders of invention in all fields of endeavours will amaze any sincere observer. All these could not have been achieved if there was epileptic power supply. Power failures threaten not only the radio broadcasting media but also business and the life of the people of Nigeria.

7.5.1. Promises Not Kept.

All the past Nigerian governments have at one time or the other, promised heaven and earth to redeem the situation but to no avail. Shortly before the second general election in the Second Republic, the then former Minister of Mines and Power, Alhaji Mohammed Ibrahim Hassan and many top NEPA officials promised the nation: "a constant supply of electricity. The whole nation witnessed a realisation of this promise for a short period. However, no sooner were the elections concluded than NEPA became the "sick baby" of the nation that it used to be, with its incessant power cuts. It was back to square one".[348]

Aware of all these problems therefore, chief BOLA IGE the then minister of Power and Steel on assumption of office during the third Republic which started in May 1999, raised the expectation of Nigerians on improved power generation and supplies in the country. Before now many Nigerians were frustrated with the services of the National Electric Power Authority. There were prolonged blackouts in all parts of the country. The Mine and Power minister, Chief Bola Ige, admitted receiving over 500 memoranda from Nigerians less than one month after assumption of office. This shows the pains Nigerians are going through over the epileptic power supply. On assumption of office, the President threw a challenge to him "If you can make it possible for us to have an uninterrupted power supply, you would have written your name in gold. The minister promised to do much more. His reply to the President was in the affirmative."[349] He assured Nigerians and said: "We are concerned that we should succeed." Just few days after this solemn promise by the Minister, power failures began to re-occur.

It was not surprising that during the "inauguration of the National Assembly by President Olusegun Obasanjo on June 4, 2000, there was a blackout. Again even the House of Representatives suffered in the hands of NEPA. They had to wait for two hours and 35 minutes on Tuesday, Dec.14, 2000 before beginning sitting as a result of a blackout. It was not the only time their crucial deliberations were disturbed

---

[348] National Concord, Lagos November 10, 1983, p.5.
[349] Ubanna, Stephen: *A Right Step Forward,* in Newswatch Magazine, Lagos March 27, 2000, vol. 31 n.12, p.25

by NEPA's epileptic supply."[350] Signs that NEPA's sickness has not been cured were shown even before some august visitors who came from all corners of the world to watch the *African Cup of Nations 2000* co-hosted by Nigeria and Ghana. In one of the matches, NEPA threw the National Stadium into darkness. NEPA blamed the incident on a fault at Akangba power transmission line, which is the source of supply to the injection substation that feeds the stadium.[351]

Internally, many companies have closed down because of incessant power disruption. Economic and social activities in the country virtually came to a standstill. Production lines in many industries were shut down for lack of power supply. In most homes, it was a tale of woes. Perishable foods cannot be preserved because fridges were out of use. Many could not listen to radio programmes again. Many radio sets depend totally on the supply of electric current; only few individuals can afford batteries. At times the electric supply is limited to urban cities. They cannot afford buying of batteries for their radio sets. They prefer forfeiting to listen to radio programmes to their two square meals.

Tijani Mohammed, a lawyer residing in Lagos summarised the situation of NEPA and that of Bola Ige after few months of the minister's promise thus: "Ige has only succeeded in restoring blackout in the country". Ige came with the zeal to revive power supply and in the first three months, he appeared to have found his focus. Unfortunately, the situation became worse."[352] In trying to reassure the citizens that they should not lose confidence in NEPA the president Olusegun Obasanjo sacked the management of the National Electric Power Authority. He accused them of non-performance. He apologised to Nigerians who had expected much from NEPA but were disappointed. He said the present power problem would be treated as "energy crisis". He assured the public that the epileptic power situation would be a thing of the past by the year 2000."[353] This never materialised.

After the cabinet reshufflement, came Chief Olusegun Agagu as the Power and Steel Minister. He gave also his own assurance of finding a lasting solution to NEPA's problem. On NEPA, he says: "The present

---

[350] ibid. p.26.
[351] ibid. 27.
[352] Ubanna Stephen, *Promise Not Kept,* in Newswatch Magazine, Lagos December 27, 1999 p.9.
[353] Ubanna Stephen, *A Right Step Forward,* in Newswatch Magazine, Lagos March 27, 2000 vol. 31 n.12, p.24

administration is committed to increase the amount of power generation from 1,600 megawatts when it took over in May 1999 to about 4,000 megawatts by the end of 2001 which will guarantee uninterrupted power supply."[354]

Acknowledging the problem of unsteady power supply, the governor of Oyo state says, the country can only move forward towards industrialisation through "improved roads and electricity supply. Industrialisation for the purpose of the future, he noted, cannot take place without putting NEPA into reckoning. More reliable sources of energy must be explored to meet the people's willingness to sustain the arduous job of diversification and increased entrepreneurship."[355] Also Chief Orji Kalu the governor of Abia State expressed his dissatisfaction with NEPA's performances. He gave NEPA eighteen months to improve power supply in the state. He threatened "If the federal government doesn't rectify the problems of NEPA in my state, we are going to import our own generating equipment and if that means breaking the law, Abia State will be the first to break the law. This is because epileptic electricity supply in the state had stagnated its industrial development."[356]

7.5.2. The Problems of National Electric Power Authority.

There is no gainsaying that NEPA has serious problems. The problems should be identified and then solutions to them should be found. What are these problems of NEPA?

i). Old generators/Lack of Maintenance.

When one looks at some of the facilities which NEPA uses in generating, transmitting and distributing power in most of Nigeria's urban centres including dead transformers which Lord Lugard left behind.

---

[354] Okoyi Lanre, *Ajaokuta Steel to Come on Stream,* in Guardian Newspaper, Lagos Monday, August 14, 2000. p.4
[355] Oseze-Langley, John, *Ekiti: Unlocking the Gordian Not,* in The Guardian Newspaper, Lagos Saturday August 12, 2000, p.19
[356] Adekeye Fola, *Shape Up, or ...* in Newswatch Magazine, Lagos May 8, 2000 vol. 31 n.18, p. 13

Each regime that comes into power promises to replace these old and dead transformers, but at the end nothing is done. The question is not now whether NEPA is dead or in coma such that it might be revived with cardio-pulmonary resuscitation. These problems should be solved immediately.

Records indicate that Nigeria has eight generating stations in various parts of the country. The three hydropower and five thermal or gas powered stations are located in various parts of the country. The hydro-stations are Kainji (760 megawatts), Jebba (540 megawatts) and Shiroro (600 megawatts). The thermal or fuel powered stations include Afam (969 megawatts), Ugheli (376 megawatts), Egbin (320 megawatts), Ijora (60 megawatts), and Sapele (720 megawatts). There are other facilities located in Jos (formerly associated with the tin mining operations) and the Oji River facility (similarly associated with the coal mining activities in the recent past around Trans-Ekulu, (Enugu). Putting all these together therefore, Nigeria could easily attain a power generating capacity of 7000 to 8000 megawatts and demand is hardly near 50 percent.[357]

When the general operational conditions and status of these stations are viewed, they are nothing to write home about. Virtually all these major stations have problems. They need major repairs. For instance "Afam thermal power station located in Rivers State was built in 1963. It has a capacity to generate 699 megawatts of electricity. The station was gutted by fire in 1997. The engineering design of the plant according to a top officials of NEPA must have been built in the 1940s. Its spare parts are rarely available in the market. Experts estimate that the station would take over N200 million to repair, which the federal government is not in a hurry to invest."[358]

The "Kainji", Nigeria's first hydropower station commissioned in 1968 is also in a dilapidated condition. It has an installed generating capacity of 760 MW. Most piece of its equipment has broken down because they had not undergone any major overhaul since they were commissioned. The situation is the same in other stations like Shiroro, Jebba, Kainij, DeltaIV, Sapele, and Utorogu.[359]

---

[357] Ubanna Stephen, *In the Heat of Cold War* in Newswatch Magazine, Lagos April 3, 2000, p.39
[358] ibid. p. 39
[359] ibid. 39

ii). Vandalisation of Equipment.

It is always reported that about hundreds of electricity meters are stolen all over Nigeria daily – from private premises, business houses and
public utilities. Based on this, the Assistant General Manager (Transmission) AGM(T) Benin, Mr. Emeka Okeke disclosed that "the NEPA
authority is willing to compensate any person who helps for the arrest
of vandals who are causing havoc to NEPA installation. NEPA is prepared to give communities cash reward if they could report any person
found to be vandalising NEPA installations in their district."[360] Due to
this constant vandalizing, the National Electric Power Authority
(NEPA), in Shomolu District, Oyo state, took another measure by deciding to hire the services of local hunters in to curb the disturbing ne-
farious activities of vandals in the area. According to the District
Mangaer of NEPA, Abiodun Ajifowolbaje, "the incessant vandalising
of NEPA line in the town was becoming most unbearable because of
the huge costs of replacing vandalised materials and the millions of
naira being lost in form of revenue from the affected industrial companies and other customers." Going further he said, "the hunters have
been given specific instructions to be very vigilant and not to handle
the assignment with kid gloves because the vandals see the theft of
NEPA lines as a purely business venture, and as such would not hesitate to crush anyone they see as a threat to their illegal activities."[361]
   The problems of NEPA are not only these difficulties arising from
the lack of maintenance of the already existing equipment, but there
are also man-made elements, which account for its woes and problems. Akinola Taiwo, an engineer and former staff of NEPA says that
the problem of NEPA lies in the activities of saboteurs. There are
saboteurs in generation, saboteurs in transmission and saboteurs in
distribution. He classified the saboteurs into groups:
   The first group, are those who are supplying and importing genera-
tors into the country. They do everything possible to see that NEPA
does not succeed.

---

[360] Onoiribholo Francis, *Fire Destroys Two NEPA High Tension Towers* in Post Express Newspapers, Abuja 16, June 2000, p.6.
[361] The Guardian Newspaper, Lagos Wednesday August 30, 2000, p.3

The second group, are those who have been used to loot NEPA's treasury and who are no longer able to be there.

The third are the disgruntled engineers who by whatever reasons are no longer in the service. These groups do everything possible to frustrate the system from forging ahead.[362]

7.5.3. The Alternative to National Electric Power Authority.

People have started looking for solutions to this epileptic supply of light by the National Electric Power Authority. The Lagos State government has started making plan for alternative power supply or what it calls "The Independent Power Provider" (IPP). Many other states have indicated their interest in toeing the same line. Light should be provided to Nigerians as a right and not as a privilege, so that life can become meaningful to all. At least, the rural areas will open up. They could then listen to their radio sets without the headache of how to buy new batteries or replace their old ones. Poverty alleviation programmes on radio without the means, would not provide enduring "millions" change in any nation. Light for all, is what the people want. Whatever may be the case, effort should be geared towards finding solutions to these problems.

---

[362] Ubanna Stephen, *In the Heat of Cold War* in Newswatch Magazine, Lagos April 3, 2000, p.40.

EVALUATION AND CONCLUSION.

8. The Necessity of Integrating Traditional and Modern Communication Systems.

We should also bear in mind that in Nigeria, just like in most African countries, communication takes place on two levels. The flow of information in urban areas is based on modern techniques while in rural areas, it is based on traditional forms of communication. Pye, in his book, "Communication Patterns and the Problems of Representative Government in Non-Western Societies", rightly observes: "Communication in non-western societies is at two levels: that of the urban elite on one hand and that of the rural masses on the other hand. He observes that in big cities, we can find the means of information based on western models and techniques to respond to the elite in the cities and to political personages. In the interior of the countries, the process of communication still rests on the traditional forms of communication and techniques to respond to the needs of those who are less western".[363]

There is then need to identify systematically the relationship and similarities in function between the traditional media channels and the western media channels of communication. They are challenges, which need commitment and foresight in those who are genuinely convinced of the potentials and relevance of traditional media in the process of development. There is always a basic link between modern and traditional media, from the viewpoint of their mutual influence or reciprocal and complementary support.

The harmonisation of the two systems of communication will then remove the sceptical attitude of old people against the modern means of communication. Till today old men in the rural areas are lamenting bitterly on the overshadowing of the modern means of communication against the traditional one. They assert that, today radio sets are like the fireplace of olden days. People sit around the radio listening to the

---

[363] Pye Lucian, *Communication Patterns and the Problems of Representative Government in Non- Western Societies* in Public Opinion Quarterly, Chicago 1956, p.250.

programme beamed onto them by an unknown, mysterious voice from nowhere in particular. Charles Mungoshi writes also that it is the same situation that an old man was lamenting when he: "Intensively quizzes a young man who has introduced a radio in a village. He wants to know whose voices are coming from that machine, and he wonders if the machine will not damage the heads of the people of the village since the voice comes from someone who does not know the village or care for it. The old man is suspicious right from the start. He fears that a mere machine has usurped his traditional, indigenous communication space".[364]

Here the old man is worried about the birth of a new type of communication in which the children were reduced to mere recipients of messages or information without being participants. There is no doubt that such fear is not unfounded. Old men in the rural areas have always claimed that since the introduction of radio sets, children no longer sit around the fire to listen to folk tales, riddles and the oral histories of their origins. Children sit around the radio set to hear stories from people whom they do not know, and who may not necessarily wield the same respect as the traditional communicators living in the community.

Efforts should be doubled to find a formula that forges a relationship between traditional and modern forms of communication without damaging the traditional ways and obstructing the necessary march towards modernity. When this is achieved, the people will participate actively in the communication process, which is an essential ingredient for a successful communication. A new approach or model is obviously necessary in the communication system of the Igbo people.

We are aware that the whole world is today viewed as a global village. People are now interested not only in the politics of their clan or tribe but also in the politics of their country and other nations. In other words, as a village/nation grows, it needs more and more information. Now, the functions of the *watchman* or town-crier increases. He will need to tell not only of things happening in his vicinity, but also things happening a few kilometres away, then villagers become aware that happenings on the other side of the world could mean danger or opportunity for them and their village. This type of change should lead to an overhauling of the means of communication. The communica-

---

[364] Chenjerai Hove, op. cit., p.13.

tion media in the time of our forefathers, cannot march with what we have today. Man started searching for other means of communication. Today we are witnessing other means of communication: satellite telecommunication has greatly extended the range and availability of communications services, bringing global telephone, radio and television broadcasting to many countries. Through computer networks, there has been the remote linkage of users to computers, and of computers to one another. The basic challenges facing the policy makers and communication practitioners today is to find means of preserving the relationship between traditional and modern forms of communication without damaging the traditional ways or obstructing the necessary march towards modernity. Improved communications have brought about new ideas and changes in every aspect of life. For instance, when there are disasters {plane crash, flood, and civil unrest} or wars in any part of the world, there would be instant pictures around the world showing what is happening. For instance, it took only thirty-five minutes after the assassination of President John F. Kennedy in 1993 for the whole world to know about it. All the radio and television stations carried the news in contrary to what happened in 1865, when President Abraham Lincoln was assassinated. It took over eight months for the same proportion of American public to learn of it.

Again, the "Internet" is another widespread network worthy of mention. It has pages containing text, pictures, sounds and even video. One can view pages of the Internet all over the world. It does not matter where the pages are physically placed; which means that an Internet user in Nigeria can view a site in Frankfurt (Germany) or in London and vice versa. There are many areas in which Internet is proving useful, especially with regard to communication: E-mail, for sending and receiving messages; this is the most popular form of traffic on the Internet. With the Internet, electronic publishing takes on a new meaning. Ideas and opinions roam freely on the Internet. The aim is to inform, analyse, influence, entertain and educate. A significant proportion of information on the Internet is useful for teaching and learning. The Internet allows you to look for information such as: products, persons, services, previous records, current information, etc. The Internet communicates by promoting the sharing of knowledge and information. It reduces the cost of interaction and collaboration. All these point to the fact that the Internet provides a unique opportunity to bridge the gap between the developed and undeveloped nations.

Should we embrace all these Information technologies whole and entire? Should we take advantage of them before they start taking advantage of us? Should we discard our old means of communication to embrace these new technologies? Today, this Information Technology is very useful and powerful. However, power in the wrong hand is dangerous. As the process of structural and ideological incorporation deepens and as modern means of communication virtually sweeps the world, we need to sit back and reflect on the interplay between the traditional and modern means of communication. This is because of the major impact these media have had and are still having in our society. For any of them to qualify as useful, it must be socially relevant.

It is necessary, therefore, in the concluding part of this work to integrate the indigenous traditional and modern means of communication. The call for an integration of the two systems is predicated on a vision of a society that does not have to remain in perpetual conflict with those things, which it can accommodate and also on the need to streamline our communication policy and system for a greater effectiveness. Macbride in his own observation says: "In their early stages of development, different communication media operated more or less in isolation from each other. Each had its own objectives to satisfy the needs, real or assumed, of its particular audience for information, entertainment and culture. Gradually however, we are witnessing the blurring of frontiers between different forms of communication. Numerous connections and relationships have been established between them, while at the same time they are aiming at more diversified audiences".[365]

For instance in Nigeria, many forms of print and electronic media have been introduced. Fifty years since broadcasting services reached Nigeria through the British Empire service, a lot has been achieved in terms of the increase in the number of acquired radio receivers and in the number of persons who are exposed to radio messages. However, the present structure and function of both systems in Nigerian society can be effectively improved upon. The systems can be better organised and restructured to achieve the wishes of the greater society. The need to combine both traditional and modern communication technol-

---

[365] Macbride Sean, op. cit. p.81

ogy for a better and more effective reach has been highlighted by the UNESCO Intergovernmental Conference on Communication Policies for Africa, where it stated: "Member states should include in their national communication policies, measures designed to ensure that greater use of traditional forms of communication for various social, educational and cultural purposes, and their integration with modern communication media, in their national development projects".[366]

This recommendation has been further supported by the African Council on Communication and Education (A.C.C.E) at its 4th Biennial Conference in Lome, Togo in 1984 where it also recommends "a multi-media approach to the communication problems in Africa and the exploration into the possibility of mixing traditional and modern media with a view to determining the situations which are supportive of specific types of media combinations."[367] The Council made it clear that before choosing the media of communication for any society, the primary considerations should be its appropriateness to the geographical and social environment of the society in which it will be used. There are certain areas in which the traditional and the modern media should go into dialogue in order to work together. These areas include: Freedom of speech and respect for the elders, Orators as minister/ commissioner for information, use of drums in broadcasting houses.

8.1. Freedom of Speech and Respect for the Elders.

In the African traditional society, everyone has the freedom to voice out his opinion in village meetings or when there is such occasion. In such gatherings, each person says his mind. The true stands of things are then known. Every person believes in saying the truth and nothing but the truth. Truth in the traditional African society is very sacred. This is the reason why the Africans are at times very sceptical and are often suspicious of advanced communication technologies. In some areas in Nigeria, radio is seen as an object of suspicion. On many occasions, *News Bulletin* broadcast either from radio or television houses

---

[366] UNESCO: Intergovernmental Conference on Communication Policies in Africa, Yaounde, Cameroon 22-23 July 1980. Final Report, Paris: Unesco, January 1980.
[367] African Council on Communication and Education (A.C.C.E), Paris 1982, p33.

are not verified and at last some turn out to be false. The public are at times misinformed on the happenings in the society. For instance the CNN TV station, broadcasting to the billions of viewers all over the world in the evening of the "America Presidential Election 2000" said that everything was now over. It went further to declare the Republican candidate, B.W. Bush as the winner of the election, whereas the electoral officer had not made any official declaration. The winner of the election was to be declared weeks after the court and counter court cases. So for any broadcasting station to succeed among the African people, it must borrow a leaf from the traditional media by way of verifying its information before dishing it out to the public. There are also some who refer to the radio as "the machine that speaks but accepts no reply". In his book Kongi Harvest, Wole Soyinka writes:

"Who but a lunatic
Will bandy words with boxes
With government redifussion sets
Which talk and talk and never
Take a lone reply."[368]

The western media must imbibe the element of objectivity and feedback seen in the African traditional communication system, if it is to strive in the African society.

8.2. Orators as Minister for Information.

In African society, majority of the traditional broadcasters or town criers are known to be orators in their respective villages. Orators are chosen to address the village gathering whenever there are important events in the village. They are always called upon by the traditional chief or king of their villages to convince the people of the necessity or importance of something. For instance, they are used to convince the people on importance of paying their taxes or going to war with the neighbouring village. This means they know the temperament of their people, how and when to talk to them. The Nigerian government

---

[368] Soyinka Wole, Kogi's Harvest. London 1979, p.12,

in their appointments should emulate these qualities. They should try to appoint an orator for the post of minister or commissioner for information, {even in local council appointments}, such an orator will get the public well informed of governments activities. This he can execute through traditional means (ekwe, drum, ogene) or radio. This position has been held over the years by eloquent orators and broadcasters in Nigeria (Okoko Ndem, Chukwuma Ogbonna, Paddy Eke, Uchechukwu Chukwumerije, Jerry Gana etc). This demonstrates the recognition by the modern nation state of the supremacy of the spoken word and the traditional communication arts in pre-colonial Africa.

8.3. Talking Drums/Drummer.

The talking drums indeed constitute the nexus or nucleus of medium of communication to the people. People have come to compare it with other broadcasting media like radio, which also communicate messages over long distances. The drum has served as strategic modes of mass communication in traditional African setting. The drummer himself occupies also a very important position within the communication hierarchy in traditional society. It is the drummer that informs and educates the public. He was virtually in charge of the communication portfolio. He is thus a communicator or media functionary. The idea of informing and educating was considered a divine responsibility, meant to eschew ignorance, and to be freely discharged without human encumbrance. The drummer, like the information officer, is the society's alert signal, the early warning signal of impending crises: war, fire. He informs and at the same time mobilises the people into action. Any external act of interference in such crucial duties is clearly not in the interest of society. That is why it is a prohibition to provoke the drummer while he performs his communication duties.

Some of the experts in drumming should be then employed in the broadcasting houses to beat the drum before any major events that are coming up like news bulletin or important announcements to the public. It is partly due to its linguistic and communicative relevance, as well as its resonance within the modern mass media that the beat of the talking drummer is heard in the drum prelude to news broadcast in some radio stations. This is because when people hear the talking drum they seem to pay special attention to it. The drumbeat alerts all the listeners to listen to the news or announcements coming up. Again, significantly, the names "Drum" and "Talking Drums" have been adopted as names of magazines, journals, and communication companies in contemporary Africa. The importance of drum and drummer should not be neglected in modern means of communication.

A combination of traditional and modern communication systems is required to achieve a greater communication system in the society. When these are achieved, it is hoped that Nigeria in general and Enugu State in particular will get into a new era of communication explosion.

SOURCES AND SELECTED BIBLIOGRAPHY:

CHURCH'S DOCUMENTS:

Vatican Council II, Decree on the Media of Social Communication, Inter Mirifica, 12th April 1963.

Vatican Council II, Pastoral Constitution on the Church in the Modern World, Gaudium Et Spes, 7th December 1965.

Pastoral Instruction on Social Communication, Communio Et Progressio, 23rd May 1971

Leo XIII, Encyclical, Libertas Praestantissimum, 20th June 1888.
----- Encyclical, Rerum Novarum, 15th May, 1891.

Pius XIII, Radio Message, 1 June 1941, (AAS 33 1941).

John XXIII, Encyclical, Mater Et Magistra, 15th may 1961.
-----, Encyclical, Pacem In Terris, 11th April 1963.

Paul VI, Encyclical, Evangelii Nuntiandi, 8 December 1975.
Evangelization in the Modern World, Evangelii Nuntiandi, 8th December 1975.

John Paul II, Message for the 33rd World Communications Day, n.4, January 24, 1999.
-----, Address to the Jubilee of Journalists, n.2, June 4, 2000.
-----, Message for the 35th World Communications Day, May 27, 2001.
-----, Church in Africa, Ecclesia in Africa, 14th September 1995
-----, Church in America, Ecclesia in America, 22nd January 1999

Die Kirche Lateinamerikas: (Dokumente der II. und III. Generalversammlung des Lateinameikanischen Episkopates in Medellin und Puebla, 6. September 1968 / 13. Februar 1979.

SELECTED BOOKS:

Achebe, Chinua: Things Fall Apart, London 1958.

Adigwe, H.: The Beginnings of the Catholic Church among the Igbos of South Eastern Nigeria, 1885-1930, Vienna 1966.

Affenyi, Dadzé Gifty: State Radio / Public Radio Stations? Or Public Service in Panos, Paris 1970

Afigbo, A.E.: Ropes of Sand, Ibadan 1981.

-----, The Warrant Chiefs, London 1970.

-----, *Towards A History of the Igbo Speaking People* in Igbo Language and Culture, Ibadan 1982.

Aggarwala N.: *Press Freedom: A Third World View* in Development Communication Report, July 1977.

Ainslie, Rosalyn: The Press in Africa: Communications and Past and Present, Walker, New York 1966.

Akpan, N.U.: The Struggle for Secession, 1966-1970: A Personal Account of the Nigerian Civil War. London 1972.

Anene, J. C.: Southern Nigeria in Transition 1885-1906, Cambridge 1966.

Ansah P.V.: *Privatisation of Radio – Implications and Challenges* in Kwame (ed). Independent Broadcasting in Ghana, Ghana 1994.

Ansah Paul: *Broadcasting and Multilingualism* in George Wendell ed. Making Broadcasting Useful: The African Experience, Manchester 1986.

Arinze, Francis: Sacrifice in Ibo Religion, Ibadan 1940.

Asuzu, Boniface: Communication Media in Nigeria Today, Paris 1987.

Bako, George: "Re-organisation and Future Development of Radio Broadcasting in Nigeria, Ibadan 1982.

Basden, G.T.: Among the Ibos of Nigeria, London 1966.

-----, Niger Ibos, London 1966.

Bates, Anthony: Broadcasting in Education: An Evaluation, London 1989.

Bloom and Ottong: Changing African: An Introduction to Sociology, London 1992.

Bobbet, David:(ed.) World Radio and TV Handbook, The Directory of International Broadcasting vol. 53, United Kingdom 1999.

Bowren, Andrew: The Cultural Dimension of Communication for Development, Hague 1974.

Brann C.M.B: Language in Education and Society in Nigeria: A Comparative Bibliography and Research Guide, Quebec 1975.

Cantril H., and Allport G.W.: The Pyschology of Radio, London 1935.

Chenjerai, Hove: *"Oral Traditions Claim a Place in Modern Mass Media"* in Media Development, Journal of the World Association for Christian Communication vol. XLIV, London 1997.

Christensen Philip: African Conference on Radio Education Harare, Ministry of Education and Culture, London 1990.

Collins, Nicholas: *Stealing Stories* in Media Development, Journal of the Association for Christian Communication vol. XLIV, London 1997.

Connolly, Patrick: Language Use in the Nigeria Mass Media. Unpublished Survey, Lagos 1975.

Crowder, Michael: West Africa under Colonial Rule London 1970.

Crowe, S.E.: The Berlin West African Conference *1884–1885,* Westport 1984.

Daniela, Frank: Dimensionen der Programmkonzeption entwicklungsorientierter Hörfunkarbeit, Konstanz 1994.

De St. Jorre J.: The Nigerian Civil War, London 1972.

Dilim, Okafor-Omali: A Nigerian Villager in two Worlds, London 1965.

Dunn, T.A: Notes on Things Fall Apart (Chinua Achebe.) Essex 1981.

Duylie, Dayo: Media and Mass Communication in Nigeria, Ibadan 1979.

Edeani, David Omazo: Press Ownership and Control in Nigeria, in Ugboajah Frank, ed., Mass Communication, Culture and Society in West Africa, München 1985.

Edeani, David: *"West African Mass Communication Research at Major Turning",* in Gazette vol. 41, London 1998.

Eiler, Franz-Josef: Communicating in Community: An Introduction to Social Communication, Manila 1994.

Ejiofor, Lambert: lgbo Kingdoms Power and Control, Nigeria 1982.

Emerson, R: From Empire to Nation, Cambridge 1982.

Fearing B.F.: *Towards a Psychological Theory of Human Communication* in Journal of Personality vol.22, Chicago 1953.

Freire Paulo: Education: The Practice of Freedom, London 1967.

Gans, Herbert, J.: People and Plans, Essays on Urban Problems and Solution, USA 1968.

Gatter, Frank Thomas: Protokolle und Generakte der Berliner Afrika – Konferenz *1884 – 1885*, Bremen 1984.

Gerard Wanjobi: *Orality and Reading Tradition in African in the Context of the Emerging World of Social Communications* in Raymond B and Marcazzan T. (ed) *Publishing at the Services of Evangelisation*. Nairobi 1996.

Girard, Bruce:(ed.). A Passion For Radio: Radio Waves and Community, Montréal/New York 1992.

Gould and Kolb William: (e.d). A Dictionary of the Social Sciences, New York 1964.

Gould J. and Kolb, W.L. (e.ds.): A Dictionary of the Social Sciences, London 1964.

Green, M.M.: lgbo Village Affairs, London 1964.

Groth, A.J: Comparative Politics, A Distributive Approach, London 1971.

Hale J.: Radio Power: Propaganda and International Broadcasting. London 1975.

Head, Sydney: World-Broadcasting Systems–A Comparative Analysis, Wadsworth 1985.

Heads, S.W.: *Trends in Tropical African Societies,* in Gerbner. G. (ed.) Mass Media Policies and Changing Cultures, London 1977.

-----, Arm in einer reichen Stadt: IKO – Verlag für Interkulturelle Kommunikation, Frankfurt am Main. 1992.

-----, Begründung von Menschenrechten aus der Sicht unterschiedlicher Kulturen, IKO – Verlag für Interkulturelle Kommunikation Frankfurt am Main 1991,

-----, Der Mensch zwischen gesellschaftlichen Plausibilitäten und Glaubensgewissheit, Darmstadt, Verlag. Steinkopf, 1986.

-----, Die Vernunft in den Kulturen, IKO – Verlag für Interkulturelle Kommunikation, Frankfurt am Main, 1995.
-----, Ethische Implikationen veränderter Rahmenbedingungen in der sozialen Arbeit, IKO – Verlag für Interkulturelle Kommunikation, Frankfurt am Main, 2000.

-----, Ethische Kriterien für die Bewertung von Unternehmen, IKO – Verlag für Interkulturelle Kommunikation, Frankfurt am Main, 1997.

-----, Ethische Vernunft und technische Rationalität: IKO – Verlag für Interkulturelle Kommunikation, Frankfurt am Main, 1992.

-----, Irrationale Technikadaptation als Herausforderung an Ethik, Recht und Kultur. IKO – Verlag für Interkulturelle Kommunikation, Frankfurt am Main, 1997.

-----, Universale Menschenrechte im Widerspruch der Kulturen, IKO – Verlag für Interkulturelle Kommunikation, Frankfurt am Main, 1994.

Humphreys, Peter: Media and Media Policy in Germany, Oxford/Providence 1994.

Ike Obiora & Ndidi Nnoli Edozien: Understanding African: Traditional Legal Reasoning Jurisprudence &Justice in Igobland, Enugu 2001.
Ike, Obiora: *The Social, Political and Economic Situation of Nigeria: A Critical Survey*, in Wer Befreit ist, kann befreien, Hoffmann Johannes (ed.) Band 5 Frankfurt am Main 1997.

International Broadcasting Vol. 53 United Kingdom 1999.

International Centre for Research on Bilingualism Bibliography and Research Guide, Quebec 1975.

Isichei, Elizabeth: The History of Igbo People, London 1976.

-----, The Ibo People and the Europeans, London 1970.

Jones G.I.: Report of the Position, Status and influence of Chief and Traditional Rulers in the Easter Region of Nigeria, Enugu 1957.

Karikari (ed.) Independent Broadcasting in Ghana, Ghana 1994,

Kirk-Greene, A.H.M.: Crisis and Conflict in Nigeria: A Documentary Sourcebook 1966-1970, vol. 11, July 1967 – January 1970, London 1971.

Koch, Jörg: Die Vermarktung privater und lokaler Hörfunk – und TV Sender in Deutschland und den USA, München / Nürnberg, 1996.

Kromah, G.V.: *The Utilisation of Broadcasting for National Development in Liberia* in George Wendell ed. Making Broadcasting Useful: The African Experience, Manchester 1986.

Kwame Karikari (ed.): Independent Broadcasting in Ghana: Implications and Challenges, Legon-Ghana 1994.

Lloyd, Libby: Towards a Democratic Radio Broadcast Media in South Africa, Montréal, AMARC 1991.

Lo-Bamijoko, Joy Nwosu: Preliminary Study of the Classification and Tuning, London 1982.

Lugard, F.D.: Report on the Amalgamation of Northern and Southern Nigeria and Administration *1912-1919,* London 1920.

Mackay, Ian.K.: Broadcasting in Nigeria, Ibadan 1964.

Maletzke, G.: Psychologie der Massenkommunikation, Uelzen 1978.

Mata, Marita: Pillar Radio, Women in Grassroots Communication. London 1994.

Maureen Chigbo: *Justice at Last* in Newswatch Magazine vol. 31, no.3 Lagos February 2000.

Mbiti, J.S.: African Religions and Philosophy, London 1977.

McNellyn John: *Perspectives on the Role of Mass Communication in The Development Process,* in Berlo D. (ed). Mass Communication and the Development of Nations, Michingan State 1968.

McQuail, D.: Towards Sociology of Mass Communication, London 1983.

Meek C.K.: Law and Authority in Nigeria Tribe. London 1950.

Mensah, Aida Opoku: *Deregulation of Radio in Africa-Political Expediency or Development Strategy?* in Inter Media, 1982.

Mill, J.S.: The Liberal Arts Press, New York 1956.

Milton Ralph: Radio Programming: A basic Training Manual, London 1968.

Milton, E.C.: A Survey of the Technical Development of the Nigerian Broadcasting Corporation, Lagos 1955.

Moemeka A: *Socio-Cultural Environment of Communication in Traditional Nigeria An Ethnographic Exploration* in: Communication Socialis, 16(1983), Grünewald.
Moemeka, Andrew: Local Radio: Community Education for Development, Zaria 1981.

Naigow, Peter: *The Role of Radio in National Development:* in Joseph Wollie, A Case study of Liberia, Ghana 1983.

Naran, Kala K.: African Conference on Radio Education, Ministry of Education and Culture, Harare -Zimbabwe 1990.

Ndiokwere, Nathaniel: The African Church, Today and Tomorrow, Enugu 1994.

Ndolo Ikechukwu: Radio Broadcasting and the Language Problems of Socio-Political Integration in Nigeria, Washington 1987.

Nwabara, S.N: Iboland: A Century of Contact with Britain 1860-1960, London 1977.

Nwakwo, Robert: *Educational Uses of Broadcasting*, in Sydney Head (ed.), Broadcasting in Africa: A Continental Survey of Radio and Television, Philadelphia 1974.

Nwala, Uzodinma: Igbo Philosophy, Lagos 1985.

Nwankwo Arthur and Ifejika Samuel: The Making of a Nation: Biafra. London, 1969.

Nwbara S: Iboland: A Century of Contact with Britain 1860 – 1960, London 1977.

Nyamnjoh, Francis: Media Ownership and Control in Cameroon, in Media Development: Journal of the World Association for Christian Communication, London, 4/1998, 31

Obazele Patrick: *Challenges of Radio Journalism and Management of Broadcasting in Nigeria* in Olatunji Dare (ed.) Journalism in Nigeria (Issues and Perspectives), Lagos 1996.
Obiechina, N.E.: *Amos Tutuola and Oral Tradition* in Presence Africaine No.65, New Bilingual Edition, Paris 1956.

Ogbondah, Chris W.: *Colonial laws: Model for contemporary African press laws?* in International Third World Studies Journal and Review, vol. 1, no.1. London 1989.

Ogbondah, Chris W.: Military Regimes and the Press in Nigeria. (1966-1993), America 1994.

Ogochukwu, Basil: On Legal and Ethical Framework for the Pluralist Operation of Radio in PANOS, Paris 1980.

Ogundimu, Folu Folarin: *Private Enterprise Broadcasting: Nigeria and Uganda*, in Gazette vol. 58 no. 1996.

Okigbo Charles: *Nigerian Radio News and the New Information Order*, in Gazette vol.41: 141-150 (1988).

Okonkwo Jermoe Ikechukwu: Folks-media and the new era of evangeliszation: The Igbo perspective, in Communicatio Socialis Heft 3, 31.Jg, Grünewald 1998.

Okonkwo, Jerome: The History and Some Problems of Television Service in Anambra State in Nigeria, Frankfurt /Main 1986.

Okwu, Frank: *Developing Indigenous Communication in Nigeria*, in Journal of Communication, 29(4) Chicago 1979.

Okwu, Frank: Mass Communication, Culture and Society in West Africa, Paris 1985.

Olorunnisola, Anthony: *When tribal wars are mass mediated: Re-evaluating the policy of non-interference*, in Gazette vol. 56, No.2, London 1995, p.127.

Olu, Ladele: History of the Nigerian Broadcasting Corporation, Ibandan 1964.
Olu, Ladele: Nigerian Broadcasting Corporation Committee Report, Nigeria 1974.

Omu Fred: Press and Politics in Nigeria 1880 – 1937, London 1978.

275

Omu, Fred: *The dilemma of press freedom in colonial Africa: The West African example, in* Journal of African History, vol. 9, London 1968.

Onwubiko, K.B.C.: *"The Catholic Church and The Development of Education in Eastern Nigeria (1885-1984)"* in Obi. C.A., (ed.) A Hundred Years of the Catholic Church in Eastern Nigeria 1885-1985, Onitsha 1985.

Onwubiko, K.B.C.: A History of West Africa 1800- Present Day, Book 2, Nigeria 1984.

Oreh,. O: *Modes of Communication,* in Reading in African Humanities, Enugu 1980.

Ottenberg, S.: *Ibo Receptivity to Change* in Herskovits, M.J. (ed.) Continuity and Change in African Cultures, Chicago 1959.

Perham, Margery: Native Administration in Nigeria, London 1962.

Philippart Michael: *The Church and the New Broadcasting Pluralism in Africa,,* in Information Bulletin CAMECO, Aachen 1/1995.

Pungente, John: Getting Started on the Media Education, London 1985.

Pye, Lucian: Communication Patterns and the Problems of Representative Government in Non- Western Societies in Public Opinion Quartely, Chicago 1956

Radhika, E. Parameswaran: *Colonial Interventions and the Postcolonial Situation in India,* in Gazette *vol.59 (1)* London 1997.
Ranney, Austin: The Governing of Men, Illinois 1958.
Richard Lander: Records of Clapperton's Last Expedition to Africa, London 1830.

Robert .A. White: *Community Radio as An Alternative to Traditional Broadcasting,* in Media Development, 30(3) London 1983.

Rocher G.: Changing Africa: An Introduction to Sociology, London 1992.

Sean, Macbride: Many Voices One World, Paris 1980.

Shorter, Aylward: Songs and Symbols of Initiation, Nairobi 1987.

Shorter, Aylward: The African Synod, A Personal Response to the Outline Document, Nairobi 1991.

Simon Ottenberg: *Ibo Oracles and Intergroup Relations* in South - Western Journal of Anthropology vol XIV, 3, London 1958.

Sofola, J.A.: African Culture and African Personality–What Makes an African, African? Nigeria 1973.

Soyinka, Wole: Kogi's Harvest. London 1979.

Srinivas, Melkote: Communication for Development in the Third World. Theory and Practice from 1950's to 1990's, London 1991.

Starling Anyanwu: The Igbo Family Life and Cultural Change, Marburg 1976.

Turner, L.W: and Byron, F.A.W.: *Broadcasting Survey of the British West African Colonies* in Mackay Ian, K. Broadcasting in Nigeria, Ibadan 1964.

Uchendu, C.V: The Igbo of South-Eastern Nigeria, New York 1965.

-----, Law of Southern Nigerian New York 1900.

-----, The Igbos of Southern Nigeria, New York 1965.

Ugboajah, (ed.) Mass Communication, Culture and Society in West Africa, Paris 1985.

Ugboajah, Frank: Communication Policies in Nigeria, Paris 1980.

Uka, U.L.: The Mass Media System in Nigeria: A Study in Structure, Management and Functional Roles in Crisis Situations. Ohio State University, 1977.

Uzodinma Nwala: Igbo Philosophy, Lagos 1985.

White, Robert A.: Radio to Support Rural Organisation: Conditions for Success. Unpublished Lecture, Gregorian University Rome 1995.

Wilcox, Dennis: Mass Media in Black Africa: Philosophy and Control, Cape Town 1977.

OTHER DOCUMENTS:

Anambra Broadcasting Corporation Handbook, Enugu 1980.

Annual Report: A Civil Liberty Organisation (CLO) Report on the State of Human Rights in Nigeria, 1995.

British Broadcasting Empire, London 1936.

Federal Ministry of Information: Reports of the Constitution Drafting Committee Vol.11, Lagos 1976.

Federal Republic of Nigeria: Supplement to Official Gazette Extraordinary, 4 Sept. 1992: A316.

Federal Republic of Nigeria: The 1998 Federal Constitution.

Federal Republic of Nigeria: The 1999 Federal Constitution.

Gazette vol.56 No.2, 1995, The British Broadcasting Corporation's Transcript, February 8, 1995.

General Instruction from Foreign Office (British): CSO 1/14 Despatch No. 2 of 18.04.1891.
History of the Nigerian Broadcasting Corporation, Lagos 1977.

House of Representative Debates, Lagos August 1-5, 1954.

House of Representative Debates, The Third Session March 6-25, Lagos 1954.

Intergovernmental Conference on Communication Policies in Africa „AFRICOM", Working Paper, Paris 1980, p.22.

Journal of Anthropology vol xiv n.3, London 1958.

Journal of Personality vol.22, Chicago 1953.

Journal of the World Association for Christian Communication, 4/1998, 31.

Native Courts Proclamation No.9 of 1900, London.

Policy Paper on "Community Radio in Africa" issued by Stem van Afrika, Hilversum (The Nitherlands) – October 1994.

Supplement to Official Gazette extraordinary, Federal Republic of Nigeria, Feb. 13, 1984.

Supplement to Official Gazette Extraordinary, Federal Republic of Nigeria, April 4, 1984.

UNESCO: Intergovernmenatl Conference on Communication policies in Africa, Paris 1980. (AFRICOM Working Paper).
UNESCO: Intergovernmental Conference on Communication Policies in Africa,

Yaounde, Cameroon 22-23 July 1980. Final Report, Paris: Unesco, January 1980.

Webster's Third New International Dictionary of the English Language, (1768), vol.1A-G, Encyclopaedia Britannica, Inc., Chicago 1981.

MAGAZINE /NEWSPAPERS:

Census News: A house Magazine of the National Population Commission, vol. 3 no. 1, Lagos September 1992.

Daily Express Newspaper, Lagos August 31 1961.

Daily Times Newspaper, Lagos October 24 1984.

Daily Times Newspaper, Lagos February 9, 1995.

National Concord Newspaper, Lagos February 16 1984.

National Concord Newspaper, Lagos July 3, 1984.

National Concord Newspaper, Lagos November 10, 1983.

Newswatch Magazine, Lagos August 14, 1995.

Newswatch Magazine, Lagos August 29, 1994.

Newswatch Magazine, Lagos August 29.

Newswatch Magazine, Lagos December 27, 1999.

Newswatch Magazine, Lagos November 1986.

Newswatch Magazine, Lagos April 3, 2000.

Newswatch Magazine, Lagos March 27, vol. 31 n.12, 2000.

Newswatch Magazine, Lagos May 8, vol. 31 n.18, 2000.

Newswatch Magazine, Lagos Nov. 24 1997.

Newswatch Magazine, Lagos Nov. 24 1997.

Newswatch Magazine, Lagos March 13, vol. 21, no. 11 1995.

Post Express Newspapers, Abuja 16 June 2000.

Sunday Concord Newspaper, Lagos June 27, 1993.

The Guardian Newspaper, Lagos Monday, August 14, 2000.

The Guardian Newspaper, Lagos Saturday, August 12, 2000.

The Guardian Newspaper, Lagos Wednesday August 30, 2000.

The Punch Newspaper, Lagos July 4, 1984.

The Punch Newspaper, Lagos July 8, 1984.

The Vanguard Newspaper, Lagos December 31 1997.

The Vanguard Newspaper, Lagos November 4   1998.

West Africa Magazine, Lagos April 20, 1987.

West Africa Magazine, Lagos September 23, 1985.

ABBREVIATIONS:

ABS   Anambra Broadcasting Service.

ACCE   African Council on Communication and Education.

AFRICOM   African Inter Governmental Conference and Communication.

AIT   African International Television.

BBC   British Broadcasting Corporation.

BCB   Broadcasting corporation of Biafra

CDS   Committee for Protection of Journalists.

EBS   Enugu Broadcasting Service.

ECBS   East Central Broadcasting Service.

ENBC   Eastern Nigerian Broadcasting Corporation

FRCN   Federal Radio Corporation of Nigeria.

IPP   Independent Power Provider.

MIT   Minaji Television International.

NBC   Nigerian Broadcasting Commission.

NEPA   National Electric Power Authority

NGE   Nigerian Guild of Editors.

NPO   Nigerian Press Organisation.

NTA   Nigerian Television Authority.

NUJ   Nigerian Union of Journalists.

RDS   Radio Distribution Service.

VOA   Voice of America.

VOB   Voice of Biafra

VON   Voice of Nigeria.

WNTV-BS   Western Nigerian Television - Broadcasting Service.

282

APPENDIX I: Questionnaire

1. **Family Status**
   a. Married
   b. Single
   c. Divorced

2. **How old are you?**
   a. 18-30
   b. 31-50
   c. 50--

3. **Have you Children?**
   a. Yes.
   b. No.

4. **Where are you living?**
   a. City
   b. Town
   c. Village

5. **Whom are you living with?**
   a. Parents
   a. Parents
   c. Friend
   d. In School
   e. Alone.

6. **How many languages do you know or speak?**
   a. Igbo
   b. Hausa
   c. Yoruba
   d. Efik

e. English

f. German

g. French

7. What is your qualification?

....

8. What is your profession?

a. Civil Servant

b. Clergy / Religious

c. Businness / Professional

d. Teacher / Student

e. Farmer / Other

9. To what extent are you informed about the happenings in the society?

a. Very well informed

b. Well informed

c. Adequately informed

d. This can be improved upon

e. Misinformed

f. Very badly misinformed.

10. In what area of life are you not getting enough information?

a. In economical affairs

b. In political affairs

c. In social affairs

d. In religious affairs

e. In cultural affairs.

11. For now, what is/are your main source of information?

11.1. In economical matters?

a. Radio

b. Television

c. Newspaper.

d. Others.

11.2. In religious matters?

a. Sermons in the church.

b. Religious seminar/symposium.

c. Ecclesiastical newspapers.

d. Pastoral letters.

e. Encyclical letters from the Pope.

f. Diocesan/parish bulletins.

11.3. In political matters?

a. Newspapers.

b. Radio.

c. Television.

d. From the people.

12. On what field/area would you like to hear/learn more about?

a. Political matters.

b. Economical matters.

c. Religious matters.

d. Cultural matters.

e. All the above.

13. Why would you like to know more in these matters?

....

14. Have you discussed this areas of your interest/choice with any of your family members or with your friends?

....

15. Have they different opinion from yours?

....

16. Are other people in your area better informed about happenings in the society than yours?
    a. Yes.
    b. No.
    c. I do not know.

17. If yes, do you think that they have other source of information than yourself?

    ....

18. Have you relations or friends wha are living abroad?
    a. Yes.
    b. No.

19. If yes, what do they tell you about Nigerian image abroad?

    ....

20. From what point of view were they talking about Nigeria abroad?

    ....

21. What is the quickest and widest means of communication especially in our society where roads, telephones and telecommunications system are unreliable?
    a. Newspaper.
    b. Radio.
    c. Television.
    d. Cartoon/Thearte.

22. Do you have time to listen to radio station and for how long?
    a. Yes.
    b. No.
    c. Not sure.
    d. Other opinion.

23. **Should broadcasting be left alone to governments?**
    a. Yes.
    b. No.
    c. Not sure.
    d. Other opinion.

24. **Have governmental electronic media lived up to peoples satisfaction?**
    a. Yes.
    b. No.
    c. Not sure.
    d. Other opinion.

25. **Have the above electronic media lived up to peoples' expectations?**
    a. Yes.
    b. No.
    c. Not sure.
    d. Other opinion.

26. **Do you think that community radio can provide alternative voice in the society?**
    a. Yes.
    b. No.
    c. Not sure.
    d. Other opinion.

27. **Is it possible that a community radio can ensure greater accessibility to the common people without being compelled by purely profit considerations?**
    a. Yes.
    b. No.
    c. Not sure.
    d. Other opinion.

28. What do you understand by a "community radio"?, one owned by:
a. The government.
b. The church.
c. Non-governmental organisation.
d. Groups of individuals.
e. a+b+c+d.
f. b+c+d.
g. c+d.

29. What areas of life would you like community radio to emphasis and why?
a. Cultural awareness.
b. Political awareness.
c. Social welfare.
d. Religious awareness.
f. Economic welfare.
g. All the above.
h. None of the above.

30. Which radio station do you receive in your area?
....

31. Which is/are your favourable programmes?
....

32. When do you have time to listen to radio programmes?
a. Early mornings.
b. Afternoons.
c. Evenings.
d. Nights.
e. No time.

33. Which programmes do you listen to most?
a. News.

b. Music.

c. Annoucements.

d. Good wishes.

e. Entertainment.

f. Any other.

34. At what time of the day is the reception clearer?

a. Mornings.

b. Afternoons.

c. Nights.

35. In what languages do you prefer to listen to radio?

a. Igbo.

b. English.

c. Both.

d. Other local languages.

36. Do you prefer :

a. Local programmes.

b. Foreign programmes.

c. All the above.

d. Mixed.

e. None of the above.

37. Do you support church presence in the mass media?

a. Yes.

b. No.

c. Not sure.

d. Other opinion.

38. How can the church be present in modern mass media pluralism?

a. Printing media.

b. Electronic media.

c. All the above.

39. **Which organ do you think the church can use to effect this purpose?**
   a. Radio station.
   b. Television.
   c. Newspaper.
   d. All the above.
   c. None of the above.

40. **Should the church establish it's own radio station or collaborate with other groups and if with other groups, which of the following?**
   a. Other religious denominations.
   b. Non-governmental organisations.
   c. Government.
   d. All the above.
   e. None of the above.

41. **Do you think that a community radio station will contribute postively to the development of the society?**
   a. Yes.
   b. No.
   c. Not sure.

42. **Seeing the nature of our society today, do you think that community radio will actively be the voice of the voiceless?**
   a. Yes.
   b. No.
   c. Not sure.

43. **Which area do you think that a community radio will emphasis more?**
   a. News and information sharing.
   b. Political reporting on governmet activities.
   c. Environment and social situation.
   d. Information on health situation.
   e. Human right of the people.
   f. Developmental education.

PONTIFICAL COUNCIL FOR SOCIAL COMMUNICATIONS: ETHICS IN COMMUNICATIONS.

(Vatican City, June 4, 2000, World Communications Day, Jubilee of Journalists.)

INTRODUCTION

1. Great good and great evil come from the use people make of the media of social communication. Although it typically said—and we often shall say here—that "media" do this or that, these are not blind forces of nature beyond human control. For even though acts of communicating often do have unintended consequences, nevertheless people choose whether to use the media for good or evil ends, in a good or evil way.

These choices, central to the ethical question, are made not only by those who receive communication—viewers, listeners, readers—but especially by those who control the instruments of social communication and determine their structures, policies, and content. They include public officials and corporate executives, members of governing boards, owners, publishers and station managers, editors, news directors, producers, writers, correspondents, and others. For them, the ethical question is particularly acute: Are the media being used for good or evil?

2. The impact of social communication can hardly be exaggerated. Here people come into contact with other people and with events, form their opinions and values. Not only do they transmit and receive information and ideas through these instruments but often they experience living itself as an experience of media (cf. Pontifical Council for Social Communications, *Aetatis Novae*, 2).

Technological change rapidly is making the media of communication even more pervasive and powerful. "The advent of the information society is a real cultural revolution" (Pontifical Council for Culture, *Toward a Pastoral Approach To Culture*, 9); and the twentieth century's dazzling innovations may have been only a prologue to what this new century will bring.

The range and diversity of media accessible to people in well-to-do countries already are astonishing: books and periodicals, television and radio, films and videos, audio recordings, electronic communication transmitted over the airwaves, over cable and satellite, via the Internet. The contents of this vast outpouring range from hard news to pure entertainment, prayer to pornography, contemplation to violence. Depending on how they use media, people can grow in sympathy and compassion or become isolated in a narcissistic, self-referential world of stimuli with near-narcotic effects. Not even those who shun the media can avoid contact with others who are deeply influenced by them.

3. Along with these reasons, the Church has reasons of her own for being interested in the means of social communication. Viewed in the light of faith, the history of human communication can be seen as a long journey from Babel, site and symbol of communication's collapse (cf. *Gn* 11:4-8), to Pentecost and the gift of tongues (cf. *Acts* 2:5-11)

Indeed, all human communication is grounded in the communication among Father, Son, and Spirit. But more than that, Trinitarian communion reaches out to humankind: The Son is the Word, eternally "spoken" by the Father; and in and through Jesus Christ, Son and Word made flesh, God communicates himself and his salvation to women and men. "In many and various ways God spoke of old to our fathers by the prophets; but in these last days he has spoken to us by a Son" (*Heb* 1:1-2). Communication in and by the Church finds its starting point in the communion of love among the divine Persons and their communication with us.

4. The Church's approach to the means of social communication is fundamentally positive, encouraging. She does not simply stand in judgment and condemn; rather, she considers these instruments to be not only products of human genius but also great gifts of God and true signs of the times (cf. *Inter Mirifica*, 1; *Evangelii Nuntiandi*, 45; *Redemptoris Missio*, 37). She desires to support those who are professionally involved in communication by setting out positive principles to assist them in their work, while fostering a dialogue in which all interested parties—today, that means nearly everyone—can participate. These purposes underlie the present document.

We say again: The media do nothing by themselves; they are instruments, tools, used as people choose to use them. In reflecting upon the means of social communication, we must face honestly the "most essential" question raised by technological progress: whether, as a result of it, the human person "is becoming truly better, that is to say more mature spiritually, more aware of the dignity of his humanity, more responsible, more open to others, especially the neediest and the weakest, and readier to give and to aid all" (Pope John Paul II, *Redemptor Hominis*, 15).

We take it for granted that the vast majority of people involved in social communication in any capacity are conscientious individuals who want to do the right thing. Public officials, policy-makers, and corporate executives desire to respect and promote the public interest as they understand it. Readers and listeners and viewers want to use their time well for personal growth and development so that they can lead happier, more productive lives. Parents are anxious that what enters their homes through media be in their children's interests. Most professional communicators desire to use their talents to serve the human family, and are troubled by the growing economic and ideological pressures to lower ethical standards present in many sectors of the media. The contents of the countless choices made by all these people concerning the media are different from group to group and individual to individual, but the choices all have ethical weight and are subject to ethical evaluation. To choose rightly, those choosing need to "know the principles of the moral order and apply them faithfully" (*Inter Mirifica*, 4).

5. The Church brings several things to this conversation. She brings a long tradition of moral wisdom, rooted in divine revelation and human reflection (cf. Pope John Paul II, *Fides et Ratio*, 36-48). Part of this is a substantial and growing body of social teaching, whose theological orientation is an important corrective to "the 'atheistic' solution, which deprives man of one of his basic dimensions, namely the spiritual one, and to permissive and consumerist solutions, which under various pretexts seek to convince man that he is free from every law and from God himself" (Pope John Paul II, *Centesimus Annus*, 55). More than simply passing judgment, this tradition offers itself in service to the media. For example, "the Church's culture of wisdom can save the media culture of information from becoming a meaningless accumulation of facts" (Pope John Paul II, Message for the 33rd World Communications Day, 1999).

The Church also brings something else to the conversation. Her special contribution to human affairs, including the world of social communication, is "precisely her vision of the dignity of the person revealed in all its fullness in the mystery of the Incarnate Word" (*Centesimus Annus*, 47) In the words of the Second Vatican Council, "Christ the Lord, Christ the new Adam, in the very revelation of the mystery of the Father and of his love, fully reveals man to himself and brings to light his most high calling" (*Gaudium et Spes*, 22).

II: SOCIAL COMMUNICATION THAT SERVES THE HUMAN PERSON

6. Following the Council's Pastoral Constitution on the Church in the Modern World, *Gaudium et Spes* (cf. nos. 30-31), the Pastoral Instruction on Social Communications *Communio et Progressio* makes it clear that the media are called to serve human dignity by helping people live well and function as persons in community. Media do this by encouraging men and women to be conscious of their dignity, enter into the thoughts and feelings of others, cultivate a sense of mutual responsibility, and grow in personal freedom, in respect for others' freedom, and in the capacity for dialogue.

Social communication has immense power to promote human happiness and fulfilment. Without pretending to do more than give an overview, we note here, as we have done elsewhere (cf. Pontifical Council for Social Communications, *Ethics in Advertising*, 4-8), some economic, political, cultural, educational, and religious benefits.

7. *Economic.* The market is not a norm of morality or a source of moral value, and market economics can be abused; but the market can serve the person (cf. *Centesimus Annus*, 34), and media play an indispensable role in a market economy. Social communication supports business and commerce, helps spur economic growth, employment, and prosperity, encourages improvements in the quality of existing goods and services and the development of new ones, fosters responsible competition that serves the public interest, and enables people to make informed choices by telling them about the availability and features of products.

In short, today's complex national and international economic systems could not function without the media. Remove them, and crucial economic structures would collapse, with great harm to countless people and to society.

8. *Political.* Social communication benefits society by facilitating informed citizen participation in the political process. The media draw people together for the pursuit of shared purposes and goals, thus helping to form and sustain authentic political communities. Media are indispensable in today's democratic societies. They supply information about issues and events, office holders and candidates for office. They enable leaders to communicate quickly and directly with the public about urgent matters. They are important instruments of accountability, turning the spotlight on incompetence, corruption, and abuses of trust, while also calling attention to instances of competence, public-spiritedness, and devotion to duty.

9. *Cultural.* The means of social communication offer people access to literature, drama, music, and art otherwise unavailable to them, and so promote human development in respect to knowledge and wisdom and beauty. We speak not only of presentations of classic works and the fruits of scholarship, but also of wholesome popular entertainment and useful information that draw families together, help people solve everyday problems, raise the spirits of the sick, shut-ins, and the elderly, and relieve the tedium of life.

Media also make it possible for ethnic groups to cherish and celebrate their cultural traditions, share them with others, and transmit them to new generations. In particular, they introduce children and young people to their cultural heritage. Communicators, like artists, serve the common good by preserving and enriching the cultural heritage of nations and peoples (cf. Pope John Paul II, *Letter to Artists*, 4).

10. *Educational.* The media are important tools of education in many contexts, from school to workplace, and at many stages in life. Preschoolers being introduced to the rudiments of reading and mathematics, young people seeking vocational training or degrees, elderly persons pursuing new learning in their latter years—these and many others have access via these means to a rich and growing panoply of educational resources.

Media are standard instructional tools in many classrooms. And beyond the classroom walls, the instruments of communication, including the Internet, conquer barriers of distance and isolation, bringing learning opportunities to villagers in remote areas, cloistered religious, the home-bound, prisoners, and many others.

11. *Religious.* Many people's religious lives are greatly enriched through the media. They carry news and information about religious events, ideas, and personalities; they serve as vehicles for evangelization and catechesis. Day in and day out, they provide inspiration, encouragement, and opportunities for worship to persons confined to their homes or to institutions.

Sometimes, too, media contribute to people's spiritual enrichment in extraordinary ways. For example, huge audiences around the world view and, in a sense, participate in important events in the life of the Church regularly telecast via satellite from Rome. And, over the years, media have brought the words and images of the Holy Father's pastoral visits to countless millions.

12. In all these settings—economic, political, cultural, educational, religious—as well as others, the media can be used to build and sustain human community. And indeed all communication ought to be open to community among persons.

Communication seeks the well being and fulfilment of community members in respect to the common good of all. But consultation and dialogue are needed to discern this common good. Therefore it is imperative for the parties to social communication to engage in such dialogue and submit themselves to the truth about what is good. This is how the media can meet their obligation to "witness to the truth about life, about human dignity, about the true meaning of our freedom and mutual interdependence" (Pope John Paul II, Message for the 33rd World Communications Day, 1999).

III: SOCIAL COMMUNICATION THAT VIOLATES THE GOOD OF THE PERSON

13. The media also can be used to block community and injure the integral good of persons: by alienating people or marginalizing and isolating them; drawing them into perverse communities organized around false, destructive values; fostering hostility and conflict, demonizing others and creating a mentality of "us" against "them"; pre-

senting what is base and degrading in a glamorous light, while ignoring or belittling what uplifts and ennobles; spreading misinformation and disinformation, fostering trivialization and banality. Stereotyping—based on race and ethnicity, sex and age and other factors, including religion—is distressingly common in media. Often, too, social communication overlooks what is genuinely new and important, including the good news of the Gospel, and concentrates on the fashionable or faddish. Abuses exist in each of the areas just mentioned.

14. *Economic.* The media sometimes are used to build and sustain economic systems that serve acquisitiveness and greed. Neoliberalism is a case in point: "Based on a purely economic conception of man", it "considers profit and the law of the market as its only parameters, to the detriment of the dignity of and the respect due to individuals and peoples" (Pope John Paul II, *Ecclesia in America*, 156). In such circumstances, means of communication that ought to benefit all are exploited for the advantage of the few.

The process of globalization "can create unusual opportunities for greater prosperity" (*Centesimus Annus*, 58); but side by side with it, and even as part of it, some nations and peoples suffer exploitation and marginalization, falling further and further behind in the struggle for development. These expanding pockets of privation in the midst of plenty are seedbeds of envy, resentment, tension, and conflict. This underlines the need for "effective international agencies which will oversee and direct the economy to the common good" (*Centesimus Annus*, 58).

Faced with grave injustices, it is not enough for communicators simply to say that their job is to report things as they are. That undoubtedly is their job. But some instances of human suffering are largely ignored by media even as others are reported; and insofar as this reflects a decision by communicators, it reflects indefensible selectivity. Even more fundamentally, communication structures and policies and the allocation of technology are factors helping to make some people "information rich" and others "information poor" at a time when prosperity, and even survival, depend on information.

In such ways, then, media often contribute to the injustices and imbalances that give rise to suffering they report. "It is necessary to break down the barriers and monopolies which leave so many countries on the margins of development, and to provide all individuals and nations with the basic conditions which will enable them to share in development" (*Centesimus Annus*, 35). Communications and information technology, along with training in its use, is one such basic condition.

15. *Political.* Unscrupulous politicians use media for demagoguery and deception in support of unjust policies and oppressive regimes. They misrepresent opponents and systematically distort and suppress the truth by propaganda and "spin". Rather than drawing people together, media then serve to drive them apart, creating tensions and suspicions that set the stage for conflict.

Even in countries with democratic systems, it is all too common for political leaders to manipulate public opinion through the media instead of fostering informed participation in the political process. The conventions of democracy are observed, but techniques borrowed from advertising and public relations are deployed on behalf of policies that exploit particular groups and violate fundamental rights, including the right to life (cf. Pope John Paul II, *Evangelium Vitae*, 70).

Often, too, the media popularize the ethical relativism and utilitarianism that underlie today's culture of death. They participate in the contemporary "conspiracy against life" by "lending credit to that culture which presents recourse to contraception, sterilization, abortion and even euthanasia as a mark of progress and a victory of freedom, while depicting as enemies of freedom and progress those positions which are unreservedly pro-life" (*Evangelium Vitae*, 17).

16. *Cultural.* Critics frequently decry the superficiality and bad taste of media, and although they are not obliged to be sombre and dull, they should not be tawdry and demeaning either. It is no excuse to say the media reflect popular standards; for they also powerfully influence popular standards and so have a serious duty to uplift, not degrade, them.

The problem takes various forms. Instead of explaining complex matters carefully and truthfully, news media avoid or oversimplify them. Entertainment media feature presentations of a corrupting, dehumanizing kind, including exploitative treatments of sexuality and violence. It is grossly irresponsible to ignore or dismiss the fact that "pornography and sadistic violence debase sexuality, corrode human relationships, exploit individuals—especially women and young people, undermine marriage and family life, foster anti-social behaviour and weaken the moral fibre of society itself" (Pontifical Council for Social

Communications, *Pornography and Violence in the Communications Media: A Pastoral Response*, 10).

On the international level, cultural domination imposed through the means of social communication also is a serious, growing problem. Traditional cultural expressions are virtually excluded from access to popular media in some places and face extinction; meanwhile the values of affluent, secularized societies increasingly supplant the traditional values of societies less wealthy and powerful. In considering these matters, particular attention should go to providing children and young people with media presentations that put them in living contact with their cultural heritage.

Communication across cultural lines is desirable. Societies can and should learn from one another. But transcultural communication should not be at the expense of the less powerful. Today "even the least-widespread cultures are no longer isolated. They benefit from an increase in contacts, but they also suffer from the pressures of a powerful trend toward uniformity" (*Toward a Pastoral Approach To Culture*, 33). That so much communication now flows in one direction only—from developed nations to the developing and the poor—raises serious ethical questions. Have the rich nothing to learn from the poor? Are the powerful deaf to the voices of the weak?

17. **Educational.** Instead of promoting learning, media can distract people and cause them to waste time. Children and young people are especially harmed in this way, but adults also suffer from exposure to banal, trashy presentations. Among the causes of this abuse of trust by communicators is greed that puts profits before persons.

Sometimes, too, media are used as tools of indoctrination, with the aim of controlling what people know and denying them access to information the authorities do not want them to have. This is a perversion of genuine education, which seeks to expand people's knowledge and skills and help them pursue worthy purposes, not narrow their horizons and harness their energies in the service of ideology.

18. *Religious.* In the relationship between the means of social communication and religion there are temptations on both sides. On the side of the media, these include ignoring or marginalizing religious ideas and experience; treating religion with incomprehension, perhaps even contempt, as an object of curiosity that does not merit serious attention; promoting religious fads at the expense of traditional faith;

treating legitimate religious groups with hostility; weighing religion and religious experience by secular standards of what is appropriate, and favoring religious views that conform to secular tastes over those that do not; trying to imprison transcendence within the confines of rationalism and scepticism. Today's media often mirror the post-modern state of a human spirit "locked within the confines of its own immanence without reference of any kind to the transcendent" (*Fides et Ratio*, 81).

The temptations on the side of religion include taking an exclusively judgmental and negative view of media; failing to understand that reasonable standards of good media practice like objectivity and even-handedness may preclude special treatment for religion's institutional interests; presenting religious messages in an emotional, manipulative style, as if they were products competing in a glutted marketplace; using media as instruments for control and domination; practicing unnecessary secrecy and otherwise offending against truth; downplaying the Gospel's demand for conversion, repentance, and amendment of life, while substituting a bland religiosity that asks little of people; encouraging fundamentalism, fanaticism, and religious exclusivism that foment disdain and hostility toward others.

19. In short, the media can be used for good or for evil—it is a matter of choice. "It can never be forgotten that communication through the media is not a utilitarian exercise intended simply to motivate, persuade or sell. Still less is it a vehicle for ideology. The media can at times reduce human beings to units of consumption or competing interest groups, or manipulate viewers and readers and listeners as mere ciphers from whom some advantage is sought, whether product sales or political support; and these things destroy community. It is the task of communication to bring people together and enrich their lives, not isolate and exploit them. The means of social communication, properly used, can help to create and sustain a human community based on justice and charity; and, in so far as they do that, they will be signs of hope" (Pope John Paul II, Message for the 32nd World Communications Day, 1998).

IV: SOME RELEVANT ETHICAL PRINCIPLES

20. Ethical principles and norms relevant in other fields also apply to social communication. Principles of social ethics like solidarity, subsidiarity, justice and equity, and accountability in the use of public resources and the performance of roles of public trust are always applicable. Communication must always be truthful, since truth is essential to individual liberty and to authentic community among persons.
Ethics in social communication is concerned not just with what appears on cinema and television screens, on radio broadcasts, on the printed page and the Internet, but with a great deal else besides. The ethical dimension relates not just to the content of communication (the message) and the process of communication (how the communicating is done) but to fundamental structural and systemic issues, often involving large questions of policy bearing upon the distribution of sophisticated technology and product (who shall be information rich and who shall be information poor?). These questions point to other questions with economic and political implications for ownership and control. At least in open societies with market economies, the largest ethical question of all may be how to balance profit against service to the public interest understood according to an inclusive conception of the common good.
Even to reasonable people of good will it is not always immediately clear how to apply ethical principles and norms to particular cases; reflection, discussion, and dialogue are needed. We offer what follows with the hope of encouraging such reflection and dialogue—among communication policy makers, professional communicators, ethicists and moralists, recipients of communication, and others concerned.
21. In all three areas—message, process, structural and systemic issues—the fundamental ethical principle is this: The human person and the human community are the end and measure of the use of the media of social communication; communication should be by persons to persons for the integral development of persons.
Integral development requires a sufficiency of material goods and products, but it also requires attention to the "inner dimension" (*Sollicitudo Rei Socialis*, 29; cf. 46). Everyone deserves the opportunity to grow and flourish in respect to the full range of physical, intellectual, emotional, moral, and spiritual goods. Individuals have irreducible

dignity and importance, and may never be sacrificed to collective interests.

22. A second principle is complementary to the first: The good of persons cannot be realized apart from the common good of the communities to which they belong. This common good should be understood in inclusive terms, as the sum total of worthy shared purposes to whose pursuit community members jointly commit themselves and which the community exists to serve.

Thus, while social communication rightly looks to the needs and interests of particular groups, it should not do so in a way that sets one group against another—for example, in the name of class conflict, exaggerated nationalism, racial supremacy, ethnic cleansing, and the like. The virtue of solidarity, "a firm and persevering determination to commit oneself to the common good" (*Sollicitudo Rei Socialis*, 38), ought to govern all areas of social life—economic, political, cultural, religious.

Communicators and communication policy makers must serve the real needs and interests both of individuals and of groups, at all levels and of all kinds. There is a pressing need for equity at the international level, where the maldistribution of material goods between North and South is exacerbated by a maldistribution of communication resources and information technology upon which productivity and prosperity greatly depend. Similar problems also exist within wealthy countries, "where the constant transformation of the methods of production and consumption devalues certain acquired skills and professional expertise" and "those who fail to keep up with the times can easily be marginalized" (*Centesimus Annus*, 33).

Clearly, then, there is a need for broad participation in making decisions not only about the messages and processes of social communication but also about systemic issues and the allocation of resources. The decision makers have a serious moral duty to recognize the needs and interests of those who are particularly vulnerable —the poor, the elderly and unborn, children and youth, the oppressed and marginalized, women and minorities, the sick and disabled—as well as families and religious groups. Today especially, the international community and international communications interests should take a generous and inclusive approach to nations and regions where what the means of social communication do—or fail to do—bears a share of the blame for the perpetuation of evils like poverty, illiteracy, political repression and violations of human rights, intergroup and interreligious conflicts, and the suppression of indigenous cultures.

23. Even so, we continue to believe that "the solution to problems arising from unregulated commercialization and privatization does not lie in state control of media but in more regulation according to criteria of public service and in greater public accountability. It should be noted in this connection that, although the legal and political frameworks within which media operate in some countries are currently changing strikingly for the better, elsewhere government intervention remains an instrument of oppression and exclusion" (*Aetatis Novae*, 5).

The presumption should always be in favour of freedom of expression, for "when people follow their natural inclination to exchange ideas and declare their opinions, they are not merely making use of a right. They are also performing a social duty" (*Communio et Progressio*, 45). Still, considered from an ethical perspective, this presumption is not an absolute, indefeasible norm. There are obvious instances—for example, libel and slander, messages that seek to foster hatred and conflict among individuals and groups, obscenity and pornography, the morbid depiction of violence—where no right to communicate exists. Plainly, too, free expression should always observe principles like truth, fairness, and respect for privacy.

Professional communicators should be actively involved in developing and enforcing ethical codes of behaviour for their profession, in cooperation with public representatives. Religious bodies and other groups likewise deserve to be part of this continuing effort.

24. Another relevant principle, already mentioned, concerns public participation in making decisions about communications policy. At all levels, this participation should be organized, systematic, and genuinely representative, not skewed in favour of particular groups. This principle applies even, and perhaps especially, where media are privately owned and operated for profit. In the interests of public participation, communicators "must seek to communicate with people, and not just speak to them. This involves learning about people's needs, being aware of their struggles and presenting all forms of communication with the sensitivity that human dignity requires" (Pope John Paul

II, Address to Communications Specialists, Los Angeles, September 15, 1987).
Circulation, broadcast ratings, and "box office", along with market research, are sometimes said to be the best indicators of public sentiment—in fact, the only ones necessary for the law of the market to operate. No doubt the market's voice can be heard in these ways. But decisions about media content and policy should not be left only to the market and to economic factors—profits—since these cannot be counted on to safeguard either the public interest as a whole or, especially, the legitimate interests of minorities.
To some extent, this objection may be answered by the concept of the "niche", according to which particular periodicals, programs, stations, and channels are directed to particular audiences. The approach is legitimate, up to a point. But diversification and specialization—organizing media to correspond to audiences broken down into ever-smaller units based largely on economic factors and patterns of consumption—should not be carried too far. Media of social communication must remain an 'Areopagus' (cf. *Redemptoris Missio*, 37)—a forum for exchanging ideas and information, drawing individuals and groups together, fostering solidarity and peace. The Internet in particular raises concerns about some of the "radically new consequences it brings: a loss of the intrinsic value of items of information, an undifferentiated uniformity in messages that are reduced to pure information, a lack of responsible feedback and a certain discouragement of interpersonal relationships" (*Toward a Pastoral Approach To Culture*, 9).
25. Professional communicators are not the only ones with ethical duties. Audiences—recipients—have obligations, too. Communicators attempting to meet their responsibilities deserve audiences conscientious about theirs.
The first duty of recipients of social communication is to be discerning and selective. They should inform themselves about media—their structures, mode of operation, contents—and make responsible choices, according to ethically sound criteria, about what to read or watch or listen to. Today everybody needs some form of continuing media education, whether by personal study or participation in an organized program or both. More than just teaching about techniques,

media education helps people form standards of good taste and truthful moral judgment, an aspect of conscience formation.

Through her schools and formation programs the Church should provide media education of this kind (cf. *Aetatis Novae*, 28; *Communio et Progressio*, 107). Directed originally to institutes of consecrated life, the following words have a broader application: *"A community, aware of the influence of the media, should learn to use them for personal and community growth, with the evangelical clarity and inner freedom of those who have learned to know Christ* (cf. *Gal* 4:17-23). The media propose, and often impose, a mentality and model of life in constant contrast with the Gospel. In this connection, in many areas one hears of the desire for deeper formation in receiving and using the media, both critically and fruitfully" (Congregation for Institutes of Consecrated Life and Societies of Apostolic Life, *Fraternal Life in Community*, 34).

Similarly, parents have a serious duty to help their children learn how to evaluate and use the media, by forming their consciences correctly and developing their critical faculties (cf. *Familiaris Consortio*, 76). For their children's sake, as well as their own, parents must learn and practice the skills of discerning viewers and listeners and readers, acting as models of prudent use of media in the home. According to their age and circumstances, children and young people should be open to formation regarding media, resisting the easy path of uncritical passivity, peer pressure, and commercial exploitation. Families—parents and children together—will find it helpful to come together in groups to study and discuss the problems and opportunities created by social communication.

26. Besides promoting media education, the institutions, agencies, and programs of the Church have other important responsibilities in regard to social communication. First and foremost, the Church's practice of communication should be exemplary, reflecting the highest standards of truthfulness, accountability, sensitivity to human rights, and other relevant principles and norms. Beyond that, the Church's own media should be committed to communicating the fullness of the truth about the meaning of human life and history, especially as it is contained in God's revealed word and expressed by the teaching of the Magisterium. Pastors should encourage use of media to spread the Gospel (cf. Code of Canon Law, Canon 822.1).

Those who represent the Church must be honest and straightforward in their relations with journalists. Even though the questions they ask are "sometimes embarrassing or disappointing, especially when they in no way correspond to the message we have to get across", one must bear in mind that "these disconcerting questions are often asked by most of our contemporaries" (*Towards a Pastoral Approach to Culture*, 34). For the Church to speak credibly to people today, those who speak for her have to give credible, truthful answers to these seemingly awkward questions.

Catholics, like other citizens, have the right of free expression, including the right of access to the media for this purpose. The right of expression includes expressing opinions about the good of the Church, with due regard for the integrity of faith and morals, respect for the pastors, and consideration for the common good and the dignity of persons (cf. Canon 212.3; Canon 227). No one, however, has a right to speak for the Church, or imply he or she does, unless properly designated; and personal opinions should not be presented as the Church's teaching (cf. Canon 227).

The Church would be well served if more of those who hold offices and perform functions in her name received communication training. This is true not only of seminarians, persons in formation in religious communities, and young lay Catholics, but Church personnel generally. Provided the media are "neutral, open and honest", they offer well-prepared Christians "a frontline missionary role" and it is important that the latter be "well-trained and supported". Pastors also should offer their people guidance regarding media and their sometimes discordant and even destructive messages (cf. Canon 822.2, 3).

Similar considerations apply to internal communication in the Church. A two-way flow of information and views between pastors and faithful, freedom of expression sensitive to the well being of the community and to the role of the Magisterium in fostering it, and responsible public opinion all are important expressions of "the fundamental right of dialogue and information within the Church" (*Aetatis Novae*, 10; cf. *Communio et Progressio*, 20).

The right of expression must be exercised with deference to revealed truth and the Church's teaching, and with respect for others' ecclesial rights (cf. Canon 212.1, .2, .3, Canon 220). Like other communities and institutions, the Church sometimes needs—in fact, is sometimes obliged—to practice secrecy and confidentiality. But this should not be for the sake of manipulation and control. Within the communion of faith, "holders of office, who are invested with a sacred power, are, in fact, dedicated to promoting the interests of their brethren, so that all who belong to the People of God, and are consequently endowed with true Christian dignity, may through their free and well-ordered efforts toward a common good, attain to salvation" (*Lumen Gentium*, 18). Right practice in communication is one of the ways of realizing this vision.

V: CONCLUSION

27. As the third millennium of the Christian era begins, humankind is well along in creating a global network for the instantaneous transmission of information, ideas, and value judgments in science, commerce, education, entertainment, politics, the arts, religion, and every other field.

This network already is directly accessible to many people in their homes and schools and workplaces—indeed, wherever they may be. It is commonplace to view events, from sports to wars, happening in real time on the other side of the planet. People can tap directly into quantities of data beyond the reach of many scholars and students just a short time ago. An individual can ascend to heights of human genius and virtue, or plunge to the depths of human degradation, while sitting alone at a keyboard and screen. Communication technology constantly achieves new breakthroughs, with enormous potential for good and ill. As interactivity increases, the distinction between communicators and recipients blurs. Continuing research is needed into the impact, and especially the ethical implications, of new and emerging media.

28. But despite their immense power, the means of communication are, and will remain, only media—that is to say: instruments, tools, available for both good and evil uses. The choice is ours. The media do not call for a new ethic; they call for the application of established principles to new circumstances. And this is a task in which everyone has a role to play. Ethics in the media is not the business only of specialists, whether they be specialists in social communication or specialists in moral philosophy; rather, the reflection and dialogue that

this document seeks to encourage and assist must be broad and inclusive.

29. Social communication can join people in communities of sympathy and shared interest. Will these communities be informed by justice, decency, and respect for human rights; will they be committed to the common good? Or will they be selfish and inward-looking, committed to the benefit of particular groups—economic, racial, political, even religious—at others' expense? Will new technology serve all nations and peoples, while respecting the cultural traditions of each; or will it be a tool to enrich the rich and empower the powerful? We have to choose.

The means of communication also can be used to separate and isolate. More and more, technology allows people to assemble packages of information and services uniquely designed for them. There are real advantages in that, but it raises an inescapable question: Will the audience of the future be a multitude of audiences of one? While the new technology can enhance individual autonomy, it has other, less desirable implications. Instead being a global community, might the 'web' of the future turn out to be a vast, fragmented network of isolated individuals—human bees in their cells—interacting with data instead of with one another? What would become of solidarity—what would become of love—in a world like that?

In the best of circumstances, human communication has serious limitations, is more or less imperfect and in danger of failing. It is hard for people consistently to communicate honestly with one another, in a way that does no harm and serves the best interests of all. In the world of media, moreover, the inherent difficulties of communicating often are magnified by ideology, by the desire for profit and political control, by rivalries and conflicts between groups, and by other social ills. Today's media vastly increase the outreach of social communication—its quantity, its speed; they do not make the reaching out of mind to mind and heart to heart any less fragile, less sensitive, less prone to fail.

30. As we have said, the special contributions which the Church brings to the discussion of these matters are a vision of human persons and their incomparable dignity and inviolable rights, and a vision of human community whose members are joined by the virtue of solidarity in pursuit of the common good of all. The need for these two vi-

sions is especially pressing "at a time when we are faced with the patent inadequacy of perspectives in which the ephemeral is affirmed as a value and the possibility of discovering the real meaning of life is cast into doubt"; lacking them, "many people stumble through life to the very edge of the abyss without knowing where they are going" (*Fides et Ratio*, 6).

In the face of this crisis, the Church stands forth as an "expert in humanity" whose expertise "leads her necessarily to extend her religious mission to the various fields" of human endeavor (*Sollicitudo Rei Socialis*, 41; cf. Pope Paul VI, *Populorum Progressio*, 13). She may not keep the truth about the human person and the human community to herself; she must share it freely, always aware that people can say no to the truth—and to her.

Attempting to foster and support high ethical standards in the use of the means of social communication, the Church seeks dialogue and collaboration with others: with public officials, who have a particular duty to protect and promote the common good of the political community; with men and women from the world of culture and the arts; with scholars and teachers engaged in forming the communicators and audiences of the future; with members of other churches and religious groups, who share her desire that media be used for the glory of God and the service of the human race (cf. Pontifical Council for Social Communications, *Criteria for Ecumenical and Inter-Religious Cooperation in Communications*); and especially with professional communicators—writers, editors, reporters, correspondents, performers, producers, technical personnel—together with owners, administrators, and policy makers in this field.

31. Along with its limitations, human communication has in it something of God's creative activity. "With loving regard, the divine Artist passes on to the human artist"—and, we might say, to the communicator as well—"a spark of his own surpassing wisdom, calling him to share in his creative power"; in coming to understand this, artists and communicators "come to a full understanding of themselves, their vocation and their mission" (*Letter to Artists*, 1).

The Christian communicator in particular has a prophetic task, a vocation: to speak out against the false gods and idols of the day—materialism, hedonism, consumerism, narrow nationalism, and the rest—holding up for all to see a body of moral truth based on human dignity and rights, the preferential option for the poor, the universal destination of goods, love of enemies, and unconditional respect for all human life from conception to natural death; and seeking the more perfect realization of the Kingdom in this world while remaining aware that, at the end of time, Jesus will restore all things and return them to the Father (cf. *1 Cor* 15:24).

32. While these reflections are addressed to all persons of good will, not just Catholics, it is appropriate, in bringing them to a close, to speak of Jesus as a model for communicators. "In these last days" God the Father "has spoken to us by a Son" (*Heb* 1:2); and this Son communicates to us now and always the Father's love and the ultimate meaning of our lives.

"While he was on earth Christ revealed himself as the perfect communicator. Through his incarnation, he utterly identified himself with those who were to receive his communication, and he gave his message not only in words but in the whole manner of his life. He spoke from within, that is to say, from out of the press of his people. He preached the divine message without fear or compromise. He adjusted to his people's way of talking and to their patterns of thought. And he spoke out of the predicament of their time" (*Communio et Progressio,* 11).

Throughout Jesus' public life crowds flocked to hear him preach and teach (cf. *Mt* 8:1,18; *Mk* 2:2,4.1; *Lk* 5:1, etc.), and he taught them "as one who had authority" (*Mt* 7:29; cf. *Mk* 1:22; *Lk* 4:32). He told them about the Father and at the same time referred them to himself, explaining, "I am the way, and the truth, and the life" (*Jn* 14:6) and "he who has seen me has seen the Father" (*Jn* 14:9). He did not waste time on idle speech or on vindicating himself, not even when he was accused and condemned (cf. *Mt* 26:63, 27:12-14; *Mk* 15:5, 15:61). For his "food" was to do the will of the Father who sent him (*Jn* 4:34), and all he said and did was spoken and done in reference to that.

Often Jesus' teaching took the form of parables and vivid stories expressing profound truths in simple, everyday terms. Not only his words but his deeds, especially his miracles, were acts of communication, pointing to his identity and manifesting the power of God (cf. *Evangelii Nuntiandi,* 12). In his communications he showed respect for his listeners, sympathy for their situation and needs, compassion for their suffering (e.g., *Lk* 7:13), and resolute determination to tell them what they needed to hear, in a way that would command their attention and help them receive the message, without coercion or compromise, deception or manipulation. He invited others to open their minds and hearts to him, knowing this was how they would be drawn to him and his Father (e.g., *Jn* 3:1-15, 4:7-26).

Jesus taught that communication is a moral act: "For out of the abundance of the heart the mouth speaks. The good man out of his good treasure brings forth good, and the evil man out of his evil treasure brings forth evil. I tell you, on the day of judgment men will render an account for every careless word they utter; for by your words you will be justified, and by your words you will be condemned" (*Mt* 12:34-37). He cautioned sternly against scandalizing the "little ones", and warned that for one who did, "it would be better... if a great millstone were hung round his neck and he were thrown into the sea" (*Mk* 9:42; cf. *Mt* 18:6, *Lk* 17:2). He was altogether candid, a man of whom it could be said that "no guile was found on his lips"; and further: "When he was reviled, he did not revile in return; when he suffered, he did not threaten; but he trusted to him who judges justly" (*1 Pt* 2:22-23). He insisted on candour and truthfulness in others, while condemning hypocrisy, dishonesty—any kind of communication that was bent and perverse: "Let what you say be simply 'Yes' or 'No'; anything more than this comes from evil" (*Mt* 5:37).

33. Jesus is the model and the standard of our communicating. For those involved in social communication, whether as policy makers or professional communicators or recipients or in any other role, the conclusion is clear: "Therefore, putting away falsehood, let every one speak the truth with his neighbor, for we are members one of another... Let no evil talk come out of your mouths, but only such as is good for edifying, as fits the occasion, that it may impart grace to those who hear" (*Eph* 4:25,29). Serving the human person, building up human community grounded in solidarity and justice and love, and speaking the truth about human life and its final fulfilment in God were, are, and will remain at the heart of ethics in the media.

311

APPENDIX III: EXCERPTS FROM

CONGREGATION FOR CATHOLIC EDUCATION: GUIDE
TO THE TRAINING OF FUTURE PRIESTS CONCERNING
THE INSTRUMENTS OF SOCIAL COMMUNICATION.

*(Rome, from the Offices of the Congregation for Catholic Education,
19th March 1986, Feast of St. Joseph.)*

INTRODUCTION

1. *Human communication, a gift of God.* God, the Supreme Good,
incessantly communicates his gifts to men and women, the objects of
his particular solicitude and love, in anticipation of the time when he
will communicate himself more fully to them in the beatific vision.
More than that: in order that his image in his human creatures might
increasingly reflect the divine perfection (cf. *Mt* 5, 48), he has willed
to associate them in his own work, making them, in their turn, messengers and dispensers of the same gifts to their brothers and sisters
and to all humanity.
By a necessity of their nature, in fact, men and women, from the earliest moments of their existence, took to communicating their spiritual
goods to their fellows, (Plus XII's, *Miranda prorsus*, 24-25.) by means of
signs which were perceptible to the senses. Then little by little, with
the passage of time, they discovered and invented means and vehicles
of communication which increasingly overcame the original limitations imposed by space and time. The point has now been reached
where, by a constant acceleration in technological development,
worldwide and instantaneous communication has become possible between the members of the human race, and the instruments which
permit this exchange evolve more refined and sophisticated forms at
an astonishing rate (e.g. informatics, telematics).
   2. *Revelation and communication.* The Church could not fail to be
interested in such a providential development, since it is charged with
the task of transmitting the truths of divine revelation to all humanity.
God, in fact, having "in many and various ways spoken of old by the
prophets; in our own time has spoken to us by his son" (*Heb* 1,1-2)

and he arranged "that the things he had once revealed for the salvation of all peoples should remain in their entirety, and be transmitted to all generations". Therefore Christ the Lord... commanded the apostles to preach the gospel to all... This was faithfully done: it was done by the apostles who handed on, by the spoken word of their preaching, by the example they gave, by the institutions they established, what they themselves had received - whether from the lips of Christ, from his way of life and from his works...; it was done by those apostles and other men associated with the apostles who... committed the message of salvation to writing.

"In order that the full and living Gospel might always be preserved in the Church the apostles left bishops as their successors. They gave them 'their own position as teaching authority'".(VATICAN COUNCIL II, *Dei verbum*, 4 and 7.)

3. *From "communication" to "communion"*. In more recent times the Church has considered even the instruments of social communication as providential means for the accomplishment of its mission to "preach from the housetops" (*Lk* 12, 3), "to all nations" (*Mk* 16, 15), "to the end of the earth" (*Acts* 1, 8), the word of salvation. It has concerned itself, moreover, with educating and caring for the human person, the whole person, both as humankind and as Christian. The Church has, in fact, welcomed with open arms those instruments as "marvellous inventions of today which have a powerful effect on people's minds" (VATICAN COUNCIL II, *Inter mirifica*, 1.) and as "wonderful fruits of human work and ingenuity, the gift of God from whom every good comes" (Pius XII, *Miranda prorsus*, 1.)

Aware, however, of the cultural and moral ambivalence sometimes displayed by media programmes, the Church "with watchful care" (Pius XI, *Vigilanti cura*, 1.) has exerted itself to circumvent every " use (of them) contrary to the Creator's plan" (VATICAN COUNCIL II, *Inter mirifica*, 2.) and such as might cause damage or ruin to his creatures.

The Church's post-conciliar teaching points out that, ideally, "communication" should result in "communion", whether the communication is interpersonal or "mass". The teaching makes an analogy with two divine exemplars of perfect communication-communion. The first is Jesus Christ, "the perfect Communicator", in Whom the incarnate Word made his own "the nature of those who were to receive his communication and gave his message not only in words but in the whole manner of his life. He spoke from within, from out of the press of his people. He adjusted to his people's way of talking and to their patterns of thought. And he spoke out of the predicament of their time...

4. The instruments of social communication and the ministerial priesthood. In the past few decades, the instruments of social communication have come to the point of exercising an enormous and profound influence on practically every aspect, sector and relationship of society. The new problems arising from this growing influence have resulted in the emergence of many teachings, exhortations and norms from the Church's teaching authority. These have been intended for the protection and benefit not only of the faithful and of each man of good will, but also of all those who are called to exercise the priestly ministry in the contemporary world.

In conformity with these official guidelines issued by the Church, this Congregation, since 1970, in the *Ratio Fundamentalis Institutionis Sacerdotalis*, has given general indications on matters relating to the instruments of social communication, and has gone on to lay down that future priests should be trained in the seminary in the correct use of these instruments. This provision had a threefold purpose, namely, that the seminarians might impose discipline on their own personal use of the media, that they might be able to train the faithful in their turn to exercise similar self-discipline, and that they might learn how to use the media in their apostolate *(Ratio Fundamentalis Institutionis Sacerdotalis, 68.)*

The following year, the Pastoral Instruction *Communio et Progressio* went over the same ground. It said: "*If students for the priesthood and religious in training wish to be part of modern life and also to be at all effective in their apostolate, they should know how the media work upon the fabric of society, and also the technique of their use. This knowledge should be an integral part of their ordinary education*" *(Pastoral Instruction Communio et Progressio, 111.)*

5. The present situation. The guidelines given in the *Ratio Fundamentalis* were therefore to be borne in mind by the competent episcopal conferences while preparing the *Ratio* for their respective countries, so that they might be put into effect in a specific way in each seminary's regulations and study programmes.

Since it was a question of inserting a totally new element into the seminary curriculum, difficulties were, of course, to be expected. The Congregation, appreciating this, initiated an inquiry in 1977 in all seminaries, major and minor, to ascertain whether and to what extent its directive to introduce a training programme in the field of social communications had been understood and implemented.

From the replies received, it emerged that in the majority of the centres of ecclesiastical formation, the matter had been indeed adverted to; however, definitive and organic programmes were still almost totally lacking, either because the specific object and scope of any programme was poorly understood, or because there had been a failure to distinguish between the aims and levels which had been visualized in the proposal. A further difficulty was that qualified staff to prepare and carry out the training programme in communications were in short supply. Yet another factor was an absence of technical aid and economic means.

6. *This Guide.* These insufficiencies have not been eliminated with the passage of the years, and the advances in human communication in the meantime have meant that the training institutes have fallen even farther behind. For this reason, the Congregation, while recognizing with approval the solid advances made in various seminaries and teaching institutes dependent on ecclesiastical authority, has decided, after consultation with the Pontifical Commission for Social Communications, to issue the present Guide, in which it will offer certain items of advice, with proposals and directives. These must necessarily be of a rather general character, given the shifting ground to be traversed in a field of such rapid change and development, as well as the diversity of local situations to be considered; (*Communio et Progressio,* 183.), but the object is to lay down reliable guidelines without delay, so that the directives and suggestions of the Church's teaching authority and the provisions in the *Ratio Fundamentalis* are carried out precisely and efficiently. The Guide is addressed, in the first place, to the bishops' conferences and to their Excellencies the bishops of the dioceses in territories of common law; then, to superiors and teachers in seminaries. The people directly affected by the specific initiation and training of which the Guide treats are intended to be principally the students of major and minor seminaries in the above-mentioned territories. The document, however, can also be of service to seminaries and institutes of priestly training which are not dependent on the Congregation for Catholic Education.

7. *The object.* The proper and direct object of the initiation and specific education with which the Guide is concerned is in the first place those media of communication of our day often referred to as the *mass media*, (*Acta Synodalia* S.ti Concilii Oecumenici Vaticani II, Vol. V, Periodus Prima, Pars III, p. 375) or as *diffusion techniques*, or mass communication, or audiovisuals. They are also called by various other, more or less inadequate, names, but the Decree *Inter mirifica*, later followed by the new *Code of Canon Law*, (Canons 761, 779, 804, 822, 823, 1063 and 1369 666 and 747) has more properly called them "instruments of social communication": "the press, the cinema, the radio, the television and the other instruments *with similar characteristics"* (no. 1). They are in fact distinguished by their high-level technical emphasis, by their specially outstanding suitability for achieving communication, which is the primary factor in the phenomenon of *socialization (Mater et Magistra,* 58) which is such a feature of today.

The social and cultural, as well as the moral and pastoral problems connected with these instruments are also an object of the Guide. First among these would be those which arise in more general human communication, and then those arising from the technology employed, especially, today, from microelectronics.

However, as well as this proper and direct object of the present *Guide,* pastoral necessity requires that we occasionally concern ourselves also with the study and practice of other media and instruments of expression and communication, such as the theatre, the figurative arts, and so forth, even if these are outside the limits which we have indicated above.

8. *Editorial criteria.* The Guide avoids treating technical questions and theories about the *mass media* and the social and cultural phenomena connected with them; something, anyhow, on which experts are often in disagreement. As well as this, it abstains from treating at length of what the Church's teaching authority has been teaching and laying down on communications matters for the past five decades.

A) COMMON PRINCIPLES.

9. *Three levels.* It will make good sense to begin the course of instruction in media matters and to continue it along three different levels.

At the first, or basic, level, attention is to be focused on the receivers, which is to say, all readers, viewers and listeners of *mass media* (*Inter mirifica*, 16). Since every student must be classified as a receiver, training from this aspect must be given to all of them without distinction.

The formation given at the second level is "pastoral", and is to be given to all future priests, since it has to do with their future priestly ministry. In that ministry, they are going to require to be able to train the faithful, in their turn, in the right use of *mass media*; they will also need to know how they can themselves use the media to the best advantage for the purposes of their apostolate.

On the third level is "specialist" training, and it will affect "those who already work in the *mass media*, or who, giving evidence of special talent, are being prepared to work in the field" (*Communio et Progressio*, 106 and 111; Inter Mirifica no. 22). Also to be considered on this third level will be those who are preparing to teach and give training in *mass media* on the first two levels.

10. *Maintaining distinctions*. It will be well, at each level, to be quite precise about what is being studied. Clear distinctions are to be made between the questions which have properly to do with the instruments of social communication, and other questions which do not touch these instruments directly. The following advice is offered:

a) Close attention should be paid - in so far as the differences in languages allow, - to the correct use of terms; and the different accepted meanings authorized by the various authors and schools will have to be kept in mind. Precision will, of course, be specially necessary with the juridical meaning which conciliar terminology has assumed in the new *Code of Canon Law*.

b) In particular, only the daily press or periodicals of information, the cinema, the radio, television and other media having the same technological characteristics, are to be regarded and treated as "instruments of social communication". They are to be distinguished from other means of expression which, for all their importance, do not fit the description (for instance, the theatre); also from communications activities employing similar techniques (for instance, book publishing), and those which are complementary to the "instruments" properly so-called, such as discs, cassettes, slides, group-media, multimedia, minimedia (mentioned in no. 7).

c) Keeping in mind the accelerated evolution, worldwide, of the social communications technology in the direction of telechronics and telematics, of which the *mass media* are at once the object, vehicle and mirror, it is clear that no one medium should be treated in the training course as if the others did not exist (e.g. cinema alone or television alone, with no mention of the printed word). Similarly, it would be a mistake to deal with some particular aspect of a medium in isolation (e.g. the culture and civilization of "the image"). The media ought to be treated all together and as a whole, and all the questions and angles dealt with by the best-known authors should be looked at, such as "the world dialogue", "the global village", "one-dimensional man", "computer-conditioned man"...

d) Finally, among these and other socio-cultural macrophenomena, it will be necessary to give most space to the questions concerning information, propaganda, advertising, public opinion, and the use of leisure, in so far as these have specific connections with the media.

11. *Integral training.* At the first two levels of formation especially, the basic and the pastoral, care will have to be taken to give the students a formation to *mass media* which is all of one piece, with its limits and content clearly defined, and the appropriate attention devoted to didactic practice. Thus:

a) What is to be attempted in every case is to form and conserve a fully human personality in the receivers, making them receptive of those psycho-sociological and ethico-cultural values with which the *mass media* involve themselves so unremittingly, providing occasion for the growth or withering of that personality. The students are to be assisted towards Christian maturity, so that, by using the *mass media* responsibly, they will then know how to live the whole of their priestly lives in a rich and productive way.

b) Side by side with the teaching of theory there must be provision of practical experience in the use of the tools of social communication. This will help the students to acquire, as they mature, a knowledge of the cultural and political, religious and moral trends in the current productions and programming. It will also enable them to evaluate, critically and realistically, the modern techniques. To make all this possible, the seminaries and institutes of instruction need to be supplied with the proper equipment.

12. *Soundness of doctrine.* It is necessary that the training in social communications shall be begun and continued in a context which is doctrinally sound and safe, with no superficiality or improvisation on the part of the teachers (cf. *Appendix* I, no. 35). Therefore...

a) It will not be sufficient that the teachers in the basic course of initiation are simply practitioners or technicians of a particular *mass medium*, even though, as such, they may be of the highest professional competence. They will need also to have a thorough grasp of the whole range of problems, cultural and technical, profane and religious; and preferably this should have been acquired by frequenting the second level (pastoral) course.

b) The teachers in the second level course especially must be well-informed regarding what the most highly qualified scholars in the different cultural situations have researched, formulated and published. But, in imparting this knowledge to the students, they must distinguish clearly between what is certain and proven and what is hypothetical and open to discussion. They will distinguish the transitory from the definitive, the particular from the general, and the facts from their ideological interpretations. This will be specially important whenever particular norms for moral behaviour and pastoral practice are derived from theories and proposals.

c) It is necessary that all shall make themselves familiar with the considerable volume of official Church teaching on social communications, that they shall accept it trustfully and teach it faithfully. This teaching collected into one place in *Appendix* I offers a great deal of material for study and reflection. Among the principal documents to which a Catholic teacher of *mass media* should constantly refer are the following: Pius XI's Encyclical on Cinema (1936), *Vigilanti Cura*; the two Discourses on the Ideal Film (1955) and the Encyclical *Miranda prorsus* (1957) of Pius XII; the Letter of the Secretariat of State to the *Semaine Sociale de Nancy* (1955); the conciliar Decree *Inter mirifica* (1963); the Pastoral Instruction *Communio et Progressio* (1971); the canons on the instruments of social communication in the new *Code of Canon Law* (1983); and the Messages issued by the Supreme Pontiffs year by year for World Communications Day.

13. *Necessary Aids.* The Congregation wishes that in the various linguistic and cultural areas, suitable books and texts shall be quickly and carefully prepared and distributed, to be used in the first two levels of

social communications training in the seminaries. They will contain the Church's official teaching, accompanied by study notes and well organized bibliographies indicating the literature published throughout the world on the various aspects of the subject.

B) PARTICULAR NORMS

I. THE FIRST LEVEL (BASIC): THE TRAINING OF RECEIVERS

14. *Purpose.* The initial introduction and basic training ought to enlighten the students, refine their critical sense, and form their conscience, so as to save them falling prey to the facile suggestions and manipulations perpetrated by the *mass media*, particularly where these may offend against truth or morality. The idea is to give the students a sound doctrinal and ascetical training, so that they will be well-equipped "to take responsibility for the manner in which they receive, by their free and personal choice, whatever is presented by the media... preferring things that are worthwhile in terms of virtue, knowledge and art; avoiding whatever may cause or occasion spiritual detriment to oneself or which, through bad example, can lead others astray; refraining from whatever impedes good communications and promotes the evil kind" (*Inter mirifica*, 9).

15. *Division of responsibility in student training.* The family, *(Inter mirifica,* 10, *Communio et Progressio,* 67) the catechism class (*Directorium Catechistieum Generale,* 11th April 1971: AAS, 64 [1972], p. 97, see also *Inter mirifica,* 16; *Communio et Progressio,* 108, 130-131.) and the school, particularly the Catholic school, whether primary, secondary, or higher, are expected to provide the basic training for the receivers, conjointly and at the appropriate time (*Communio et Progressio,* 67). In the school, the *mass media* will be dealt with either incidentally, in the course of teaching the various ordinary subjects, or - at least in the middle and higher schools - in classes set aside for the subject itself. But in cases where students entering the seminary are found to be lacking in this basic training, the seminary itself will have to supply it. In any case, the seminary will not confine itself to giving classes in *mass media* in the course of its ordinary curriculum, but will, in addition, arrange for courses, conferences, seminars, exercises (*Ratio fundamentalis,* no. 89, and *Communio et Pro-*

gressio, 66) and talks... all designed to inculcate principles and norms which will be useful:

1. in aiding the student to make well-informed choices, by himself, - both quantitive and qualitative - among the programmes available to him;

2. in insuring that the student will make profitable and responsible use of his listening and viewing time, and

3. in exercising the student, according to the level at which he is studying and the maturity which he has reached, in making well-reasoned critical judgements on the messages and values - cultural and religious, explicit or implicit - which are proposed, or systematically ignored, by media programmes.

16. *Cultural aspect.* The student will require to know something about the technical aspects of each medium, otherwise he cannot hope to understand its "language" correctly. They should be carefully instructed also regarding the economic, political or ideological structures which, in the different national and cultural areas, may affect the media of social communications at the level of production, distribution or consumption, or may condition the messages coming from them, either in quantity or quality (*Communio et Progressio,* 64). But the cultural and aesthetic awareness of the student must also be sharpened, and so, at the different levels of his academic progress, he should be trained to recognize and appreciate other modes and forms of expression and communication: history, philosophy, literature, drama, the figurative arts, music; and to make the necessary comparisons and checks with what the *mass media,* that "parallel school", presents. This cultural and aesthetic formation, training and refining the good taste of the students will make it natural for them to reject as a matter of course programming of poor cultural quality or moral unseemliness (*Communio et Progressio,* 50, 53). In this connection, it goes without saying that a solid philosophical foundation will be of great benefit to the students.

17. *Religious and moral aspect.* The religious and moral aspect is of fundamental importance in the training of future priests towards that personal interior freedom, rooted in deep conviction, which will cause them to set an example, regarding *mass media,* that their people will wish to follow. In thus preparing them...

a) treatment of the moral aspects of *mass media* should not be allowed to descend to mere moralizing, nor should it be reduced to a consideration merely of sexual morality; though the special implications of this latter for those preparing for a life of celibacy should not be overlooked;

b) the emphasis should be upon the positive, showing a strong preference for what is solid and constructive over what is harmful or dangerous and therefore to be avoided;

c) in good as in bad, attention should be drawn not only to what affects the individual conscience, but also to the social relevance of a person's choices and their social effects. The students' attention shall be directed also to any "moral judgements" which shall happen to be pronounced by the competent authority (*Inter mirifica*, 9, *Communio et Progressio*, 112).

18. *Exposure to the mass media.* The students need to become acquainted with the real world about which they are being taught in class. They need also to be trained to give "the witness of a well-rounded and mature personality that can enter relationships with others without exaggerated precautions or naive imprudence, but with an open-hearted and serenely-balanced cordiality (JOHN PAUL II, Discourse to religious women, *L'Osservatore Romano*, 12th November 1978.). To achieve these aims, and to prevent them adopting a totally defensive and closed attitude to the *mass media*, it is recommended that they should accustom themselves, individually or in homogeneous groups, to wide-ranging news reports from the media about the dramas and problems of the real world outside:

a) taking due account of the different ages of the students and the different levels of cultural and moral development they have reached;

b) educating them to use the *mass media* not merely or exclusively for entertainment, but much more for information, for broadening the mind, widening the horizons, and achieving a nicely-balanced cultural and social growth. They should be drilled, by means of *forums* and other similar exercises, in analyzing, discussing and giving critical judgement on media shows and messages, especially those dealing with matters which are topical and controversial in the religious, moral or cultural fields;

19. *Necessary balance.* Situations will arise where it is found necessary to find remedies for past excessive use or misuse of the *mass me-*

dia. In such cases, the basic media training course should be conducted in a context of balanced individual and community discipline, designed to compensate for the cultural and spiritual imbalance connected with a prolonged and unbalanced use of *mass media*. The damage to be repaired will have arisen either from the content of the media programmes which may have been sometimes unseemly or of poor quality; or even from the manner of presentation, which may have resulted in the "medium" itself becoming the "message".

As an antidote to time-wasting, sometimes even alienating indulgence in superficial media programmes, the students should be guided to the love and practice of reading, study, silence and meditation. They should be encouraged, and be provided with the necessary conditions for community dialogue and prayer. This will serve to remedy the isolation and self-absorbtion caused by the unidirectional communication of the *mass media*, and will revive the authentic and absolute value proper to the Christian profession and the priestly ministry, particularly those of obedience and evangelic poverty, (*Ratio fundamentalis*, no. 49, 50) which the materialist and consumerist vision of human existence offered by the instruments of social communication very often rejects or ignores.

II. THE SECOND LEVEL: PASTORAL TRAINING.

20. *The three aims*. The social communications training of the second level, which is specifically pastoral, is to be given to all students without distinction during their philosophy and theology courses. It has three aims:

a) to train those concerned in the correct use of the instruments of social communication (and in general, of every technique of expression and communication) in their pastoral activities, when the circumstances permit it;

b) to train them to be masters and guides of others (receivers in general, educators, all those who work in the *mass media*) through instruction, catechesis, preaching, etc., and as consultants, confessors, spiritual directors;

c) and above all, to get them into a state of mind in which they will be permanently ready to make the necessary adjustments in their pastoral activity, including those demanded by the inculturation of the Christian faith and life in the different particular churches, in a world psychologically and socially conditioned by the *mass media* (*Communio et Progressio*, 111, *Ratio fundamentalis*, par. 4 and no. 88) and even already by telematics and informatics.

21. *Practical training.* The irreplaceable function of the ministry of the word in the priestly apostolate demands that the future priest shall be thoroughly trained in the theory and practice of the art of speaking. As a necessary part of his training in social communications, also, he should be instructed on the manner in which each of the instruments of social communication works (the so-called "languages" proper to the different media), and its relationship with the "messages" it is expected to transmit, and with the "receptive" characteristics of the various "audiences".

This will be achieved by methodical lessons, which will be absorbed in greater depth in sessions of critical and comparative analysis of current or recorded programme-types and publications.

Furthermore, the students should be given practical, "hands on" exercises, possibly with the help of experts from outside, in the proper use of communications equipment: speaking to microphone, movie camera, or telecamera, with special attention to performance in liturgical ceremonies, interviewing and being interviewed, writing news and feature articles and scripts for radio and television, and composing advertising copy. Discussion sessions on the merits and faults of the individual performances will be of value.

For journalistic practice, advantage should be taken of internal seminary publications, also the local press, whether religious or secular. Use should be made of closed circuit television facilities when these happen to be available locally in parish or schools. Seminary publications are to be specially encouraged and, where necessary and possible, subsidized, as they are valuable means of stimulating and exercising the students' creativity.

22. *Teaching and pastoral aids.* In this practical training in the use of *mass media*, due attention should be given also to those various other media and techniques of expression and communication which may be regarded as similar or ancillary. Theatre has pre-eminence among these. Serious efforts should be made to help the future priests understand and appreciate it, both when it is featured in *mass media*

(*Inter mirifica's* no. 14, *Communio et Progressio* no 158) programming, as it frequently is, and when opportunities are provided within the seminary for producing theatrical works and acting in them. These latter activities can contribute greatly towards refining the student's capacity for communicating in a public way, as well as for group work.

There are also, and not to be undervalued, much less ignored, the group media, multimedia, minimedia, and audiovisuals in general, - discs, audio and video-cassettes, photo-slides, small films, - which, with their relatively modest cost and simplicity of operation, have particular advantages in teaching and pastoral work, especially with catechesis and group animation.

23. *The whole person.* To achieve the other two aims of this pastoral training, it will be important not to overlook, at least in their essential points, the various socio-cultural themes: technology, telematics, cultural anthropology, sociology, economics, semiology, linguistics, psychology and pedagogy, etc. - in so far as they are connected with human communication which is achieved by use of the *mass media* and of the latest technologies.

At the same time, the religious, moral and pastoral implications of the instruments of social communication should be examined. It will be useful, in fact, to keep always in mind "the whole person", whom the *mass media* affect both as an individual and as a social being: first as a person, then as a believer and a Christian. The Church thinks of the promotion of this "whole person's" wellbeing and advancement, especially today, as its proper pastoral task (*Gaudium et Spes*, 3). The pastoral task of the priest will be to teach this person the message of salvation in an understandable way, and to motivate him/her to live accordingly.

24. *Aptitude for communication.* This theoretic and practical formation in the use of the instruments of social communication will certainly be helped forward if there exists in the seminary a favourable climate of communication among the students, and between the students and their teachers, in which it may be integrated. To this end, the following would seem to be required:

- that the students should be educated in interior silence, necessary for the spiritual as well as the intellectual life, and to shut out the enervating din of the daily clamouring media of communications;

- that the students be trained to engage in frequent interpersonal and group conversation, in which they will give special attention to correctness of language, clearness of exposition and logical argumentation. This will serve as a corrective to the passivity which can be occasioned by the unidirectional communications and images of the *mass media*;

- that the teachers, for their part, while treating of the *mass media* and other subjects, should take all possible care to express themselves with total clarity, while in no way sacrificing scientific exactness, and that they should make sure they speak in the idiom of today rather than that of earlier centuries (CONGREGATION FOR CATHOLIC EDUCATION, Document on *The theological formation of future priests*, 22nd February 1976, nos 76, 77.);

- that all concerned, without distinction, united in heart and will, should apply themselves to achieving "that communion which according to the Christian faith constitutes the primary and ultimate end of every communication" (*Communio et Progressio*, 6, 8, 11, 73, 102).

25. Aids and sources. The works of the more reputable authors should be put at the disposal of the students, and they should also be provided with relevant bulletins and magazines so that they may keep themselves *au fait* with the latest thinking and technical development in the communications field. They should be guided in critical discussion about the theses and proposals put forward in this literature, particularly when they are of a kind which can be applied to the ethico-moral behaviour of the faithful and of men in general, and to pastoral practice.

Further, recourse should be had to specialist assistance from outside, and the students should be facilitated for example, on the annual "World Day" which they themselves will prepare and celebrate (*Inter mirifica*, 18 and also *Communio et Progressio 100, 167)* - in having frequent encounters with people who work in the ecclesiastical Organisms for *mass media*: diocesan, national and even international (that is, UCIP for the printed word, OCIC for Cinema, UNDA for radio and television), and with the workers in these disciplines in their work places.

26. Courses and examinations. It is advised that this specific pastoral training, at least in part, shall be given incidentally, as occasion arises, and little by little, during instruction on humanistic, sociological, philosophical and theological subjects. However, the discipline may not be considered as merely auxiliary or optional, but during the philosophy and theology courses the lessons and exercises on social communications are to be integrated in organic courses, with examinations at the end.

III. THE THIRD LEVEL: SPECIALIST TRAINING.

27. *The candidates*. It will be right that "those who already work, or are preparing themselves to work, in communications" and who "show special aptitude and inclination" for this kind of work, shall not content themselves with the pastoral training given to all the seminarians, but shall procure for themselves "in due course one more specialized" (*Communio et Progressio*, 106 and 111.). The superiors, on their part, shall be solicitous to identify these young men and to help them and keep track of their progress.

Not only those who are preparing themselves for active journalism, or to work in cinema, radio or television, are invited to get themselves such training, but also, in some measure, those who are preparing to teach this discipline, or to direct or collaborate in diocesan or national offices for the social communications media.

28. *Centres*. To provide the specialist training for such as these, there exist in the different language areas, through the meritorious initiative of Church agencies or of individuals among the faithful, training centres which provide partial or complete courses in social communications techniques.

Where these, however, are lacking, or where, because of insufficiency of equipment or qualified staff, existing institutes of the Church are unable to provide what is required, it will be fitting that seminary students, or priests already engaged in the ministry, will prudently seek out other suitable public institutes where they can get a truly professional training (*Ecumenical directory*, no. 92, 13th April 1970: AAS, 62 [1970], p. 705).

It is the hope of this Congregation that a clergy trained in this way will effectively benefit "all men of good will... in using the instruments of social communication solely for the good of humanity, whose future depends more every day in the correct use (of these instruments)", and this especially at a time when "the People of God, their gaze fixed on the future, descry with immense trust and burning love the marvels promised them in full measure by space age" telematics (*Inter mirifica*, 24 and *Communio et Progressio*, 187. 36).

IKO - Verlag für Interkulturelle Kommunikation
Holger Ehling Publishing – Der Medienverlag
Edition Hipparchia
Frankfurt am Main • London

Frankfurt am Main
Postfach 90 04 21; D-60444 Frankfurt
Assenheimerstr. 17, D–60489 Frankfurt
Tel.: +49-(0)69-78 48 08
Fax: +49-(0)69-78 96 575
e-mail: info@iko-verlag.de

Internet: www.iko-verlag.de
Verkehrs-Nr.: 10896
VAT-Nr.: DE 111876148
Auslieferung: order@kno-va.de

London
70 c, Wrentham Avenue
London NW10 3HG, UK
e-mail: HEhling@aol.com

Aus der Reihe
„Ethik – Gesellschaft – Wirtschaft"
(hrsg. von Johannes Hoffmann)

Band 8
Claudia Döpfner
**Zur Glaubwürdigkeit ethisch-
ökologischer Geld- und Kapitalanlagen**
Eine theologisch-ethische Untersuchung
vor dem Hintergrund der Frage nach der
Glaubwürdigkeit der ökonomischen und
monetären Strukturen
2000, 256 S., € 22,00,
ISBN 3-88939-514-7

Band 9
Peter Grieble
Ethisch-ökologische Geldanlage
Einflussmöglichkeiten durch Beachtung
von ethisch-ökologischen Gesichtspunkten
bei der Anlage von Geld
2001, 390 S., € 25,80,
ISBN 3-88939-575-9

Band 10
Hans-Albert Schneider
Ethisches Rating
Begründung-Bewertungsmöglichkeit-
Evaluation
2001, 330 S., € 21,00,
ISBN 3-88939-582-1

Band 11
Franz Josef Stendebach
Wege der Menschen
Versuche zu einer Anthropologie des Alten
Testaments
2001, 348 S., € 21,50,
ISBN 3-88939-558-9

Band 12
Lucia Reisch (Ed.)
Ethical-ecological Investment
Towards Global Sustainable Development
2001, 146 S., € 16,80
ISBN 3-88939-578-3

Band 13
John Chidi Nwafor
Church and State:
The Nigerian Experience
The relationship between the Church and
the State in Nigeria in the areas of Human
Rights, Education, Religious Freedom and
Religious Tolerance
2002, 444 S., € 26,80,
ISBN 3-88939-632-1

**Bestellen Sie bitte über den Buchhandel oder direkt beim Verlag.
Gerne senden wir Ihnen unser Titelverzeichnis zu.**